VIKINGS OF THE PACIFIC

VIKINGS

TAHITIAN FLEET MOBILIZING FOR AN EXPEDITION

OF THE PACIFIC

FIRST PUBLISHED AS *VIKINGS OF THE SUNRISE*

Peter H. Buck

THE UNIVERSITY OF CHICAGO PRESS

CHICAGO AND LONDON

THE UNIVERSITY OF CHICAGO PRESS, CHICAGO 60637
The University of Chicago Press, Ltd., London
Whitcombe and Tombes Ltd., Christchurch, New Zealand

© 1938 by J. B. Lippincott Company. First published 1938
by Frederick A. Stokes Company. © 1959 by The University
of Chicago. Fifth Impression 1972. Printed in the United
States of America

International Standard Book Number: 0-226-07950-3
Library of Congress Catalog Card Number: 59-16101

FOREWORD

IN WRITING *Vikings of the Pacific* (originally entitled *Vikings of the Sunrise*), Peter Buck drew on his Maori heritage, his experience as a physician, and his field work as an anthropologist to present the dramatic story of the Polynesians. The book communicates the quality of Polynesian life in a manner which has not been equaled. It is now twenty years since *Vikings of the Sunrise* first appeared. No book has replaced it, and it continues to find an appreciative audience with a new generation of readers.

Peter Buck was a remarkable man and a biographical note may be of interest. He was born at Urenui, Taranaki, New Zealand, in 1880, of an Irish father and a Maori mother. He attended Te Aute College, from which he graduated in 1898, and received his medical degree from New Zealand University in 1910. Buck served his Maori people as Medical Health Officer from 1905 to 1909, and as a member of the New Zealand Parliament from 1909 to 1914. With the outbreak of World War I, he joined the Maori Battalion as a medical officer, seeing active service in Egypt, Gallipoli, France, and Belgium. On his return to New Zealand he became Director of Maori Hygiene from 1919 to 1927. In the meantime, he developed an increasingly serious interest in anthropology, which finally led him to give up his medical career and to accept an appointment as Ethnologist on the staff of Bishop Museum in Honolulu. He served in this capacity from 1927 to 1936, when he became Director of Bishop Museum, a post which he held until his death on December 1, 1951. Among the many honors which he received during his life was a knighthood, bestowed in 1946.

The anthropology of the peoples of the Pacific has, of course, progressed considerably since the first publication of *Vikings of the Sunrise*. In the light of present knowledge, a few points in the book require comment.

Recent work on both blood groups and morphology indicates that the genetic composition and antecedents of the peoples of Oceania are considerably more complicated than is implied in the brief sketch in Chapter II. The Melanesians, whom Buck contrasts with the Polynesians, seem to be the result of a series of racial strains which migrated out of Asia, and can hardly be classed under the convenient rubric of Negroids, despite the dark color of their skin. Distinctive as the Polynesians are, both they and the peoples of Micronesia also have an ancestry whose complexities have not yet been determined.

The migration route of the Polynesians into their vast island domain likewise is a matter of speculation rather than demonstrated fact. Their food plants (save the sweet potato), language, and much of their culture are clearly of Asiatic origin, but whether these seafarers came by way of Micronesia or entered Oceania along the north coast of New Guinea must remain an open question. However, it can be said that a balanced view of the evidence does not provide substance for Heyerdahl's belief in the origin of the Polynesians in the New World.

Buck's concluding chapter is a quite reasonable alternative to Heyerdahl's views as to the origin of South American culture elements in Polynesia.

In Chapter XXI, one point concerning food plants needs correction. The Micronesian islands, including the larger and wetter atolls, are capable of growing breadfruit and bananas, and Buck's explanation of the introduction of the distinctive Asiatic complex of food plants into Polynesia is redundant. There is every probability that the Polynesians carried their food plants, as well as their domestic animals—pigs, chickens, and dogs—with them from their Asiatic homeland.

Finally, when Buck wrote his book the archaeology of the Pacific islands had barely commenced. The field is still in its infancy, but the archaeological work accomplished since World War II indicates that the Oceanic islands were settled earlier than previously thought and that the time scale of human settlement of the Pacific will be greatly revised in the next few years.

None of the points mentioned above seriously impairs the worth of the book. Let the reader enjoy it and judge for himself.

ALEXANDER SPOEHR
Director
Bishop Museum

PROLOGUE

A REGIONAL survey of Polynesia was undertaken by the Bernice P. Bishop Museum under the guidance of its Director, Professor Herbert E. Gregory. Research work was rendered possible by financial assistance from Bayard Dominick, Yale University, the Rockefeller Foundation, and various generous friends of the Museum in Hawaii. The Museum contributed out of its own funds and adopted the policy of publishing the reports as soon as possible.

The project was so appealing to one of Polynesian blood that I relinquished my position as Director of Maori Hygiene in New Zealand and joined the staff of the Bishop Museum as an ethnologist to aid in the fieldwork. The reports of fieldworkers are of necessity somewhat technical, and, though of the greatest value to science, they do not reach the general reader. This work is an attempt to make known to the general public some of the romance associated with the settlement of Polynesia by a stone-age people who deserve to rank among the world's great navigators.

I have tried to tell the tale from the evidence in Polynesian myths regarding the creation of man and of islands, and in legends and traditions of the great seafaring ancestors and their voyages. Though the story is not intended for critical anthropologists, I have mentioned various customs and usages that I deem of interest to them and to the general reader. I have introduced personal incidents, wherever possible, to give the story a more human atmosphere.

I have drawn freely from the works published by the Museum, and I am greatly indebted to the staff of the Museum for their assistance and above all for their criticism. While it is invidious to select from so many advisers, I must acknowledge my gratitude to Frances E. Williams, editor on the Museum staff. She has among other things corrected my mixed tenses and moods due to writing in English and thinking in Polynesian.

Of Polynesian words and names, I have kept to the spelling of the particular group and used the hamza or inverted comma for consonants that have been dropped, even though the present written language takes no note of them. The inclusion of the glottal in *Hawai'i* shows more clearly its affinity with *Havai'i* in central Polynesia than the present official spelling of *Hawaii*.

I am grateful to Bob Davis of the New York *Sun* for encouraging me to make this presentation of the Polynesian romance to the English-reading public. The *Sun's* man has travelled 1,250,000 miles around the world without reference to the rising or the setting of the sun. He has written nine travel books and his opinion that there was need for a book dealing with old-time travels across the Pacific in the trail of the rising sun has greatly stimulated the production of this work.

I may be criticized for applying the term vikings to the Polynesian ancestors, but the term has come to mean bold, intrepid mariners and so is not the monopoly of the hardy Norsemen of the North Atlantic. To the Polynesians, the sunset symbolized death and the spirit land to which they returned, but the sunrise was the symbol of life, hope, and new lands that awaited discovery. I am hopeful that *Vikings of the Sunrise* will reach my kinsmen in the scattered isles of Polynesia and draw us together in the bond of the spirit. We have new problems before us, but we have a glorious heritage, for we come of the blood that conquered the Pacific with stone-age vessels that sailed ever toward the sunrise.

PETER H. BUCK

Bernice P. Bishop Museum
Honolulu, Hawaii

CONTENTS

THE POLYNESIAN TRIANGLE WITH THE NORTHERN MICRONESIAN

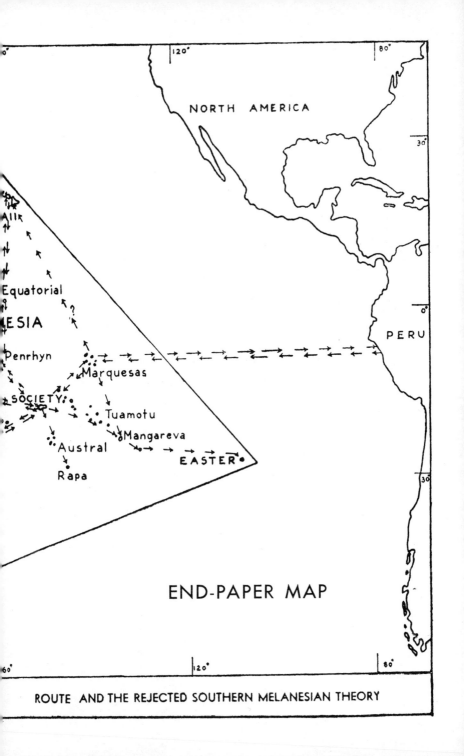

END-PAPER MAP

ROUTE AND THE REJECTED SOUTHERN MELANESIAN THEORY

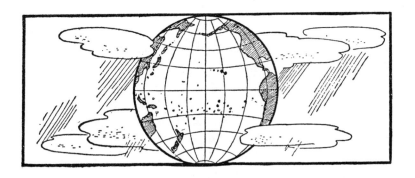

I. THE GREAT OCEAN

The fame of your canoes can never be dimmed
The canoes which crossed the ocean depths,
The purple sea, the Great-Ocean-of-Kiwa,
Which lay stretched before them.

MAORI LAMENT

THE Mediterranean Sea, locked in by land on all sides
like a lake, except for its narrow western opening between
the Pillars of Hercules, was the great sea of the Caucasian
ancients. On the shores of the 'Purple Sea', as Homer called
it, early civilizations rose and fell. The Phœnician sailors
who reached the zenith of seacraft in that area ran no risk
of being lost on wide expanses of angry waters. On their
most daring expeditions they hugged the western coasts of
Spain and France and slipped across the English Channel
to exploit the tin mines of Cornwall. Even if 'once upon
a time' they groped their way around the continent of Africa,
it is doubtful whether that particular Odyssey ever lost
sight of land. They could call in at any time to replenish
food supplies and water and drop anchor near land until
storms passed by. They followed the shoreline and had no
need of consulting the stars above the open seas. In spite
of having metal tools with which to build seagoing ships,
the Phœnicians were coastwise folk.

When history dawned on the shores of the North Sea, it

revealed a hardy race of seamen, who boldly set forth on the cold waters of its upper bounds. The Vikings, with their winged helmets and metal battle-axes, rowed their long ships down the western shoreline of the North Sea to harry the coasts of Britain and Scotland. They took no short cuts through the open sea that lay on their starboard side.

More courageous Vikings sailed out of the narrow seas into the unknown north Atlantic. They discovered and colonized Iceland and Greenland. On a voyage to Greenland, a Viking was driven to the west and reported sighting an island upon which he did not land. Leif Ericsson, a son of Eric the Red, intrigued by the tale of land to the west, sailed forth in 1003 A.D. and reached the eastern coast of North America. He coasted south to some part of what is now New England and named it Vineland. This was a dazzling achievement, and yet the Vikings, with all the courage needed to breed deep-sea sailors, kept to the familiar northern seas and were not lured by the beckoning stars toward the wider expanses of the southern ocean.

The widest part of the Atlantic was eventually crossed by Christopher Columbus in 1492. Europe was attracted by reports of the wealth of the Great Khan and the riches of Cipango and far-away Cathay. The transport of goods by land took too long, and so Columbus, inspired by a superb conviction that the world was round, sought to shorten the time of transport by sailing west across the Atlantic to reach the distant east. He set forth with a letter from Ferdinand and Isabella of Spain to the Great Khan to establish commercial contact between India and Spain. The seamen did not share their leader's theory about the shape of the world, and, as they sailed farther and farther from land, their fears of dropping over the edge of a square world brought them to the verge of mutiny. Only by falsifying his reports of the distances sailed each day could Columbus allay the fears of his crew until the sighting of an island brought timely relief. The island lay off the coast of an undreamed-of continent that had interposed itself between Europe and the India of their search. The name West Indies, applied to the island and others in its vicinity, embodies the record of a wonderful mistake.

Startling and momentous as were the discovery of a vast new continent and the confirmation of Columbus' new theory, the conquest of the seas by Europeans had scarcely begun. Between America and Asia stretched the largest of all oceans, beside which the explorations on other oceans seem puny by comparison. When later Balboa stood 'silent upon a peak in Darien' and gazed on the Pacific with a 'wild surmise', he was justified, for he was the first European to behold the Great Ocean stretching out to infinity from the shores of the new continent. Yet long before Columbus made his great voyage, a stone-age people, in efficient crafts, had crossed the Pacific from continent to continent across its widest part and had colonized every habitable island within its vast interior.

After the discovery of America, the continent was explored, settled, and exploited by Europeans. It gave refuge to those seeking freedom from the oppression of the older countries, and tales of wealth and rich resources lured adventurers, traders, and buccaneers. New lands were developed on the eastern shores of North America in addition to the older gold-seeking colonies in South America. Commerce grew, and the maritime centre of gravity which had swung from the Mediterranean Sea to the North Sea, passed on to the Atlantic Ocean.

Finally European interest and curiosity expanded westward to embrace the Pacific. Belated exploration of the Pacific by European navigators, equipped at least with compass and sextant, opened up new commercial prospects. Spanish, Portuguese, Dutch, Americans, and British, all made their contributions in rediscoveries and imposed their own names on islands already named by the original native discoverers. Great Britain, by colonizing Australia, Tasmania, and New Zealand, supplied the present human boundaries to the south Pacific. Between Australia and Asia, Holland established her rule over a large indigenous population. Great Britain and France extended their influence to the southeast corner of the continent of Asia. Spain, after colonizing the Philippines and Marianas Islands, relinquished her possessions and left the United States to puzzle over a problem. The Asiatic western boundary remained under the power of the original Mongoloid settlers, but Russia crept in on the extreme north. The western coast of South America had been infused by peoples of Spanish stock. The western coast of North America had been peopled by Anglo-Saxons who spread from the Atlantic coast and maintained contact with the eastern seaboard through railways.

Today the shores of the Pacific are peopled by teeming millions beside which the population of Europe dwindles ever into less importance. Increased trade and an ever-increasing population in eastern Asia are causing the centre of world interest to swing from the Atlantic to the Pacific. Small islands in its vast interior, hitherto of no economic interest, have assumed an extraordinary value because of their strategic position with regard to airway transport. Great countries have come to realize that islands in the Pacific can be used as outposts of defence for their huge continental holdings. The Pacific has assumed a vast importance. Let us consider the land boundaries of the Pacific.

The Pacific Ocean is bounded on the west by the continent of Asia and on the southwest by the closely set islands of Indonesia and the large island of New Guinea. South of New Guinea lies the continent of Australia, and southeast of New Guinea stretch the high islands of Melanesia, extending nearly 2000 miles into the Pacific to end in Fiji. Geologists hold that the islands of Indonesia, New Guinea, and Melanesia are continental islands which form a southeastern extension of the ancient land mass of Asia with which they were connected in remote ages. They have had their various ups and downs, and at the dawn of human history they formed a broken Asiatic corridor into the Pacific.

The eastern boundary of the Pacific is formed by the western coast of the two Americas, which stretch in unbroken continuity from Bering Sea to Cape Horn. Bering Strait in the north interposes but thirty-six miles of water between Asia and America. In past geological times, this ocean gap may have been further closed by a land bridge, whose broken-down pillars may be represented by the Diomede Islands. Farther to the south, the Alaska Peninsula, the Aleutian chain of islands, the Komondorski, and the Bering Islands form a series of stepping-stones from Asia to America. Even without these land bridges, the frozen sea in winter could provide a broad pathway for the migrations of early man without any need for a knowledge of seacraft.

After man appeared on this earth of ours, he grew and multiplied. When numbers grew too large for the food supplies of the region originally occupied, groups were forced to venture farther afield. Some groups were forced to move by the surge of hordes behind them; others ventured voluntarily, lured by attractive prospects before them. They hunted for fish, birds, and animals and gathered leaves, fruit, seeds, and roots that they found to be edible. Ever-present hunger stimulated them to invent improved methods of acquiring food. In the course of time, they learned to culti-vate edible food plants and to tame animals. When forced to move onward into unoccupied lands, they took their cultivable food plants and domesticated animals with them.

Early man probably originated somewhere in ancient Asia, and, through causes as yet but dimly understood, developed into different types. These have been grouped into three main divisions: Mongoloid, Negroid, and Europoid (Cau-casian). The Mongoloids peopled the entire eastern coast of Asia, spreading north to cross dry-shod over the narrow northern extremity of the Pacific and colonizing the two Americas from Alaska to Cape Horn. In the age-long wand-erings before the southern outposts were established, they skirted wide rivers and mountain ranges, but ever they travelled on foot to the regions they were destined to occupy. Thus the continental boundaries stretching for thousands of miles on either side of the Great Ocean were peopled primarily by pedestrians of Mongoloid stock.

The Negroids early divided into two branches: the Conti-nental Negroids who moved west and south into Africa, and the Oceanic Negroids who wandered east and were forced by peoples behind them down the Asiatic corridor into the Pacific. Each of the Negroid branches had a pygmy or Negrito branch. The Negrito branch of the Oceanic Neg-roids is held to have been the earliest group to be pushed off the mainland of Asia. They were shoved aside by later waves of people and survive today in the Malay Peninsula, the Andaman Islands, and the mountains of the Philippines and New Guinea.

The next people to move down the Asiatic corridor were the Australian aborigines, who reached New Guinea and crossed to Australia. They belong to Dravidian stock, and their nearest relatives are the Veddas of Ceylon. Their hair is straight or wavy but never frizzy or woolly. In spite of their dark colour, scientific investigation as to their blood grouping proves conclusively that they are not Negroids but that their next of kin are among the races of the north and west of the Mediterranean area. Wood Jones sums up the problem by saying that Australia received its primitive animals such as the monotremes and marsupials when Australia was connected with the Asiatic land masses, but became separated 'before the higher mammals, like cats and deer, and rabbits and monkeys had arrived in southern Asia'. Australia was, therefore, 'an island continent before man or any of his poor relations could avail themselves of land bridges'. The Australian aborigines, with their women and their dogs, must, therefore, have reached Australia by sea, 'not as a castaway, but as the navigator of a seaworthy boat'. The aborigine deserves all honour for his achievement early in the stone age.

Next down the Asiatic corridor came the Oceanic Negroids who, by massing in New Guinea, drove the Negritos into the mountain fastnesses and perhaps completed the evacuation of the Australian aborigines. In response to the urge to seek out new lands, a section of the Negroids moved down along the chain of continental islands now known as Melanesia to the southeast of New Guinea. Those who remained behind are known as the Papuans and those who moved on are designated as Melanesians. Between the high volcanic islands the sea distances are comparatively short and could be crossed by primitive craft without venturing into wide ocean expanses. And so by land and by short voyages, the Melanesian seamen reached Fiji at the eastern end of the broken Asiatic corridor.

The most travelled group of the Negroids are those who by will or accident found their way to the island of Tasmania, south of Australia. The Tasmanians have woolly hair and come of a stock distinct from the Australian aboriginals. The people most like them in physical appearance are the Melanesians of New Caledonia. The evidence is all against the hypothesis that the Tasmanians traversed by foot the entire length of the Australian continent to arrive at Bass Strait which separates Tasmania from Australia. A long sea voyage from New Caledonia to Tasmania seems equally impossible. It appears certain, however, that the Tasmanians must have reached the eastern coast of Australia by some form of craft from a Melanesian island and perhaps by short coastal voyages reached Bass Strait and crossed over to the unoccupied island of Tasmania. They successfully survived the ordeals of the sea, but they were brutally exterminated by the Europoids who came centuries later.

The Europoids migrated from the Asiatic centre westward into Europe, and types exist in India, hither Asia, and northern Africa. Except for the Australian aborigines and the equally puzzling Ainu of Japan, the Europoids apparently had little to do with the early peopling of the Pacific boundaries. Their main hordes had turned their backs on the Orient and arrived at the Occident. Thus East remained East and West became West.

The western and eastern boundaries of the Great Ocean were thus settled by landsmen. The Asiatic corridor was peopled also by landsmen who were coastwise folk. They had neither sufficient push from behind nor the inward urge of the spirit to take to the open sea that lay beyond Fiji. The contention that Melanesians penetrated into the central and eastern Pacific rests on skeletal material to which Melanesian ownership is unproved. The widely-spaced islands between Fiji and South America remained unvisited by man until late in the world's history. They are included in a vast triangular area with its points at Hawai'i in the north, New Zealand in the south, and Easter Island in the east. This area, now known as the Polynesian Triangle, lies with its base to the west inviting entry and its apex far on the path of the rising sun, 2030 miles from South America. The scattered specks of land within the triangle are oceanic islands separated by abysmal depths. Never within the period of human migrations have they been joined together to offer an easy path to footmen.

For untold centuries after the boundaries of the Pacific had been peopled by man, these islands remained isolated and unoccupied save by land shells, insects, reptiles, and birds. Even the native flora was meagre as regards potential food for man. The coconut palm, the banana, and the breadfruit, now so characteristic of the oceanic flora, awaited human transport. The westerly winds and the constant trades blew over empty seas, for no primitive navigator had yet dared to raise a matting sail to waft him to waiting islands. Years after countless years, the Pleiades rose on the eastern horizon, but no man hailed their coming with dance and song as the sign of the new year. The stars rose and travelled across the sky, but no craft groped its way across unknown waters by their aid. The moon waxed and waned, but its phases went unstudied. Fish spawned, increased, and went their unhampered way through reef channels into silent and unlit lagoons. The Ocean Maid in her tumultuous moods vented her wrath against inanimate rock and reef, for no conqueror had yet appeared to mark her heaving bosom with the wake of the voyaging canoe or to dig into her yielding body with the dripping blade of the deep-sea paddle. Pedestrians had reached the eastern bounds of the Asiatic corridor and could walk no farther. The hanging skies to the east of the Fijis remained unpierced. Beyond the eastern horizon, earth, sea, and sky awaited the coming of a breed of men who not only had an effective form of ocean transport but who had the courage to dare and both the will and the skill to conquer. The uncharted seas awaited the coming of the Polynesian navigators.

2 . THE MANNER OF MEN

Waves of the ocean are breasted by the bow of the canoe,
Waves of men are surmounted by human courage.

MAORI PROVERB

WHAT manner of men were they who, by surpassing the achievements of the Phœnicians in the Mediterranean and the Vikings of the north Atlantic, are worthy of being called the supreme navigators of history?

The tourist's opinion as to race distinction, based so often on personal prejudices, is of little worth. It is only fair to human beings that they should be studied with the same courtesy that is extended to plants, insects, fish, birds, and lower mammals. What would we think of an alleged botanist who stated that a plant was a new species of a particular genus without publishing a careful description of the plant and giving his reasons for assigning it to its place in the plant kingdom? Yet a statement has been made in an official Government handbook that the Samoans are the purest branch of the Polynesians. Those who realize the amount of careful work that must be done cannot but be astounded at the confidence of lay statements which apparently issue from some form of popular inspiration that requires no proof. No statement as to the manner of men can be accepted by intelligent people unless it is based upon a sufficiently large number of measurements of the physical characters of the human body and careful observations as to the form of hair, eyes, nose, skin colour, and other general features.

Much importance has been attached to what has been termed the cephalic index. This index is merely the ratio of the greatest breadth of the head from side to side to the greatest length from before back. If the breadth is 75 per cent of the length or less, the head is proportionally long. If it is 80 per cent and more, it is proportionally short or, what is the same thing, broad. People are thus classified as long headed (dolichocephalic) and short or broad headed (brachycephalic). The heads between 75 and 80 per cent fall into a kind of no man's land that can be exploited from either trench. The classifications are established from exact measurements made by trained observers with special instruments designed for the purpose. The same need for meticulous accuracy applies to the measurements of the nose, face, and other parts of the human body. Among any group of people there is a wide range, and it is necessary to measure a sufficiently large number of individuals to correct individual abnormalities. The opinions of untrained men without a scientific technique are worthless. There is only one way by which we can arrive at an understanding of the physical characters of a people and that is by measurements, measurements, and yet more measurements.

Human beings, as the result of innumerable measurements and careful observations by trained scientists, may be divided into the three main divisions already mentioned: Negroids, Mongoloids, and Europoids. Without going into tiresome details, let us take a few outstanding characters that distinguish the three divisions. The Negroid is characterized by a long head, woolly hair, black skin, short wide nose with a depressed bridge, and thin calves. The Mongoloid has a short head, straight, wiry black hair, flat face, and above all the Mongoloid fold formed by extra tissue pushing down the skin of the upper eyelid at its inner angle and so covering the little red gland that is responsible for the secretion of tears. The Europoids, formerly termed Caucasians, seem to serve as a convenient category into which are cast those who cannot be classified as Negroids or Mongoloids. In head form they range from long to short, in stature from tall to short, and in complexion from blonde to brunette. They are best distinguished by what they have not. They have not the woolly hair and broad nose of the Negroid nor the flat face and drooping inner eyefold of the Mongoloid.

Until recent years our knowledge of the racial character-istics of the Polynesians was extremely scanty. Students had to rely on the comparatively few skulls that had been secretly filched from burial places and had found their way into modern mausoleums provided by museums. Professor J. H. Scott wrote a paper in 1893 on New Zealand and Chatham Island skeletal material compiled from his collection in the Otago Medical School. I remember well when a fellow Maori student and I first entered the taboo precincts of the Medical School and saw at the top of the stairs a notice offering various prices for Maori skulls, pelves, and complete skeletons. We read it with horror and almost abandoned our quest for western medical knowledge.

After acquiring a knowledge of human anatomy, however, I determined to contribute to the material on Polynesian somatology by measuring the heads of a number of my living countrymen. Six years as a member of Parliament and four years' service as medical officer with New Zealand troops during the Great War temporarily distracted me. With the end of the war and my appointment as one of two medical officers to the troop ship which was to bring the Maori Pioneer Battalion back to their homeland, I at last had a unique opportunity for measuring a number of Polynesian heads. After great difficulty, I acquired a Flower's craniometer, and on the voyage out to New Zealand I measured the heads of 424 full-blooded Maoris.

Bishop Museum of Honolulu, Hawai'i, was the first scientific institution to study the problem of measuring living Polynesians on a comprehensive scale. For its programme of research work on the native people of Polynesia, commenced in 1920 through the Bayard Dominick fund and aided later by the Rockefeller Foundation and local patrons, the field workers were equipped with instruments and cards and worked out a uniform method of procedure. The cards returned by expeditions were collated by Dr. Louis Sullivan and after his death in 1925 by Dr. H. L. Shapiro. The studies compiled up to date, including my Maori material, have been based on the measurements of 2500 living people from representative parts of Polynesia. Additional measurements have been made, but the results have not yet been published.

The taking of measurements in the field is rather difficult for the student specializing in some other branch of the study of man, such as functionalism. People have to be brought together and their interest maintained during the long monotonous process of recording data and measuring. Individuals with a very dark skin or an unusually broad nose are susceptible to the witticisms of the waiting audience. Interest in a strange technique wanes, and those who have satisfied their curiosity but have not been measured are apt to go off fishing. On the island of Mangaia in the Cook group, where I temporarily occupied the position of magistrate, I was able to mobilize the inhabitants by means of native police and to measure them in the courthouse. The measurements taken at that time illustrate how great may be individual variation of cephalic index within a culturally homogenous group. The Mangaians measured in the courthouse all had long heads with narrow breadth averaging 156 millimetres, whereas on the nearby island of Atiu in the same group the natives previously measured had very broad heads, some of them over 160 millimetres. My wife filled in the cards as to name, age, sex, place of birth, and parentage, and I took no auditory notice of these preliminaries. Having become accustomed to the narrow breadths, I was astonished when my calipers were extended to 163 millimetres by the head breadth of an individual, and I said, 'According to the breadth of your head you ought to be an Atiuan.' 'I am', he replied.

As a result of the studies made on the living in all parts of Polynesia, it is evident that the master mariners of the Pacific must be Europoid for they are not characterized by the woolly hair, black skins, and thin lower legs of the Negroids nor by the flat face, short stature, and drooping inner eyefold of the Mongoloids. Like other Europoids, the Polynesians show a wide range of variation in head form. Shapiro has pointed out remarkable homogeneity in certain characters that result in a relatively narrow and high forehead with a wide face. In general, however, there is a preponderance of short heads in central Polynesia, in Hawai'i, and to some extent in Samoa and Tonga; and an extreme of long heads in New Zealand, which becomes modified in Mangaia and the atolls of Manihiki and Rakahanga in the Cook Islands, appears in the Marquesas, eastern Tuamotus, Mangareva, and becomes extreme in the eastern outpost of

Easter Island. The tendency in the past has been to attribute the long heads to intermixture with the Negroid population of Melanesia and the short heads to intercourse with the Mongoloids of Indonesia. However, it is unlikely that head form alone should be affected by intermixture and that other physical characters should remain unchanged. If the New Zealanders have a Negroid strain, they should have woollier hair and wider noses than their Mongoloid-infected cousins in central Polynesia, yet the Maoris have the narrowest noses in Polynesia! The long-headed element among the present Polynesians have been regarded as proof that a group of Melanesians preceded the Polynesian voyagers and settled the far-flung islands of the Pacific as far as Easter Island, where long heads are dominant. This simple belief is based on unthatched skulls and is unsupported by any further physical or cultural evidence.

A. C. Haddon states that an analysis of the mixed population of Indonesia indicates that certain long-headed elements occur in a vast setting of Mongoloid short heads. This long-headed element as represented by the Battas and Dyaks has been conveniently termed Indonesian. The Indonesians probably originated along the lower valley of the Ganges and moved eastward into Indonesia centuries after the migration of the Australian aborigine. The short-headed Mongoloids probably migrated south at a still later period and dominated the Indonesians by force of numbers. The resultant intermixture between the long-headed Indonesians and the short-headed Mongoloids was supposed to produce theProto-Polynesians or the ancestors of the seafarers of the Pacific.

That this intermixture took place with invading hordes of Mongoloids in Indonesia may be admitted. It may even be possible that a Mongoloid vanguard followed the Polynesians into Micronesia, but the physical traces are surprisingly few. That intermixture took place between the Melanesians and Polynesians may also be admitted, but it appears that this mixture was due to a later westward movement of Polynesians from Tonga and Samoa rather than to contact with Melanesians by the original Polynesian migrants on their way through Melanesian islands.

The significance of head form may be left to the specialists to decide, when the measurements of the entire area come to be analyzed. Both long and short heads may have been inherited from a varied Europoid ancestry. Sufficient for the day is the fact that a tall, athletic people without woolly hair or a Mongoloid eyefold had the ability and courage to penetrate into the hitherto untraversed seaways of the central and eastern Pacific.

3 · WHENCE CAME THEY?

We came from Hawaiki-the-Great
From Hawaiki-the-Long, from Hawaiki-the-Distant.

MAORI LEGEND

HAWAIKI is a symbol of the distant home whence came the ancestors of the first discoverers of the heart of the Pacific. The peoples on the western base of the Polynesian triangle at Samoa and Tonga speak of Pulotu as the land to which the soul of man returns 'along the slippery path, the sliding path of death'. Most of those who penetrated farther into the triangle cherish the memory of a homeland in distant Hawaiki. From Hawaiki, their ancestors set out on the trail of the rising sun, and to Hawaiki the souls of their dead return along the golden train cast on the ocean by the dying rays of the setting sun. It is as it should be; the morning sun for youth and adventure, the setting sun for age and rest.

Whither the souls of our ancestors arrived we may not know, for the Maori poet says, 'They have passed along the path that beckons the thousands, the path that calls the myriads, the path that sends no messenger to the rear.' On almost every island from Samoa to Easter, from Hawai‘i to New Zealand, there is a traditional departing-place-of-spirits, from which the human soul sets out on its return journey to the west. There is no recorded instance of the Polynesian myth-makers forcing the tired soul to continue exploration to the east. They conceded the spirit homing instincts and allowed it to return to a western homeland.

Such an indefinite idea of a land of origin does not satisfy those of another culture who have studied us. From a wider horizon of comparative study, they can interpret our language, myths, traditions, genealogies, and historical narratives in a manner that is impossible to a native people embedded in the isolation created by lack of written records. How could we know that our word *ra* for the sun, by coinciding with *ra* in Ammon Ra, the Egyptian sun god, could be accepted as evidence that we came from Egypt? A Maori reference to dwelling in the Land of Uru has been interpreted as pointing to a sojourn in Ur of the Chaldees in Mesopotamia. Perhaps it is beside the point to remark that Uru in the dialect of the tale merely means west. The occurrence of names similar to Polynesian for a district named Ora and a port named Mana in the ancient kingdom of Irania has been suggested as proof that we once dwelt in Baluchistan. A tradition of living in Irihia has moved us a stage farther east into Vrihia, an ancient name for a part of India. A Rarotongan legend states that an ancestor named Tu-te-rangi-marama dwelt in the land of Atia-te-varinga-nui which means Atia-where-*vari*-was-abundant. In Rarotonga, the word *vari* means mud, but a connection has been seen between *vari* and the south Indian word *padi* meaning rice. It has thus been thought that the Polynesian ancestors lived in a land where rice was grown in mud and that after they had left the rice lands behind them, they applied the word *vari* to the mud of taro swamps. Percy Smith, founder of the Polynesian Society, believed that Atia was located in the basin of the Ganges. Perhaps the location is right, but the name Atia looks suspiciously like a Polynesian form of Asia. And so by isolated words and place names students have tried to prove that we travelled from the Land of the Pharaohs to India en route to the shores of the Pacific.

Another approach to elucidating the past has been the interpretation of Polynesian genealogies. Probably no people have been prouder of their lineages than the mariners of the Pacific. In Polynesian mythology, the god Tane moulded the first woman out of earth, brought her to life by magic power, and made her the mother of the first human being. The descendants of this first union thus partook of divine attributes by direct physiological inheritance. This may appear irrational to scientists who claim descent from anthropoid apes, but it gave great confidence to chiefly leaders, who in moments of stress could call upon their divine ancestors for assistance whereas western man may expect little help from his remote arboreal progenitors. Faith in the Divine breeds confidence and dissipates fear, which after all is what man needs when facing the unknown. The European applied his faith to guiding him into a safe haven in the journey after death, but the Polynesian applied his faith to inspire confidence in this life to voyage into unknown seas.

The oral transmission and memorizing of genealogies was a routine part of the Polynesian system of education. Succession to chieftainship rested on priority of birth in the senior male line, which was closer to the famous ancestors, the culture heroes, and the gods themselves than were the junior lines. The relationship terms which grouped parents, uncles and aunts, and senior cousins under a similar term were meant to bind people together in a unity of co-operation and blood kinship. The finer degrees of Physiological relationship were distinguished by a knowledge of genealogies.

Thus kinship terms and genealogies form one inseparable unit in the structure of Polynesian society. Even the commoner could trace his lineage and family connections for generations with a certainty which a family of position in western society might envy. The chiefs and priests could trace their ancestry back to the gods. The experts took pride in reciting lineages before public gatherings, and the audience admired such demonstrations of classical knowledge. In New Zealand, the expert sometimes demonstrated with a beautifully carved, notched stick, touching the successive knobs as he recited the ancestors in chronological sequence. In the Marquesas, a knotted braid of coconut fibre was used in a similar manner, each knot representing an ancestor. Usually the fingers of the outstretched hand were ticked off as each ancestor's name was spoken.

The recital of genealogies was an established technique in social life and served as a chronology of historical events associated with the sequence of ancestors. How far back this sequence may be relied upon depends not only on the limitations of human memory but also on the interruptions that may have occurred to direct and orderly transmission of titles. Most islands have their own genealogies covering the period from the present back approximately five hundred years to the arrival of the colonizing ancestors who took up their permanent abode on the island. Beyond this settlement period is the migrational period of indefinite length during which remote progenitors felt their way from island to island, exploring the unknown spaces of the sea. The names of these ancestors, who dwelt in land designated as Hawaiki, Tahiti, Vavau, 'Uporu, Manuka, Iva, and numerous others, are common to the genealogies of such widely spread groups as New Zealand, Cook, Society, Tuamotu, Austral, Marquesas, Gambier, and Hawai'i, and indicate a common ancestry within historic time for all Polynesian peoples.

Beyond the period of heroic ancestors and their voyages, the genealogies take us into the realm of sheer myth. The lineage of heroes and demigods link up with the gods. The gods themselves carry back the genealogies in ordered sequence to various natural phenomena that were personified as if they were actual human ancestors. Thus we have the Void, Abyss, Night, Gloom, Dawn, Light, Thought, Conception, and various other ideas recited as a genealogy, not because the learned men really thought that they were human ancestors, but because the genealogical recital was the literary technique for recording not only historical events but also the order in which nature presumably came into being.

Genealogies, after they pass the settlement period and the latter part of the migrational period, cannot be relied upon for the exact or even approximate times at which the Polynesian ancestors occupied various mainlands and island groups in their voyages from Asia to the scattered islands of Polynesia. Even within the settlement period all manner of contradictions occur. Rarotongan genealogies state that the ancestor, Tangiia, who was the last ancestor to arrive at Rarotonga, landed on the island twenty-six generations back from 1900. Accepting twenty-five years as the average span of a generation, Tangiia must have arrived about 1250 A.D. Genealogies of the neighbouring island of Mangaia state that the sons of the god Rongo occupied that island for the first time seventeen generations back from 1900, thereby placing the origin of man on Mangaia two hundred and twenty-five years after the last settlement in nearby Rarotonga. Thus it is evident that when human memory failed, the gods crossed the forgotten years and came closer to the sons of men.

The longer genealogies have been studied by European scholars, whose faith in these feats of memory has led them to overlook certain flaws which exist in the alleged human sequences. In some, the names of various lands at which the ancestors sojourned have been included, perhaps accidentally, as human beings. Various qualifying terms, as long, short, large, small, have been added in a sequence to the same name, but each is treated as a generation. The method is a convenient technique for lengthening a lineage. In others again, personifications of natural phenomena that belong to a mythical period have been interpolated into the human succession. Individuals have falsified records in order to give prestige to families newly risen to power or to hide the bar sinister that somehow cannot be avoided in long descent. The Hawaiian historian, David Malo, truly said that the expert genealogist was the wash-bowl of the high chief. It may be difficult for people who learn by eye from the printed page to fully appreciate the great feats of memory accomplished by people who could learn only by ear. Yet even for a people so intellectually endowed as the Polynesians, there must be some admission of the limitations of human memory.

The Rarotongan genealogies go back for ninety-two generations to the ancestor Tu-te-rangi-marama who dwelt in a land that Percy Smith believed to be India. The arbitrary estimate of twenty-five years to a generation places him at about 450 B.C. The period of time covered by ninety-two generations is 2300 years, and the distance in space is from India to Rarotonga in the Cook Islands. It is possible that any group of people subjected to the accidents of flood and field and war for over 2000 years of time and over many thousands of miles of land and sea could keep from generation to generation an accurate record of human succession by memory alone? With all my love for my mother's stock, my father's unbelieving blood gives me pause.

We may sum up the present position by saying that in remote ages the ancestors of the Polynesian people probably did live in some part of India and worked east, but myths and legends transmitted orally do not reach back that far. They must have sojourned in Indonesia in order to reach the Pacific; the Polynesian language has affinities with Indonesian dialects. During their stay in Indonesia, the sea salt entered into their blood and changed them from landsmen to seamen. When the pressure of Mongoloid peoples pouring in from the mainland became oppressive, the Polynesian ancestors turned their gaze toward the eastern horizon and embarked upon one of the greatest of all adventures.

4. SHIPS AND THEIR BUILDERS

Thread it from inside, it goes outside,
Thread it from outside, it comes inside.
Tie it firmly, bind it fast

THE SHIPBUILDER'S SONG

WHEN the ancestors of the Polynesians slipped off the mainland and began to venture eastward from island to island,
they evolved of necessity an oceanic culture. They learned
to extend their fishing operations farther and farther from
the coast, and as their horizon lengthened, their fishing
canoes evolved into ships capable of transporting explorers
and their families over hundreds of miles of open sea. In the
realm of mechanical achievement, the construction of the
voyaging canoe was the material counterpart of the mental
and spiritual development of a sea-minded people who were
stimulated by the drive of adventure that knew no fear.

No knowledge is extant of the type of ships used in the
early stages of the eastward movement. It may be taken for
granted, however, that the vessels used in Polynesia were
constructed in principle on early models that had been found
to be effective. The Polynesian vessels were of two types,
the outrigger canoe and the double canoe. We have to skip
space and time to obtain in Polynesia itself some idea of the
ships and their builders.

At first sight the dugout canoe, steadied by an outrigger float, seems a simple affair. But when one considers that the tree must be felled, cut into lengths, shaped on the outside, and hollowed on the inside with adzes made of stone, the making of the simplest canoe commands respect. The tree trunks used for small fishing canoes were so narrow that the tendency to capsize had to be counteracted by the addition of an outrigger to the hull. This consisted of a long spar of light wood, which rested on the surface of the water at a little distance from the hull. It was connected to the hull usually by two cross booms which were lashed to both gunwales (top edge of hull) at one end and to the outrigger float at the other. In order that the float might lie at water level, the booms had either to be bent down to meet the float or, if they remained straight, to be attached to the float by separate wooden connectives. Much variation and ingenuity has been shown throughout Polynesia in the methods of outrigger attachment.

Canoes that went far out to sea in quest of bonito and deep-sea fish were given greater protection from overlapping waves by adding a plank to the top of the dugout hull, which increased the freeboard or height from the water's surface. For the transport of people with food and water supplies, larger vessels were made and still greater freeboard given by additional tiers of planks. For long voyages or the inter-island transport of troops, a second canoe was substituted for the float, and thus was formed the double canoe used by the Polynesians in their conquest of the Pacific.

The small dugout fishing canoes were needed by every family for procuring their food supples from mother ocean. These could be dubbed out and shaped by unskilled labour, but the planks for the larger canoes had to be split, shaped, fitted, and lashed with meticulous care and expert knowledge that only the skilled artisan could supply. Once a Samoan expert carpenter was enumerating to me the various types of Samoan canoes. He omitted the ordinary dugout termed *paopao*. 'You have left out the *paopao*', I said. He gave me a withering look as he replied, 'Is the *paopao* a canoe?'

Gradually, as our ancestors spread eastward from the large islands and narrow seaways of Indonesia into the wide ocean, they developed skill and experience in building and sailing ships. By the time they reached the central Pacific, ship-building had become vital to the culture, and the expert builders had assumed a high rank in society. In Samoa and Tonga the canoe builders were under the patronage of the god Tangaroa, the first builder of canoes and houses. In central Polynesia the builders took the god Tane as their tutelary deity. They had their own religious gathering places or *maraes* where they went through an organized ritual before undertaking a difficult task, such as the building of a voyaging canoe. When we consider their stone tools and the work before them, we must admit that they had need of all the assistance they could obtain from the unseen sources.

The psychology of the old-time craftsmen may be read between the lines of Teuira Henry's account of shipbuilding in Tahiti. When a chief contemplated a voyage for which a new canoe must be built, he commanded his subjects to plant extra food crops to feed the craftsmen he should employ and to make bark cloth, to plait mats, and to collect red feathers to be used as payment gifts. After a sufficient supply of provisions had been laid in, the chief engaged one or more master craftsmen to take charge of the work. With them he went into the forest to select trees suitable for making the various parts of the canoe. If the required tree was not found in the woods owned by the chief and his tribal group, search was made in neighbouring territory. The suitable trees from the lands of other chiefs had to be obtained by diplomatic advances and the transaction sealed by appropriate gift payments. I use the term gift payment advisedly because the Polynesian approach to business matters was indirect. A chief sent a gift of food and property to a brother chief. If it was accepted, the receiver was under obligation to grant the request for a tree later made by the sender of the gift. If he refused, he lost prestige, not only in the eyes of neighbouring tribes but also among his own people. With but rare exceptions, the Polynesian chiefs went down, if they had to, with the flag of honour lashed to the mast.

After these preliminaries, the builders took charge. Each workman had his own kit of tools consisting of carefully chipped and finely ground adzes and chisels made of basaltic rock. These were variously shaped for special uses and were lashed to short wooden handles by coconut fibre or sennit braid. The diversity and complexity of lashing designs shows the tremendous pride of the workman in his tools. On the last night of the moon the craftsmen took their adzes to the temple of their tutelary god and carefully 'put them to sleep' for the night in a special recess. At the same time, they offered up an invocation to Tane:

> Place the adze in the sacred place
> To be charged with divine power,
> To become light in the worker's hands
> And accomplish work amid flying sparks.

A feast confined to the skilled workers followed on the temple ground. A fatted pig was killed, and, as it was prepared for the oven, tufts of hair were plucked off as an offering to Tane while the craftsmen recited their motto:

> Work with alert eyes
> And swift-moving adzes.

Thus Tane received the first part of the pig. The pig was roasted whole and when it was cut up the tail was set aside for Tane. Thus Tane received the last part of the pig. These offerings were laid upon his shrine. The tutelary deity of the craft having received due recognition, his devotees could feast in the firm conviction that they would receive divine strength for the impending work.

At early dawn the still-sleeping adzes were awakened by being dipped in the sea, the element upon which their completed work was to float. As the cold water met the working edges of the adzes, the exhortation rang out,

> Awake to work for Tane,
> Great god of the artisans.

Before sunrise the artisans girded on their working loincloths and with adzes charged with the same divine spirit as themselves, they sought out the trees already selected. Tane was the god of the forests, and the trees were his children. Before laying adze to trunk, an invocation had to be offered up to Tane to placate him for the taking of his child. Some trees were the property of other gods, and the specific god had to be asked ritually for his consent to take the tree.

All Polynesia knows the tale of Rata, who felled a tree without asking permission. After lopping off the branches and peeling off the bark, he retired for the night. On returning the next day, he found the tree standing erect with no trace of human interference. Though mystified, he felled it again but hid himself near by. Then came the elves and wood fairies, the henchman of the divine owner of the tree. They surrounded the fallen giant of the forest and in mournful voices sang in unison:

> Fly hither, fly thither,
> O chips of my tree!
> Branches, take up your places,
> Watery sap, flow upwards,
> Adhesive gum, repair and heal!
> Stand! The tree stands erect!

Before Rata's startled eyes, the leaves, chips, and branches came together with orderly precision, the trunk rose on its healed stump, and the tree top soared once more above its leafy neighbours. When Rata, unable to restrain his anger at once more having his labour brought to nought, rushed out and upbraided the fairies, he was told fearlessly that he had no right to fell private property without obtaining permission from the divine owner. Rata admitted his fault, and the supernatural beings who had been arrayed against him came to his assistance. The fairies made a wonderful voyaging canoe over night, dedicated it in a shower of rain, and, sliding it down the arch of a rainbow, launched it in the lagoon before his house.

The trees were felled in the valleys and uplands, and the labour involved in lowering and hauling the trimmed trunks to the carpenter's shed was lightened by singing and chanting. The various timbers were split and shaped to form the keel and planks of the hull and decks. As the 'fast-flying adzes' of the craftsmen became hot and brittle through friction, the blades were driven into juicy banana trunks to cool off. Ever and anon, the adzes were sharpened on sandstone blocks. The planks of the hull were fitted edge to edge, carvel-built, wet mud having been smeared over the top edge of the lower plank. Misfits, indicated by mud spots on the upper plank, were trimmed down until the two edges fitted perfectly. Beaten coconut husk and breadfruit gum were used as caulking along the seams. Paired holes were bored near the edges of adjoining planks with *terebra* shells, pointed hardwood sticks, or stone chisels. Through these holes was passed the lashing of three-ply coconut husk-fibre which held together the parts of the canoe. Like the planks which it joined, this sennit braid was regarded as a symbol of Tane.

Two experts worked on each side as the canoe was built up symmetrically from the keel. In the building of the famous *Hohoio* of Hiro, the great Tahitian navigator, the chief craftsman was Hutu, who worked on the outer side on the right of the canoe, while his assistant Tau-mariari worked on the inside. Memeru, the royal craftsman from Opoa, worked on the outer side on the left, his assistant Ma'i-hae on the inner side. As they passed the braid through to each other to lash the planks, they chanted:

> What have I, O Tane,
> Tane, god of beauty!
> 'Tis sennit.
> 'Tis sennit from the host of heaven,
> 'Tis sennit of thine, O Tane!
> Thread it from the inside, it comes outside.
> Thread it from the outside, it goes inside.
> Tie it firmly, bind it fast.

This chant, as translated by Teuira Henry, describes the function of the sennit as holding the canoe together in order that 'it may go over short waves and long waves to reach near horizons and far-off horizons'. The canoe itself is referred to as Tane's canoe, which is not only complimentary but enlists the god into protecting his property. The importance of the sennit lashings is again stressed in the final words:

> This sennit of thine, O Tane,
> Make it hold, make it hold.

When all the planks were in position, the hull was washed out with fresh water, dried, and painted both outside and inside with a mixture of red earth and charcoal. For very large canoes the roof of the builder's shed had to be removed to make room for the addition of the outrigger booms, deck, bow and stern ornaments, and the deck-house. The lashing of the outrigger booms was an important event, and here again the chant calls in the aid of Tane to strengthen the lashings:

> It cannot weaken,
> It cannot loosen,
> When bound with sacred sennit.
> With thy sacred sennit, O Tane.

The completed canoe was given its own personal name and was usually dedicated to Tane. The launching of a large canoe was more important than the launching of an ocean liner or a warship from a European or American ship-building yard today. In the West, a few selected guests quietly view the event. In Polynesia, the entire population of the district took part. They prepared various foods for a feast to celebrate the occasion; and, garlanded with flowers and sweet-smelling herbs and clothed in their best garments and ornaments, they gathered on the beach to marvel at the launching of a mighty craft. Skids of rounded wood were placed under the keel and on the track to the water's edge. As the props were removed, men holding the sides began to urge the ship along the skids. The chief artisan invoked the aid of numerous gods who assisted the human efforts in impelling the vessel over the skids until, amidst the deafening shouts of the people, it slid into the lagoon and poised grace-fully upon the waves that rose to salute it. Even the western custom of christening a ship by wetting the bow with champagne suffers by comparison with the Polynesian ceremony of making the new canoe drink sea water (*inu tai*). The great ocean is metaphorically alluded to as the altar of the gods. Upon this immense altar the ship was rocked up and down until waves poured alternately over the bow and stern. When a sufficient quantity had been thus introduced into the hold, the new bailers, especially made for the ship, were plied quickly in the ejection of the water and so made acquainted with their future function. By the drinking of sea water the ship was consecrated to Tane, and, above all, it received its full introduction to the element which it had been designed to conquer.

The ship was equipped with mast, sails, paddles, bailers, and stone anchors. Some vessels had as many as three masts. The sails were made of plaited pandanus mats sewn together in triangular form with wooden yards and booms to strengthen the long sides of the triangle. They were rigged as spritsails with the apex at the base of the mast or as lateens with the yard slung from the mast and the apex forward at the bow. Just as the long ships of the Vikings of the Atlantic were equipped with oars, so were the voyaging canoes of the mariners of the Pacific fitted with paddles. The oars had the advantage of leverage against a rowlock, but had the disadvantage of forcing the rowers to turn their faces toward the wake that lay behind. Polynesian paddlers faced forward toward impending waves and ever-receding horizons, and they gazed open-eyed on the ocean vistas that unrolled before them.

Much has been written about drifts to leeward because of the drag of the outrigger float, but the counteracting effect of the deep-sea paddle has not been sufficiently taken into account. The steering paddle took the place of the rudder, and its importance was so recognized that it was given a

personal name. Polynesian legends give not only the name
of voyaging canoes but also those of the navigator and the
steering paddle he used. Maori legends mention the canoes
of the gods themselves, and invariably they give the name
of the steering paddle. The god Rehua, who dwelt in the
tenth heaven, is thus recorded in an ancient song:

> To hoe o Rehua
> Ko Rapaparapa-te-uira.

> The paddle of Rehua
> Was the Flashing-of-Lightning.

In spite of the caulking, canoes leaked so much that men
were appointed to bail out the hold as part of the ship's
routine. The bailer, in important ships, received a personal
name; Rehua's bailer was named Whakawaha-taupata. Stone
anchors with holes drilled through to take the rope were
carried on long sea voyages. During storms, a bow anchor
was dropped overboard to keep the canoes head-on to the
seas. Light anchors were also dropped to indicate the run
of currents. The anchors of important canoes had personal
names. The Arawa canoe, which sailed down to New Zealand in 1350 A.D., had two stone anchors named Toka-
parore and Tu-te-rangi-haruru.

The actual details of the construction of the various Polynesian craft have been recorded by James Hornell. In this
work I am more concerned with the mental and emotional
attitude of the Polynesians toward their ships. Their attitude
even transcends the mental and emotional and becomes
spiritual. Knowing that the timber, the tools, and the lashing
material were associated with a tutelary deity, we may dimly
envisage the dynamic force that inspired the Polynesians in
their long sea voyages, both of discovery and settlement.

In Tahiti, the god Tane was represented at one historical period by a piece of finely plaited sennit. When he was forsaken for the god 'Oro, a priest of Tane placed the symbol of his god in a coconut shell, sealed the opening, and set the vessel adrift on the wide ocean to find another home. Later he followed by canoe to seek whither his god had voyaged. Finally, on the island of Mangaia, he caught the coconut shell in a scoop-net while fishing in the lagoon. As he removed the stopper, the god, as represented by the finely braided sennit, made a chirping noise (*kio*); and the god, re-established in another land, received the name of Tane-kio. In Mangaia, the god of the artisans was Tane-mata-ariki, Tane-of-the-regal-face. He was represented by beautifully ground basaltic adzes lashed with fine sennit braid in a complicated pattern to a well-carved wooden haft. Thus stone, sennit, and wood, the fundamental materials of the craftsmen, were combined to form a symbol worthy of the deity whose divine assistance inspired the builders in their craft. The wood of Tane, shaped with adzes charged with divinity and lashed together with sacred sennit, formed a vessel endowed with spiritual power. On the canoe itself an altar to Tane was constructed, and by ritual and offerings his daily aid was assured. With such divine backing, the crew had firm confidence in facing unknown horizons. Polynesian seamen were unhampered by the mutinous fears that obsessed the crews of Columbus and later European navigators. If ships and men were lost, other navigators did not blame the gods or the sea. The lost navigator was entirely to blame for not interpreting correctly the weather signs or for overlooking some ritual observance. Later navigators followed to accomplish what others had failed to do. Faith in their gods and their ships and confidence in themselves led the Polynesians to discover and settle the Pacific.

Though double canoes held more men, provisions, and water, it is evident from traditional stories that outrigger canoes were also used on long voyages. The *Hohoio* on which Hiro made his last voyage is described as having a float (*ama*) of *tamanu* wood soaked in sea water to destroy borers, and then scraped with coral rubbers. The outrigger canoe, by affording less friction in the water, was faster; and with the wind on the outrigger side, the canoe was allowed to keel over so that she sailed with the outrigger float out of the water. Men watched with alert eyes, and if the float rose too high, they clambered out on the outrigger booms to press the float down and so prevent capsizing. Once, when I was sailing on a whaleboat in the spacious lagoon of Aitutaki in the Cook Islands, a small outrigger canoe flew past us with the outrigger float high above water and with the owner shouting exultantly at the speed of his craft. He would slow down to allow us to pass and then repeat the performance. Suddenly silence fell upon the lagoon, and, looking back, we saw a capsized canoe. The outrigger float had been allowed to rise too high. In a European community we should have gone back to render aid, but here everybody laughed heartily, and we went on. The owner had merely to stand on the outrigger float, press it down to beyond the perpendicular with a forward kick of both feet, and the hull turned right side up. In a light canoe, a few jerks back and forth emptied the water over the bow and stern, the canoe man climbed in, splashed the remaining water over the sides with the blade of his paddle, and went his way with no hurt save to his dignity. The Polynesians were amphibious and so suffered little damage from capsizing.

When Nuku sailed from Tahiti to New Zealand to fight

Manaia, he had two double canoes and one outrigger canoe. After a voyage of over 2000 miles upon an affair of honour, he finally sighted Manaia's double canoe sailing along the coast, and he gave pursuit. The outrigger canoe, acting as a fast cruiser, came up on the seaward side and forced Manaia's canoe in toward the shore while the double canoes, like battleships, lumbered up behind. Finally Manaia was forced ashore, and the battle was waged on land. After a desperate battle, peace was made between the two valiant warriors. Nuku decided to return to Tahiti, but, as the season was late, he converted his double canoes into outrigger canoes in order to make a speedier voyage.

Though the long sea voyages ceased centuries ago, a rough idea of the size of the ships may be formed from the vessels recorded by early European explorers. Various accounts indicate a general length of from sixty to eighty feet, but vessels were seen that measured a hundred feet and even more. In a sacred grove of trees on the shores of Kawhia Harbour in New Zealand there is a bare patch where legend states that the famous Tainui canoe, after its historic voyage from central Polynesia in 1350 A.D., was hauled up to rest below the shrine of Ahurei. Here it crumbled to dust, but no plants grew upon the soil that had been rendered sacred. Two stone uprights mark the spots where the bow and stern rested, and these give the canoe a length of seventy feet.

Two hulls of seventy to eighty feet with a deck between were capable of accommodating a fair number of people. Some of the war canoes of Tahiti, when setting out on a raid, held as many as a hundred warriors. On voyages for settlement, in which provisions, plants, seed, tubers, pigs, dogs, and fowl were carried in addition to women and children, the large double canoes could readily accommodate sixty or more passengers. Such a number was quite sufficient to form a nucleus to populate an island, but we know from the traditions of various island groups that the sources of population were not restricted to one voyaging ship.

The sea provisions for the voyage were usually cooked. In atoll areas, the reserve food consisted of ripe pandanus fruit grated into a coarse flour, cooked, dried, and packed in cylindrical bundles with an outer wrapping of dried pandanus leaves. Such packages are still made in the Gilbert and Marshall atolls. Beechey found that some Tuamotuan castaways, who had been blown to the east, had prepared dried pandanus flour and dried fish to provision their canoe ere setting out on their search for home. From volcanic islands, there were greater possibilities. The Samoans told me that preserved breadfruit cooked in fairly large baskets was used on the voyages. The Maoris state that sweet potatoes, cooked and dried, formed the main sustenance at sea. Dried shell fish such as the *tridacna* kept indefinitely. Fowls carried on the voyage were fed with dried coconut meat, and some were killed for food when required. A fireplace was provided on the canoes laid on a bed of sand, and firewood was carried along. Deep-sea fish including sharks were readily caught by master fishermen. The provisioning of the sea-going canoes offered no problem.

The fresh-water supplies were carried in coconut water bottles, gourds, or lengths of bamboo. The deep-sea fishermen of Hawai'i sometimes trailed their gourds in the sea to keep the water cool, but such refinements were not necessary on deep-sea voyages. We learn from the traditions of Hawai'i and New Zealand that the crews of expeditionary ships were trained beforehand in self-restraint with regard to consumption of food and water. With organized discipline, any voyaging canoe could be rationed easily for from three to four weeks, the time required to cross the widest ocean spaces between the island groups of Polynesia.

The ships and the builders played their parts, but chief, priest, and navigator, with inborn courage and a firm faith in the gods, drove the sennit-bound vessels over leagues of untraversed ocean to make safe landing on distant isles.

5 · THE EASTERN HORIZON

The handle of my steering paddle thrills to action,
My paddle named Kautu-ki-te-rangi.
It guides to the horizon but dimly discerned.
To the horizon that lifts before us,
To the horizon that ever recedes,
To the horizon that ever draws near,
To the horizon that causes doubt,
To the horizon that instils dread,
The horizon with unknown power,
The horizon not hitherto pierced.
The lowering skies above,
The raging seas below,
Oppose the untraced path
Our ship must go.

POLYNESIAN DEEP-SEA CHANTEY

THE steering paddle thrilled to action when increasing hordes poured into Indonesia from the mainland of Asia. The ways to the lands of the west were blocked, and the only paths available to our Polynesian ancestors led out to open sea. Fishing canoes and vessels used for coastwise transport between seaside villages developed into voyaging ships, and the brown-skinned sailors began their conquest of the greatest of oceans. By short voyages and numerous haltings that occupied many generations, they moved on-

42

ward 'from island unto island to the gateways of the dawn'. New horizons lifted and receded, but ever new ships manned by succeeding generations with increasing sea salt in their blood moved on. Storms threatened to overwhelm them and seas to engulf them, but the steering paddles kept them true on the eastward course.

No matter how brave and enduring a seafaring people may be, the length of their voyages is limited by the size of their ships which determines the amount of food and water that can be carried. Those who exhausted their resources perished in the open sea. Those who reached islands, where they settled or refitted, survived. Hence the voyage to Polynesia was feasible only by following island-studded routes. Two routes were possible, a southern and a northern.

The southern route, which was generally accepted as the correct one by early ethnologists, twines through the closely set islands of Indonesia, passes along the northern coast of New Guinea, and skirts the eastern fringe of the Melanesian chain to Fiji, which was thought to be the rallying place of the Polynesians, whence they scattered east, north, and south to explore and settle the far-flung islands within the Polynesian triangle. Because the name Savai'i, that of the largest island of the Samoan group, is the dialectical equivalent of Hawaiki, the traditional homeland of the Polynesians, Samoa was considered to be the island first reached by Polynesian voyagers after they had left Fiji.

However, in the light of recent comparative study of the material cultures and social organizations of Melanesia and Polynesia, it seems improbable that the great migrations into the Pacific passed through Melanesia. In general the Polynesians are physically very different from the Melanesians. Had they stopped at Melanesian islands to refit their ships and gather new supplies, it is probable that racial intermixture would have taken place and that Negroid characteristics would appear consistently among Polynesians. Isolated objects such as the elaborate mourner's dress of Tahiti and organizations such as the 'Arioi Society, also of Tahiti, which have been used as proof of Melanesian influence, are quite capable of local development.

Much of the linguistic evidence formerly cited in support of an original west to east migration of Polynesians through Melanesia has recently been proved to indicate a movement from Polynesia westward to the marginal islands of Melanesia. William Churchill studied the occurrence of Polynesian languages in Melanesia and on the strength of this study traced several lines of migration from New Guinea into various parts of Polynesia. Charles Hedley has shown that the Polynesian languages spoken in Melanesia occur on the eastern sides of islands facing Polynesia, and further studies by G. Thilenius and S. H. Ray prove that they most strongly resemble dialects of Samoa and Tonga, the Polynesian islands nearest Melanesia. Thilenius and Ray also state that they contain no archaic words as might certainly be expected had the Polynesians passed through Melanesia on their slow progress into the open sea. In addition there is little trace of word-borrowing by the Polynesians from Melanesian languages.

W. H. R. Rivers, in his study of the history of Melanesian society, considered that certain elements were due to contact and interaction of two waves of people that passed through Melanesia from west to east. He associated the burial of the dead in a sitting position with an earlier wave of migration, and burial of the dead in an extended position with a later wave. As both forms of burial were recorded in Polynesia, he inferred that both waves reached Polynesia and

MARGINAL ISLANDS (underlined) IN MELANESIA INHABITED BY POLYNESIAN-SPEAKING PEOPLE were thus composed of what we now term Polynesians. He considered the practice of brother-sister avoidance and the absolute power of a nephew over the possessions of his maternal uncle as contributions made by migrating Polynesians to the Melanesian communities through which they passed. These two social customs were widespread in Melanesia and occurred in Polynesia only in Samoa and Tonga, just outside the boundaries of Melanesia, and in Tikopia, a Polynesian community within Melanesia. Why, we may ask, did all Melanesia accept these practices which were retained by only three groups of Polynesians? We must conclude that they were of original Melanesian origin and were carried eastward only as far as the fringe of the Polynesian triangle.

At first sight the strongest evidence in favour of a southern route of migration is the chain of small islands stretching from New Guinea to Fiji along the northern edge of Melanesia. A. C. Haddon appropriately calls these islands 'marginal communities in northeastern Melanesia' and lists them as: Tikopia Anuta (Cherry Island), Duff Islands, Rennell Island (Mo Ngava), Bellona Island (Mo Ngiki), Sikaiana, Ndai, Ontong Java including Leuaniua, Nukumanu (Tasman Islands), Taku (Marqueen Islands), Kilinailu (Carteret Islands), Nissan, Tanga, and Nuguria. The inhabitants of these islands speak Polynesian dialects similar to those of Tonga and Samoa and are physically unlike the dark, frizzy-haired Melanesians. Many elements of their material culture have been introduced from Micronesia, and traditional histories of the Ellice, Gilbert, and Caroline Islands tell of voyages made by single canoes to uninhabited islands to the south. The plaiting of mats in Leuaniua and Nuguria is said to have been introduced from Tarawa in the Gilbert Islands, and the use of the loom in Nuguria, Taku, Ontong

Java, and Sikaiana was brought from the Carolines. The forked stick connecting the cross booms to the float of an outrigger canoe, used in Sikaiana, Ontong Java, and Nuku-manu, is distributed throughout Micronesia. Finally, the physical characters of the people of Ontong Java, studied by H. L. Shapiro from measurements made by H. I. Hogbin, have closest affinity with those of the people of the Caroline Islands in Micronesia. Thus we must conclude that the 'Polynesian outliers' are not stopping places on the route from New Guinea to Fiji but rather colonies which have been established by movements from the east and the north.

The northern route, which the early Polynesian navigators may have followed in their journey from west to east, leads through Micronesia, which means 'small islands'. Though there are some volcanic islands, the islands along the eastern end of the route are low coral atolls, contrasting with the mountainous islands of Melanesia. The only possible north-ern route leads through Yap, Palau, and the Caroline Islands; then it branches, one line leading northeast through the Marshall Islands toward Hawaii, and one going south-east through the Gilbert and Phœnix Islands to enter Poly-nesia north of Samoa.

Strong support in favour of the Micronesian route lies in the positive evidence against the route through Melanesia. It is unfortunate that the original population of Micronesia had been overlain by Mongoloid elements that crept in after the ancestors of the Polynesians had passed through. Yet, in spite of the imposition of a new language throughout the area, numerous Polynesian words occur to mark the ancient trail.

E. W. Gifford, in an analysis of the mythology of Tonga, found that twenty-seven elements were shared with Micro-nesia and ten with Melanesia, some of which may be due to recent contact with Fiji. He concluded, therefore, that mythology came to Tonga by way of Micronesia and not Melanesia. If we remember that much of the mythology of today was the history of yesterday, we have further evidence that deified ancestors of the Polynesians entered the central Pacific by way of the northern route.

No matter how stout of heart the wielder of the steering paddle, he could not continue indefinitely. He reached an atoll and settled down. A colony was formed and the torch of adventure was carried on by younger men of another generation. Much of the culture of the homeland in the volcanic islands of Indonesia must have been abandoned in coral atolls because certain elements did not suit the changed background or because the requisite natural resources were not available.

Much has been written about forgotten arts and crafts with the implication that the loss or lack of certain arts indicates degeneration or inferiority. It must be considered, however, that a craft depends not only on need and technical knowledge, but also on raw materials. Many unthinking people have criticized our Polynesian ancestors for their lack of pottery and loom weaving without considering the fundamental importance of the geographical distribution of raw materials. Pottery was made in Fiji; then why, ask our critics, was it not made in Tonga and Samoa? The answer is absurdly simple—there is no clay in Tonga and Samoa. Without it neither the Tongans nor the Samoans nor their kinsmen to the east could make pottery. Clay is the product of a chemical change requiring geologic ages to take place; hence it is found only on old land masses. The distribution of clay in the Pacific ends with the continental islands of Fiji. No clay is found in the coral islands of Micronesia or in the recent volcanic islands of Polynesia. Even had the Polynesian ancestors made pottery in their Indonesian homeland, the lack of clay in the islands of Micronesia through which they passed would have forced them to make new adjustments. The earth oven, for which nothing was required beyond wood and stones, sufficed for cooking. Coconut shells and wooden bowls served all other requirements for vessels. Long before our ancestors reached Polynesia, they ceased to need pottery and the memory of a useless craft did not survive. When the Maoris reached New Zealand where clay abounded, clay as a raw material meant nothing.

The loom for weaving textiles is a product of temperate climates, but it found its way into Indonesia and along the northern route to the Carolines. From there it spread direct to some of the marginal communities in northeastern Melanesia and to the neighbouring Santa Cruz Islands of Melanesia but no farther. The Melanesians were not loom weavers and consequently the craft could not reach Polynesia by way of the southern route. But if the Polynesians travelled along the northern route and passed through the Carolines, why did they not carry loom weaving into Polynesia? Possibly weaving was introduced into the Carolines after the Polynesians had passed through. However, the most vital reason is the fact that the Gilbert Islands, which form the link between the Carolines and Polynesia, had no weaving. The wild hibiscus which provided the fibres used for weaving in the Carolines did not grow in the Gilberts. The Polynesian ancestors, therefore, could not carry the loom with them during their lengthened passage through the Gilberts. When they eventually reached the high volcanic islands of Polynesia where the hibiscus would grow, they had long forgotten the art of weaving. A people with writing may resurrect a forgotten craft from written records, but the human memory will not burden itself with technical details which cannot be applied. The lack of raw material in the Gilberts proved an impassable barrier to the spread of loom weaving into Polynesia.

Further information as to the eastward route is provided by the study of projectile weapons. In Melanesia the bow and arrow was used in war and in Micronesia, the sling. The bow and arrow was known in Polynesia, but it never functioned in war except in the somewhat doubtful locality of far-eastern Mangareva. In both Tonga and Samoa it was used in sport to shoot pigeons and fish. In the Society Islands, archery was the sport of chiefs, who shot for distance with rounded arrows from a triangular stone platform. In Hawai'i, the bow and arrow was also used in sport to shoot rats. The surprise that has been expressed at the bow and arrow not having been used in war in Polynesia has been due to the blind acceptance of the theory that the Polynesian voyagers passed through Melanesia and should have obtained there a knowledge of the man-slaying possibilities of the bow, even if they had not adopted it before. The very fact that it was so unimportant in Polynesia is surely additional evidence that the Polynesians did not make the lengthy passage through Melanesia that has been attributed to them. The Tongan bow follows the Fijian pattern, and it is probable that the bow diffused through to Samoa and Tonga from Fiji and that its use for sporting purposes was carried thence to central Polynesia.

The functioning Polynesian projectile weapon was the sling. It is found throughout Polynesia but was evidently dropped in New Zealand. The Maoris were hand-to-hand fighters, and the development of short clubs shows that long-distance preliminaries with projectile weapons had gone out of favour. It is significant, however, that slingstones have been found in the Kermadec Islands to the north of New Zealand, indicating that the early colonists who called at the Kermadecs carried slings with them. Many of the Polynesian slingstones were shaped to a point at each end and thus resemble those collected in Micronesia. The use of the sling in Micronesia and Polynesia bears further evidence in favour of the northern route into Polynesia.

A specific link in affinity between the Gilbert Islands and central Polynesia is the presence in both areas of warriors' helmets. They are shaped somewhat like a Turkish fez and are made of coconut-husk fibre with a coiled technique. In central Polynesia, they occur in the Cook and the Austral Islands. In the Cook Islands, they were used as protection against slingstones, while in the Gilberts they were used in war together with the peculiar coconut-husk armour of coat with sleeves and trousers. The helmets have a prolonged flap at the back, and are so highly specialized that it is unlikely that they represent two different inventions.

Refer to the end-paper map and you will notice that the Polynesian triangle resembles the head of a spear with its point thrusting toward the rising sun. Fitted into its base is the shaft of the spear, comprised of the southern chain of volcanic islands termed Melanesia and the northern chain of atoll islands named Micronesia. As we shall argue later, the food plants and domestic animals travelled along the southern route, but our Polynesian ancestors steered their ships along the northern route from atoll to atoll toward the unpierced eastern horizon.

6. EARLY EXPLORERS AND SETTLERS

Within the circle of the sea,
It holds a fish of note.
It holds a fish
O'er which the rainbow arches,
Spanning the immensity of Ocean.
It is—my land.

AITUTAKI CHANT

THE adventurers who guided their ships into the unknown Pacific were deep-sea fishermen as well as able mariners. They angled for fish and fished for islands. By adding magic powers to their tackle, semi-mythical fishermen were enabled to raise islands up from the depths of the sea. The greatest fisherman in all Polynesia was Maui, an early discoverer who became a legendary hero. He figures in a cycle of heroic exploits which, down the ages, have been narrated by fond grandparents to their awestruck grandchildren. Each island group has its own version of the tale and its local variations; islands that he never saw have been added to Maui's original fantastic catch.

In the Maori version, Taranga gave birth to four sons. At the fifth conception, she aborted, casting the embryo in her diaper upon the sea. Tangaroa, god of the sea, took pity upon the seed of life so untimely doomed never to reach maturity. He cradled the object in the arms of the seaweed and rocked it in the gentle waves of the ocean. The embryo, contrary to all biological laws, became viable and grew into an active male child. Directed by the god who had cared for him, the boy returned to his mother's house at night and, creeping in unobserved, lay down among his sleeping brothers. In the morning, Taranga cast her maternal eye over her sleeping brood and was amazed to find a stranger present. The part of the myth that I liked best as a child was when my grandmother, playing the part of Taranga, ticked off her four sons from thumb to ring finger of one hand, saying, 'Maui-in-front, Maui-within, Maui-on-one-side, Maui-on-the-other-side'. She would gaze in pretended astonishment at the nameless little finger, exclaiming, 'But who is this? It is no child of mine.' Then up piped the precocious fifth, 'Yes, indeed, I was born of thee. Thou cast me immature upon the ocean vast, but my ancestor Tangaroa took pity upon me and raised me to maturity.' The mother pressed her nose to his and said, 'In very truth, thou art my last-born son, and so I will name thee after my top-knot of hair, Maui-tikitiki-a-Taranga.'

When Maui grew to man's estate, he accomplished many wonderful feats, but throughout his career he was an impish sprite and a trickster. In a fit of jealousy because his brother-in-law had caught more fish than he, Maui jammed him under the bow of their fishing canoe at the landing, pulled his nose, ears, and spine to greater length, and so created the first dog—Irawaru of the Maoris and Ri of the Tuamotuans. He procured fire from Mahuika in the Underworld and taught man how to obtain it by friction from the wood in which it was stored. By the use of fire, man was enabled to cook the food that he had hitherto eaten raw.

Maui voyaged to the eastern portals of the day, and, with a slip noose of human hair, he snared Ra, the Sun, as he emerged from the pit of night to commence his all too rapid daily round. Club in hand, Maui dictated terms whereby Ra consented to travel less rapidly across the dome of heaven and thus gave mankind more hours of daylight in which to procure and cultivate food.

Shortly after I entered the New Zealand Parliament as the representative of a Maori constituency, I was asked by the party whip to help in a stonewall or filibuster as it is termed in America. The object was to talk profusely on various bills so that an undesired opposition bill would not be reached on the order paper before 12.30 a.m. After that no new business could come up, and the obnoxious bill would not only lose its turn but would go down to the bottom of the order paper when such bills came up again. The bill before the House at the time I was thrust into the breach was the first Daylight Saving Bill to be introduced into New Zealand. As the speeches made from our side of the House in behalf of the bill were merely to waste the non-daylight hours leading up to midnight, the argument used to save future daylight would have puzzled any meteorologist. I was fearfully nervous at what was to be my second utterance in such a learned assembly, but in casting about for something to say, it occurred to me that the first practical Daylight Saving Bill in the Pacific had been introduced by the Polynesian demigod Maui. With all the enthusiasm of youth and the claim to distant relationship, I exploited the theme to its fullest extent, and, curiously enough, the House became interested in what they seemed to regard as a humorous contribution to a dry debate. Years afterward, New Zealand placed this second Daylight Saving Act on the statute book through the continuous efforts of Sir Thomas Sidey, on whose behalf I had enlisted the aid of Maui. Of my six years' contribution in Parliament to the welfare of my country, my surviving colleagues seem to remember only my alleged humorous interpretation of Polynesian mythology. I have never confessed until now how really serious I felt at the time.

To carry on with our story, Maui's brothers became jealous of their youngest brother. In planning a fishing expedition, they refused to allow him to go with them. In the New Zealand version, Maui concealed himself overnight under a mat in the hold of the canoe; in the Mangarevan, he assumed the form of a rat and hid under a coil of rope. When well out to sea, Maui emerged, and, in spite of their protests, he urged his brothers onward until they reached the right spot in the ocean for catching big fish. Now his brothers were able to get revenge, though for a very brief period. Maui had no bait, and, in spite of his pleadings, his brothers refused to give him any out of their own supply. The New Zealanders say that Maui smote his nose and baited his hook with the blood that flowed from the injured organ. The Mangarevans, who apparently require a solid bait, say that he plucked off one of his ears and impaled it on his hook. The curiously baited line was lowered and caught in the bottom of the sea. With much vigorous hauling in time to a magic chant, a wondrous fish in the form of part of the ocean bed was brought to the surface. In this manner, the North Island of New Zealand, Tonga, Rakahanga, Hawai'i, and other big fish were hauled up from the ocean depths and fixed in their appointed places.

When I visited the atoll of Rakahanga during a Bishop Museum expedition, it was my good fortune to see a play enacted to illustrate the fishing up of that island. The stage was the coral-gravelled village street before our host's house, on the veranda of which we occupied front stalls. The village population sat cross-legged on both sides of the street. The orchestra, which consisted of a huge drum and two slit wooden gongs, burst into rhythm, and the choir, grouped in the open courthouse opposite us, sang a chorus concerning the coming of their ancestor Huku. The eyes of the audience turned in the direction of a roofless house, evidently the stage dressing room, a few yards up the street. We followed the gaze and from around the corner of the house emerged a fisherman clad in a scanty loin cloth, his body covered with grey mud in lieu of grease paint, and a cone of bark cloth perched on his head like a dunce's cap. He had whiskers, beard, and moustaches formed of coconut husk and standing out at most unhuman angles. He occupied the middle of a split coconut leaf, which, tied fore and aft to secure it to his body, represented his fishing canoe. He was further equipped with a paddle and a short fishing rod carrying a large wooden hook. He paddled toward a coconut which lay in the middle of the stage, every now and again stopping to cast his line. He gazed fixedly over the side of his coconut-leaf canoe at the coconut and exclaimed, 'Ah, here is a growth of land at the bottom of the sea. It will grow to the surface.' The orchestra crashed and the choir informed us musically that this was the ancestor Huku from Rarotonga who, on a fishing trip, discovered an upgrowth of land. Huku turned his canoe and paddled back to Rarotonga, but on the way his feet, which protruded through the hull of the canoe, kept time on the bottom of the ocean to the dance rhythms with which the orchestra sped him on his return voyage. He struck bad weather, for the bow of his coconut leaf rose to dizzy heights and descended into abysmal troughs. Once he fell and grovelled, kicking on the ground. We thought he was lost, but the canoe righted and he finally rounded the corner of the ruined house into the safe haven of Rarotonga.

A young girl, dressed to represent an old woman, appeared on the stage and, with a few coconut leaves, erected a bower in which she ensconced herself. She was Hine-i-te-papa, the Lady-of-the-lower-level, who dwelt at the bottom of the sea. The audience again gazed down the street, and from around a house another fisherman emerged paddling a canoe similar to that of Huku. The choir informed us that this was Maui-the-last, who came to interview the Lady-of-the-lower-level. Maui paddled up to the bower and, detaching himself from his coconut leaf, made a stage-dive down to the floor of the ocean. Introducing a modern element, he knocked with his knuckles on the midrib of one of the coconut leaves forming the bower of the Lady. He instructed her as to what she should do when he and his brothers came fishing on the morrow. Then he crawled into his coconut leaf which lay on the ocean floor, came to the surface, and paddled off.

After a brief interval, a longer coconut leaf, enclosing three fishermen, appeared around the corner. The chorus announced that these were the three brothers, Maui-the-first, Maui-the-middle, and Maui-the-last, come on a fishing expedition. Near the house of the Lady, the canoe cast anchor. Maui-the-first baited his hook with a certain bait and cast his line. According to the instructions, the Lady put on a certain fish and pulled the line. Maui-the-first yelled with excitement and asked his brothers to guess what fish he had hooked. Maui-the-last, having arranged matters beforehand, easily won the guessing competition. Maui-the-middle baited his hook with a different bait and caught a different fish, but again Maui-the-last guessed right. Then Maui-the-last baited his hook with a small coconut and a twig of green leaves. When the Lady saw the bait, she inserted the hook, according to instructions, into the outgrowth of land that Huku had seen. Maui, when he felt his hook had struck, hauled on the fish. The land rose with its shoreline below the middle of the canoe. The canoe was lifted on high, but, before it broke in two, Maui-the-last stepped off the stern half onto firm land, and his two brothers in the bow half were swept away into the vortex of the sea. Here I have followed the myth and forgotten the play. In the play, the Lady stuck the hook into the coconut that had been placed in mid-stage. Maui-the-last, with exaggerated facial contortions, struggled to bring the coconut up to the surface. When it came level with the gunwale of the canoe, he stepped backward out of the split coconut leaf onto land, but his two brothers fell forward and kicked and wriggled off the stage into oblivion.

The play had three more acts which need not be detailed. Huku returned from Rarotonga to find that not only had the coral outgrowth reached the surface but that it was occupied by Maui. A fight took place in which Maui, stamping upon the land in order to spring up into the stratosphere, split the land into the two atolls of Rakahanga and Manihiki. I was shown a rock in the seaward lagoon of Rakahanga that bore the impress of Maui's foot. With such evidence, what should one do but believe?

An island that has been fished up from the bottom of the sea is naturally regarded as a fish, and the divisions of the island are often likened to the parts of a fish. Even islands in which the fishing incident is lacking may be so regarded. The island of Atiutaki, though not shaped like any known fish, is divided into head, body, fins, and tail. According to myth, this fish is anchored to the bottom of the sea by a strong vine, and its permanent position depends upon the security of the knot with which the hawser is tied. The verse at the beginning of this chapter gives a poet's thoughts concerning the story. When I stood on the highest hill in Aitutaki, I appreciated the poet's flight of imagination. The hillsides were clothed with native trees which gave place, at the base, to encircling groves of coconut palms, banana, and breadfruit trees. On the shore flats were cultivations of taro with the thatched roofs of native houses peeping through the trees. Beyond the beach, the shallower waters of the lagoon stretched out in varying distances to the encircling reef, which formed a clear-cut, wavering line bounding the island from the depths of the Pacific Ocean. The transition in colour from the green of the lagoon to the deep purple of the sea beyond the reef was striking. The eye followed the purple sea from reef to distant horizon and then the full round of the reef from the hilltop as a centre. One thrilled to the poet's thought that this was a speck of land set 'within the circle of the sea'. The circle was so vast and the fish so small that one actually took comfort from the assurance that the knot of the binding vine would hold. Arch a rainbow over the picture, and you who live in cities may perhaps envy the poet when he sings, 'It is my land'.

Maui and others who are regarded as demigods belong to an early stage of exploration. Their voyages were made so long ago that the islands they discovered cannot now be accurately located, for they lie behind, probably in hither Micronesia, along the route by which our ancestors passed into Polynesia. It is certain that Maui never reached New Zealand, but the early settlers carried the tale of his exploits with them and applied them locally.

The exploits of later adventurers, such as Rata and his immediate forbears, are associated with specific islands radiating from central Polynesia. These men are regarded as heroes and undoubtedly did explore the seas and islands of the central Pacific. Early historians and bards recognize their achievements, stressing their discovery of uninhabited lands. Kupe, who discovered New Zealand, returned to central Polynesia from that land far away to the south and reported, 'The only people I saw there were a fantail flitting about and a bell bird that tolled from the depths of the forest.' Atiu-muri, who discovered Atiu, named it 'Enua-manu, which has been translated as Land of Birds. When, in 1929, I inquired of a local chief why the island had been first named Enua-manu, he replied, 'When Atiumuri beached on the land (*enua*), the only inhabitants were *manu* (birds).' As native birds were scarce, I asked in the native language, 'What kind of *manu?*' 'Oh,' he said, 'moths and beetles.' The word *manu* was applied to any living thing with the exception of human beings and quadrupeds. Thus by emphasizing the lowliest of creatures did the poet heighten the glory of those hardy individuals who were the first humans to cross the immensity of ocean and gaze upon the sea-girt lands.

The earliest settlers who groped their way into Polynesia from the hither end of the Micronesian route cannot be too greatly lauded for their achievement. Yet, whom are we to praise? Their records have been effaced by the fingers of time, and such fragments as may have survived have been converted into myth or plagiarized by the historians of a later school. The later historians of various groups were primarily concerned in the narratives of those settlers who set out from central Polynesia after the eleventh and twelfth centuries A.D.

and gave full honour to their leaders from whom they traced their descent. They admitted, however, that various islands were already settled before these later ancestors arrived.

If we suppose that the Gilbert Islands were the last group in the Micronesian chain from which early settlers could embark for Polynesia, we can appreciate that there were three groups of volcanic islands that could be reached by voyagers setting out from that outpost—Hawai'i to the northeast, the Society Islands to the southeast, and Samoa to the south. Coral atolls that lay between formed convenient resting places, but could not serve as centres of development because of limited size and paucity of natural resources. It is significant that each of these three groups has traditions of early settlers.

Hawaiian myths tell of a race of dwarfs called Menehune who were dwelling in the islands when the ancestors of the present Hawaiians landed. The Menehune are associated with the legend of a chief named Hawai'i-loa, who sailed northeast from somewhere along the Micronesian route before it reached Polynesia. Possibly they were a group of early peoples who were wafted by winds and currents direct to Hawai'i from the Gilberts or from some island farther to the west. The probability that they had no cultivable food plants supports this theory, for had they come to Hawai'i from central Polynesia, they would certainly have brought with them the foods which were later imported by settlers from Tahiti.

The Society Islands in the centre of Polynesia were peopled by an early group called Manahune. These were real people, referred to both in legend and history, and perhaps belonging to the same period as the Menehune of Hawai'i. They could readily pass from the Gilberts, through a chain of atolls, such as the Phœnix Islands, Manihiki, Rakahanga, and Penrhyn to drop down into the leeward group of the Society Islands.

Samoan myths record an early people existing on the islands before the arrival of the descendants of Tangaloa. These people were produced from worms grown from a rotting vine. Though their mythical origin is local, we may suppose that these people were voyagers who preceded later historical settlers, probably coming from the Gilberts through the Tokelaus to find a new home. From Samoa the so-called descendants of worms went farther south and colonized Tonga, where they were given human names.

The early settlers were probably poorly equipped with cultivable food plants and domesticated animals. They may have belonged originally to the same group as the later Polynesians but, because they were of an inferior social status, were forced to leave when the growth of the population exceeded the available food supplies of a coral atoll. Forced migrations of this kind have occurred over and over again in the Tuamotu atolls and in Mangareva, as native historians tell. New Zealand was settled by peoples lacking cultivable plants and domestic animals, who may have been driven or blown from Tonga or some other island to the northward. In these migrations, the weaker peoples with the least food must have left first and the strongest left last.

So we may assume that the earliest inhabitants of Hawai'i, the Society Islands, and Samoa were the humblest members of a social group, and that when forced to leave the Gilberts they radiated north, south, and east in search of a home. They settled on the volcanic islands nearest the Gilberts and adjusted their culture to what natural resources were available. These commoners were not only ill-equipped economically and culturally, but were weaker physically than their social superiors. The distinction between chief and com-

moner in stature and physique is due not only to breeding
and selection, but to the food supply that accompanies rank.
It is small wonder that these earlier settlers were so readily
dominated by the better-equipped people who came later.
Yet, no matter what their origin or fate, they must be recognized as the first humans to penetrate into the vast and
turbulent unknown waters of the Great Ocean.

A theory has been advanced that some islands were peopled by deep-sea fishermen who were blown away while
engaged in their lawful avocation. The objection to this is
the fact that Polynesian women did not go out fishing in
canoes with their menfolk. The women's sphere of marine
activity lay within the lagoon, and their boundary was the
encircling reef. They did not pass beyond the reef except in
transit with their families on visits to nearby islands or on
organized expeditions. No canoe-load of male fishermen
could people an uninhabited island for longer than their own
lifetime. Hence, when a population including women was
found on an island, no matter how remote, it is certain that
the first settlers set out on a purposive voyage with a certain
amount of food and water. They might have missed a near
objective and been carried afar, but their range of travel was
limited by their supply of food and water and the amount of
human endurance that persisted after their supplies were
exhausted. A crew of experienced fishermen, carrying their
tackle with them, could augment their supplies from mother
ocean by trolling for bonito, shark, and other fish. In Bligh's
historic voyage of 3000 miles in an open boat from Tonga
in Polynesia to Timor in the Malay Archipelago, a Polynesian is struck by the fact that, though on occasion fish teemed
around the boat, Bligh and his severely rationed crew could
not catch one fish. They had neither line nor hook. In

Beechey's account of a Polynesian canoe which was driven six hundred miles to the east before a westerly gale, one of the men bent a ship's iron scraper into the form of a hook and caught a large shark that had been following the canoe. Samson's riddle was answered for 'Out of the eater came forth meat'.

A great deal of nonsense has been talked about the impossibility of the Polynesians sailing east against the prevailing trade winds, and this alleged impossibility has been advanced to support a theory that the Polynesians originated in America and came west into the Pacific. The foolishness of the theory will be dealt with anon. It is sufficient to say that westerly winds also prevail for a part of the year. Beechey demonstrates the force of these winds in the account mentioned above. The missionary John Williams sailed east from Samoa to the Cook Islands on a straight course without changing tack. Schooner captains in the South Seas will tell you that if they had to set out on an exploratory voyage, they would prefer to beat against the prevailing winds, because, if supplies ran low, they could sail directly home before the wind.

The early Polynesians had acquired from their ocean environment a practical knowledge of prevailing winds and their seasons. The cardinal points, termed *kaveinga*, were named after the various winds which blew through holes in the horizon. During a long sea voyage, the holes of the adverse winds were metaphorically plugged with the aid of Raka, God of the Winds. In New Zealand, the god of the winds was Tawhiri-matea. In the chant of the voyager Kahu-koka, the god was invoked to close his eye that looked to the south so that a safe voyage might be made from west to east.

CHANT OF KAHU-KOKA

Now do I direct the bow of my canoe
To the opening whence arises the sun god,
Tama-nui-te-ra, Great-son-of-the-sun.
Let me not deviate from the course
But sail direct to the land, the Homeland.

> Blow, blow, O Tawhiri-matea, God of the **Winds!**
> Arouse thy westerly wind to waft us direct
> By the sea road to the Homeland, to Hawaiki.

Close, close thine eye that looks to the south,
That thy southerly wind may sleep.
Allow us to sail o'er the Sea of Maui,
And impede us not on our course.

> She stirs, she moves, she sails!
> Ah, now shall speed Tane-kaha,
> The gallant canoe of Kahu-koka,
> Back to the bays of Hawaiki-nui,
> And so to Home.

It is clear that Kahu-koka asked for a west wind and also asked that the southeast trade be still. It is also clear to me that Kahu-koka would never have made preparation for his voyage and invoked his god until his own experience or the advice of his navigating officer assured him that the season of the westerly winds had arrived.

The first pioneers in the Pacific were followed by people whom I believe to have been of the same stock but of a higher social grade led by chiefs of rank and priests of intellect and learning. Whether they were forced to leave eastern Micronesia because of increasing pressure behind, conflict within, or the lure of adventure before, we can but surmise. Certain it is that eminent leaders directed their voyaging canoes into Polynesia on a southeast course that kept north of Samoa, and probably passed through the now-deserted Phœnix atolls or even the Tokelau group. These small atolls with sparse vegetation might serve as resting places but certainly could not appeal to ambitious leaders as permanent homes. So they sailed on until the high volcanic mountains of the leeward Society Islands loomed on the horizon before them. Here they settled, giving to the new islands the names of their previous homes—Vavau, 'Uporu, and Havai'i. As population increased and shipbuilding improved, explorers went forth from this centre to rediscover islands already occupied by the earlier voyagers, and to dominate them by organized forces and a higher development of their own culture. Thus the Society Islands became the nucleus for exploration and the dissemination of learning throughout central Polynesia.

7. THE CENTRE OF THE TRIANGLE

Havai'i, fanaura'a fenua.
Havai'i, the birthplace of lands.
TAHITIAN CHANT

THE main body of the Polynesian Expeditionary Force,
following on the trail of the Manahune vanguard, moved
into the leeward islands of a volcanic group that lay on their
eastward course. Fate, fortune, and the urge of their own
stout hearts had enabled them to penetrate into the centre
of the widely spaced oceanic islands that, centuries later,
were to be termed Polynesia (the many islands) and so give
the name Polynesians to the descendants of the original
discoverers and settlers.

The settlement of this group of islands in central Polynesia took place about the fifth century A.D. Over a thousand
years later, the credit for their discovery was given to a
British explorer named Wallace. The permanent geographical name was given by another British explorer, James Cook,
who named the whole group the Society Islands after the
Royal Society of London, under whose auspices he had made
observations on the transit of Venus, with Tahiti as his base.
These explorers of another race who came into the Pacific
less than two centuries ago have been honoured rightly, but

the original discoverers of over a thousand years before have been forgotten through lack of written records. Perhaps their descendants conferred upon them the highest possible honours by promoting them to the rank of gods.

The Society Islands are divided into a leeward and a windward group. The islands of the leeward group were named by their first discoverers, but as time rolled on, new names were given. The old classical names were used in legend and song, but the later names were used in current speech and so were adopted by the European map-makers. The ancient names of the principal islands of the leeward group are given here with their modern equivalents in parentheses: Vavau (Porapora; European version, Borabora), Uporu (Taha'a), Havai'i (Ra'iatea), and Huahine. Of the windward group, Tahiti, the principal island, lies a little over a hundred miles from Ra'iatea. Mo'orea, formerly known as Eimeo, is seven miles from Tahiti, and a number of smaller islands complete the group.

Tahiti, because of its large size and great fertility, came to support the largest population in the Society Islands, and, in later times, the political power passed from its original centre in Havai'i to Tahiti. Still later, it became the seat of the government for French Oceania, which includes not only the Society Islands, but also the Marquesas, Tuamotu, Austral, and Gambier islands. It will be more convenient to allude to the myths and legends of the group as Tahitian than to use the longer term Society Islands.

The headquarters of the Polynesian main body was established in the largest island of the leeward group, named Havai'i after an ancient homeland. From this centre various groups later dispersed to people other islands, taking with them a common basic language, the same foodstuffs and animals, a common religion, and a common cultural background of myth and tradition. Therefore all Polynesian cultures, wherever found in the wide spaces of the Polynesian triangle have common elements that can be traced back to a common period of reorganization in central Polynesia.

One basic language prevails throughout Polynesia. The vowels are consistently the same—*a*, *e*, *i*, *o*, and *u*, pronounced as in French or German—and the consonants are always followed by a vowel. Dialects have developed in various island groups by changes in consonant sounds. *R* and *v* are used in central and eastern Polynesia where *l* and *v* are used in western Polynesia. In some dialects certain consonants are not fully sounded but are represented or should be represented by an inverted comma over its place in the word. In the Society Islands, *k* and *ng* were dropped; so the name for the ancestral homeland, pronounced Havaiki in other dialects of central Polynesia, is here pronounced Havai'i. In New Zealand, where *w* is used instead of *v*, the ancient home is Hawaiki. In the Cook Islands, where *h* is dropped, it is 'Avaiki. In the Hawaiian islands, where *w* is used and *k* is dropped, the largest island of the group is named Hawai'i. In Samoa, where *s* replaces *h*, *v* is preferred to *w*, and *k* is dropped, the largest island is called Savai'i.

The food plants, the domestic animals, the raw materials and tools upon which Polynesian material culture is built, were probably first developed and tested in the leeward Society Islands and carried from there by explorers and settlers to other parts of Polynesia. We may imagine the wonder and the joy of those first voyagers from Micronesia upon beholding the lofty hills, the wide valleys, the running streams, and fertile soil of a large volcanic island after they and their ancestors had for centuries scraped a meagre exist-

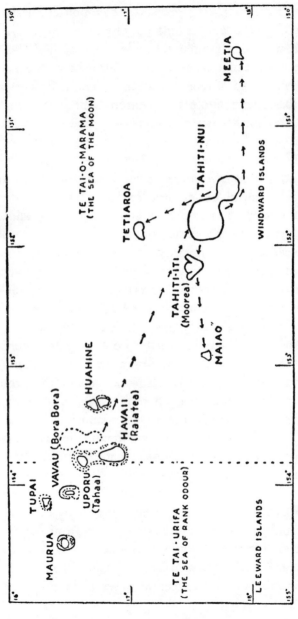

THE CENTRE OF THE TRIANGLE: SHOWING HAVAI'I, THE BIRTHPLACE OF LANDS

ence from the unfriendly sands of coral atolls. Their whole physical background was miraculously changed. We may picture dimly the interest of the older people as they explored the profusion of plants, recognizing familiar ones, naming new species, and testing the useful value of woods, barks, and leaves. Here was an abundance of wood for building houses and canoes, and barks to furnish fibre for textiles and cordage. Most useful of all was the basaltic rock, which is absent in coral atolls. Food in the atolls had been cooked in earth ovens in which the heating agent had been pieces of coral rock and *tridacna* shells that crumbled away after each cooking. The volcanic islands provided basaltic stones which could be used over and over again and so formed a permanent medium for cooking. Basalt provided material for adzes and chisels that were vastly superior to those previously made from shell. Countless possibilities opened out in the arts and crafts, and progress in the development of new and improved techniques was rapid.

In the fertile soil of the rich valleys, food plants were cultivated to support an increasing population. All the food plants cultivated in Polynesia (except the sweet potato), and the domesticated animals were brought to central Polynesia at an early period from Samoa. The manner of their spread will be discussed later. The increase of food supplies in a volcanic group materially assisted the great cultural development that took place.

An exuberant new life opened up in central Polynesia, and new adjustments and progress took place, not only in the arts and crafts but in social and religious matters. The senior families and the most intelligent priests seem to have settled down in the Opoa district of Havai'i, which became the cultural centre of the group. A school of learning was established, and, in the course of time, the school systematized the scattered fragments of myth and history that had been remembered by various voyagers from Micronesia. That systematization took place locally is borne out by the fact that the myths and legends were applied to the local area. The pattern established was ultimately carried by later voyagers in varying degrees of completeness to the remote angles of the Polynesian triangle. Tahitian mythology or theology, however, continued to evolve; and the myths, as recorded for Tahiti by Teuira Henry from the manuscripts of the Reverend Orsmond, include changes made after the long-distance mariners had left the near homeland of Havai'i.

Ta'aroa, the Creator, was self-begotten, for he had no father and no mother. He sat in a shell named Rumia, shaped like an egg, for countless ages in endless space in which there was no sky, land, sea, moon, nor stars. This was the period of continuous, countless darkness (*po tinitini*) and thick impenetrable darkness (*po ta'ota'o*). At long last Ta'aroa cracked the shell to hatch himself. He stood on the shell and called in various directions, but no sound answered from the void. He retired within Rumia into an inner shell termed Tumu-iti (Lesser-foundation), where he lay torpid for a further untold period. At last, he determined to act. He emerged and made the inner shell of Rumia into a foundation for the rock and soil of the world, and the outer shell he made into the dome of the sky which was low and confined. He breathed into the rock foundation the essence of himself and personified it as Tumu-nui to be the husband; likewise he personified the rock stratum as Paparaharaha to be the wife. Both, however, refused to obey the command of Ta'aroa to approach each other, for each had a fixed appointed place in the earth structure from which they would not move.

Then Ta'aroa created rocks, sand, and earth. He conjured up Tu, the great craftsman, to help him in the task of creation, and together they formed the myriad roots. The dome of Rumia was raised on pillars, and thus space beneath was extended. The space was termed *atea* and pervaded with a spirit personified as Atea. Land and space were increased and the underworld was set apart. Forest trees and food plants grew, and living things appeared on the land and in the sea. At the back were the mountains, personified as Tu-mou'a, with land, springs, and rivers. In front was the ocean and its rocks ruled by the ocean lord, Tino-rua. Above was Atea (Space) and below was Rua (Abyss). The land was Havai'i, the birthplace of other lands, gods, kings, and man.

Darkness brooded under the confined dome of Rumia. The gods Tu, Atea, Uru, and others were created or conjured forth by Ta'aroa in darkness. Later the stars and the winds were born. From Ta'aroa and Atea, who figures in the early part of this mythological period as a female, the god Tane was born as a viable mass without form. Skilled artisans were called to shape Tane. They came in pairs, carrying their kits of stone tools slung over their shoulders, but at the sight of the majesty of Atea, they retired in fear. Then Atea herself assumed the task of shaping Tane, and successively formed all the anatomical details associated with the human body, including the boring of the external ear passages with a fine spiral shell. After these many plastic operations, duly enumerated in myth, Tane assumed perfect form and became the god of beauty (*te atua o te purotu*). Ta'aroa exalted Tane in power, and he became the god of craftsmen. Another of the major gods, Ro'o, was born of a cloud and became the colleague and messenger of Tane. At a later period, Atea changed sex with Fa'ahotu to become a male, the sex attributed to Atea in the myths of other islands.

The Tahitian myth of the creation of man is lacking in detail. Ta'aroa with the aid of Tu, the great artisan, created Ti'i, the first human being. The word *rahu* (to create) is used, but as one of the names of Ti'i is given as Ti'i-ahu-one (Ti'i-mounded-from-earth) it is apparent that he was formed from earth. He married the goddess Hina, daughter of Te Fatu (Lord, Core) and Fa'ahotu (To-begin-to-form). The children of Ti'i and Hina intermarried in the period of darkness with the gods of that era. The children whom they conceived were the ancestors of the high chiefs entitled to wear the red feather girdles denoting the highest rank, but the children whom they simply conjured up became the progenitors of the common people.

In another version, Ti'i created a woman from earth at Atiauru, took her to wife, and committed incest with his daughter to beget the first man. Another story states that Ta'aroa married Hine-ahu-one (Earth-formed-maid) and produced Ti'i as the first man. The three versions are mentioned because we will meet them later.

In this period of confined darkness was born the famous Maui family of demigods. Ru had a daughter, Ruahea, who married Hihi-ra (Sun-ray) and gave birth to five sons, all named Maui with a qualifying term, and a daughter, Hina. The last Maui was born prematurely and was cast into the sea. The gods took pity on him and nursed him to maturity in a coral cave beneath the ocean. He developed eight heads and hence was called Maui-with-eight-heads (Maui-upo'o-varu). When he grew up he performed miracles, but in the Tahitian version he is not associated with the fishing-up of islands, as he was in other groups.

Many artisans were employed to raise the sky and let

light into the world, but all retired with their kits of stone tools when they came before the dread face of Atea, the God of Space, beneath the dome of Runia. Ru, the grandfather of the great Maui, made the first attempt to prop up the sky. He managed to raise it onto the mountain peaks where it rested on the leaves of the arrowroot, which consequently became flattened. But his physical efforts made him hump-backed and so he desisted. The task was then attempted by Tino-rua, Lord of the Ocean, but he also failed. Maui, under the name of Maui-ti'iti'i, studied the problem and decided that the way to succeed was to remove the pillars on which Rumia rested, to detach the tentacles of the Great Octopus which were holding the sky, and to relax the grip of Atea who held the earth. After trying in vain, Maui sought aid of Tane in the tenth heaven. By means of shell cutting and boring instruments and great logs for levers and props, Tane detached Atea and pushed him up on high. Thus light came into the world, and the long night of Rumia was ended. Tane then employed Ra'i-tupua, who dwelt in the Milky Way, to restore order to the upper spheres of heaven which had been dislocated by the raising of Atea to his present position high above the world. The sun, moon, and stars were set in their appointed places, and peace and order reigned above. In the lower world, temples and houses were built, and man adjusted himself to an environment which provided food on land and sea.

The land that had been established had been termed Havai'i, and the Tahitian bards seem to have taken for granted that this Havai'i was the island now known as Ra'iatea. The ocean to the west of Havai'i was termed the Sea-of-rank-odour, and the ocean to the east was the Sea-of-the-moon. The births of new lands, conjured up as was Havai'i, are described by the ancient poets as follows:

> Let more land grow from Havai'i,
> From Havai'i, the birthplace of lands.
> The quickened spirit of the dawn rides
> Upon the flying scud beyond restraining bounds
> Bear thou on! Whence beats the drum?
> It beats beyond in the western sea,
> Where the sea boils and casts up Vavau;
> Vavau, the first-born of the family,
> With the fleet that strikes both ways.

Thus Vavau (Porapora), to the drumming of the surf, emerged from the depths. Again, to the beating of the ocean drum, the smaller islands of Tupai, Maurua (Maupiti), Mapiha'a (Lord Howe Island), Putai (Scilly Island), and Papaiti (Bellingshausen) emerged in quick succession from the deep. The bard then faced east and sang:

> Bear thou on! Whence beats the drum?
> It beats beyond in the eastern sea,
> Where the drumming surf casts up Huahine,
> The land that reveres its chiefs,
> The land set in the Sea-of-the-moon.

The towering seas cast up Maiao-iti, and then the sound of the drumming waves receded to Tuamotu, Marquesas, Hawai'i, distant lands that at present do not concern us. The family of islands forming the leeward group had been born around the motherland of Havai'i.

According to mythology, the windward group was created after the religious centre of Opoa had developed in Havai'i. At that time, the present sea channel between Havai'i (Ra'iatea) and 'Uporu (Taha'a) was filled by land. For an impending ceremony, sacred restrictions were imposed at Opoa. No cock must crow, no dog bark, and neither pig

nor man must walk abroad. The wind ceased to blow, and
the sea became still. In the midst of this dread silence, a
beautiful girl named Tere-he stole secretly away to bathe in
a river that ran near her home. The gods punished the
infringement of taboo by causing her to drown. A giant eel
swallowed her whole and became possessed by her spirit.
The eel became enraged and tore up the foundation of the
land between Havai'i and 'Uporu. The loosened land floated
away on the surface of the sea like a huge fish. The head
of the fish had been at Opoa and the tail extended to 'Uporu.
As it floated out toward the horizon, the gods did not inter-
rupt their sacred ritual at Opua, but Tu, the great artisan
of Ta'aroa, took charge of the fish. He stood on its head,
which is now Taiarapu, and guided its course to the east and
south to the horizon of a new sky. The fish was Tahiti-nui
(Great Tahiti) possessed by the soul of the maid, Tere-he.
The first dorsal fin of the fish stood up and formed the highest mountain of Orohena. The second dorsal fin detached
itself and fell over the steering paddle to follow in the wake
as Tahiti-iti (Little Tahiti). It became the island of 'Ai-meo,
now called Mo'orea. The great fish dropped off other fragments which became the small islands of Meti'a and Te
Tiaroa. The little fish also dropped a fragment which became
Mai'ao-iti. Thus Great Tahiti and the smaller islands of the
windward group were established from the land fish which
floated away from Havai'i, the mother of lands. Tu, having
finished his task as pilot, returned to the religious convention
that was being held by the gods at Opoa.

Study the map on page 67, and you will see how accurately
myths have been based on geographical position. The emergence of Tahiti from the gap between Ra'iatea and Taha'a
does not require such credence as the western theory that the

moon emerged from the Pacific Ocean. The head of the fish (Taiarapu) certainly points in the direction in which the fish was piloted, and Mo'orea lies behind in its wake. I have lived at Papeete (chief town of Tahiti), visited Taiarapu, gazed across at the rugged skyline of Mo'orea, and come in and out on ocean liners, but I never realized the relative positions of the individual units composing the Society Islands until I restudied the map in the light of Tahitian mythology. The myths were composed from the verbal logs of deep-sea mariners, and the picture of the relative positions is as accurate as if the bards had had a modern chart spread out before them.

When the land of Tahiti floated down to the present location, there were brave warriors upon it, but, according to later traditions, there were no high chiefs of royal lineage among them. When Tu returned to Havai'i, Tahiti was left without gods, at least without the gods worshipped at Opoa. The early people of Tahiti were termed Manahune and were governed by warrior chiefs called *fatu*. Because the later chiefly families did not officially trace their descent through them, the term *manahune* came to mean plebeian. Tahiti was therefore termed Tahiti-manahuna, Tahiti without royal chiefs and without gods. Both high chiefs and gods have belittled the achievements of the early people who made their creation possible.

Native legend states that the land of Tahiti had been long standing; new generations were born in the land, bananas ripened, mountain plantains matured, the crowing of cocks resounded in the woods, dogs barked on the seashore, hogs' tusks turned upward, 'ava plants developed their roots, taro plants blossomed, sugar cane leaned forward, breadfruit fermented in the pits, and songs accompanying the beating of bark cloth were heard in the land.

In spite of this picture of happy contentment, the warrior leaders were uneasy regarding the stability of their fish. The fish that had swum from Havai'i might swim elsewhere. The warrior, Tafa'i, said that the sinews of the fish must be cut to render its position permanent. A number of warriors, whose names were personifications of varying moods of the ocean, hacked the land with their stone adzes but to no avail. Tafa'i then called upon the gods of the sky, the sea, and the moon to assist, but no god responded to his prayer. Tafa'i sailed south to Tupua'i in the Austral Islands to seek aid of King Marere-nui. The king asked what gods had assisted them in their efforts. Tafa'i replied, 'None! Tahiti-mana-hune stands there without gods.' The king after reflection gave Tafa'i a stone adze which bore the name of Te-pa-huru-nui-ma-te-vai-tau, and with it the sinews of the fish Tahiti were effectively divided. Formerly a chain of mountains extended throughout the length of Tahiti, but this was severed with the magic adze, and the gap forms the present isthmus of Taravoa connecting the head, Taiarapu, with the body of the fish. The throat of the fish had been cut and it became stable.

A time arrived when the gods of Opoa in Havai'i came down to the westerly winds of Tahiti, and the people fled in terror to the caves and ravines of the mountains. Like birds' peckings were the morsels of food at that time. The gods settled first on Mo'orea and then spread to Tautira in Tahiti, where their reign was tyrannous. They demanded the heads of warrior men, and the people deserted Tautira through fear of the gods. Nought remained but the birds. The people begged the gods not to destroy them, and the gods harkened to their prayers. The gods gradually spread throughout the land of Great Tahiti, and the people returned to their homes, having no more fear. Temples were erected and dedicated to them, and the people adjusted themselves to the new theology.

Myths and traditions have been freely quoted to give a picture of the Tahitian method of narrating events that occurred so far back that they have become clothed with the supernatural. If this form of literary style is interpreted in the spirit and not in the letter, we may grasp the main order of human events as they occurred in the dim past.

From the mythical account of the origin of Tahiti, it is evident that the priests at Opoa imposed severe religious restrictions upon the people. The silence imposed on cocks and dogs, confinement on pigs and man, and stillness on the wind and sea are indications of a tyrannous rule. The action of the maid Tere-he may be interpreted as a rebellion by the Manahune against these restrictions. The name Tere-he may be translated as Floating-away-through-sin, and it aptly illustrates the Polynesian method of recording events by applying them as proper names to persons who figure in the story. Her death by drowning and the struggles of the sea eel imbued with her spirit indicate that reprisals followed and an upheaval took place. As a result of the social upheaval, a section of the warlike Manahune, who worshipped the god Tu, set out in their canoes to seek a new home. The later historians admitted the association of Tu with the Manahune by allowing Tu to pilot the fish, but they stole Tu by returning him to Opoa, thus leaving the Manahune without gods. The fish that broke away from Havai'i was not the island of Tahiti but the Manahune fleet that conveyed the first inhabitants to Tahiti. Hence the first name of Tahiti was Tahiti-Manahune, Tahiti-of-the-Manahune-people. The gods who followed after were the people influenced by the priests of Opoa. They established themselves on the nearest island of Moʻorea and afterwards on the main island of Tahiti in the district of Tautira. They demanded the heads of Manahune warriors, which statement may be accepted literally as indicating that they killed many of the Manahune and conquered them. Finally, peace was made and the vanquished accepted both the rule and the gods of their conquerors.

So the priests and scholars at Opua pieced together broken records and scraps of myths to compose a Genesis that would apply to their new home and oceanic environment. They deified the leaders of early expeditions who, in the course of time, became major gods, such as Taʻaroa, Tu, Tane, Roʻo, and others. As gods, they took part in the creation of the sky dome, the earth foundation beneath it, and the things that grew on land and in water. Man was connected with the gods through genealogies, for, in truth, the gods had been human ancestors before they were made divine. In addition to gods and demigods, certain natural phenomena and evolutionary concepts were added to the pantheon in the personifications of Atea (Space), Papa (Earth foundation), Te Tumu (Source, Cause), and Faʻahotu (To being-to-form).

The mediums of family gods graduated into powerful priests, who composed appropriate invocations and a richer ritual. They developed the architecture of the temple from a simple pattern of a cleared space before a stone upright into a paved or gravelled courtyard before a raised stone platform. At Opoa, the great temple, or marae, of Taputapu-atea was erected to the new god, ʻOro, the son of Taʻaroa, and its fame spread far and wide. New temples were built in the Society Islands, but, in order to acquire religious prestige, a stone from Taputapu-atea had to be incorporated in the building. It was the leaven from which new structures derived *mana* (power).

For years I had cherished the wish to make a pilgrimage to Taputapu-atea. From Maori traditions, I knew that some of my ancestors had come from Ra'iatea, and I felt that much of our theology had emanated from Opoa and its chief temple. Fortunately, during a Bishop Museum expedition to the Cook Islands in 1929, I found myself on the northern atoll of Tongareva (Penrhyn), and my quickest means of getting back to my base at Rarotonga was by way of the Society Islands. Through the courtesy extended by the New Zealand Navy Department to scientists in the field, I was picked up at Tongareva by H.M.S. *Veronica* en route to Ra'iatea. As we steamed southeast, I could not help feeling what a vast difference the centuries had made. Here we were on a steel-clad British man-of-war, steering a course by compass, observing the sun at noon with an accurate instrument, and plotting off the position on a chart with all the islands accurately located. The number of miles per day could be absolutely controlled, and we knew the hour that we would arrive at Ra'iatea. The Manahune vanguard had sailed down this identical course centuries before in wooden vessels made with shell tools, with matting sails and man power at the paddles, no compass, no sextant, no chart, but a firm faith that they would land somewhere.

'Porapora of the muffled paddles' rose sheer from the sea before us, a magnificent sight to one who had spent even a brief month on atoll islands. Farther on, Taha'a and Ra'iatea towered into view, and beyond lay Huahine. Here before us, in the Sea-of-rank-odour and the Sea-of-the-moon, lay the great islands where Polynesian history was made. We approached Ra'iatea, the ancient Havai'i, and steamed through the capacious reef channel to tie up to a buoy in the deep lagoon before the chief village of Uturoa. The Commander went ashore to pay an official call, and I landed with him. I felt that I should reverently pick up some of the sacred soil of Havai'i from the first footprint that I made on stepping ashore. But it could not be done, for we landed on a modern wharf with wooden buildings forming the background. The old world atmosphere of Havai'i, the birthplace of lands, that I had been conjuring up in my imagination, was rudely displaced by a modern French trading village. It was all wrong.

My melancholy musings were interrupted by a familiar voice. Before me, with a welcoming smile, stood K. P. Emory, a member of the Bishop Museum staff who was to conduct an expedition into the Tuamotu Archipelago on a motor launch built at Tahiti. The boat had been completed and was being tried out on a trip from Tahiti to Ra'iatea. It had been given the ancient canoe name of *Mahina-i-te-pua* (The-crescent-wave-at-the-bow-that-bursts-into-foam-like-a-flower). Emory had been told when I would arrive at Ra'iatea and said, 'I have come to give the boat a trial and to take you to Taputapu-atea.'

The people of Ra'iatea had gathered at Uturoa to celebrate the French fête of the fall of the Bastille. In the evening, various village groups competed in singing and acting out some historical or legendary incident. One of these plays represented the origin of the little cluster of stars known as Pipiri-ma (The-twin-stars-in-Scorpio). The story goes that a selfish fisherman and his wife ate his catch of fish and sent their two children supperless to bed. The two children, therefore, ran away and ascended a mountain. Their parents pursued them. As the children stood on the mountain peak, their parents besought them to return, but the children refused. When the parents ascended the peak, the children sprang up into the sky, where they became the stars Pipiri-ma. In the play, a rather corpulent man and his wife sat beside a burning coconut leaf that represented the cooking fire. The two children lying on the ground peeked through their fingers at their parents going through the pantomime of eating fish. Finally the parents lay down to sleep, and the two children crept quietly away toward a high pole in the show ground that represented a legendary mountain. At the foot of the mountain were two chairs fixed to ropes which ran through pulleys at the top of the pole. The parents woke up and, with exaggerated wailing, followed in pursuit. As they neared the mountain, the two children were hauled up in the chairs and suspended in the heavens. The corpulent father clasped the foot of the pole and besought the children to come back. The two children produced electric torches and took evident delight in flashing them down on the upturned face of their remorseful father. The flashes of light from the modern electric torches represented the twinkling rays of the star cluster, Pipiri-ma.

Next morning we sailed down the lagoon to deserted Opoa. The old people who might have conjured back some of the religious atmosphere were still at the fête of Uturoa. Taputapu-atea stands on a low, wide cape bounded on either side by beautiful bays. The court of the temple was overgrown with weeds, but the altar (*ahu*), 141 feet long by 25 feet wide, bore witness to past grandeur. The stone platform was walled with huge slabs of coral limestone embedded in the earth, and the enclosure was filled in with loose rock through which, formerly, skulls were scattered or piled in recesses until the people had to conceal them elsewhere from

the acquisitive fingers of foreign vandals. Some of the slabs
rose twelve feet above the ground; some had fallen, revealing
an inner row of lower wall slabs which showed that a larger
platform had been built around and above a smaller structure. Thus modern decay revealed the evidence of previous
growth whereby the first temple of Feoro had become
Vai'otaha and finally had risen in size and importance to
become the international marae of Taputapu-atea. Near the
temple was an upright stone pillar, nine feet high, termed
the White-rock-of-investiture (Te Papa-tea-ia-ruea). Here
the head of the royal line of Opoa, girdled with a red feather
belt and seated on his wooden seat of honour, was raised
to the top of the pillar as part of the ceremony of investiture.
Close to the beach was another marae on which the human
sacrifices brought by canoe were laid to await their turn in
the temple ritual of Taputapu-atea.

We took pictures of speechless stone and inanimate rock.
I had made my pilgrimage to Taputapu-atea, but the dead
could not speak to me. It was sad to the verge of tears. I
felt a profound regret, a regret for—I know not what. Was
it for the beating of the temple drums or the shouting of
the populace as the king was raised on high? Was it for
the human sacrifices of olden times? It was for none of
these individually but for something at the back of them
all, some living spirit and divine courage that existed in
ancient times and of which Taputapu-atea was a mute symbol. It was something that we Polynesians have lost and
cannot find, something that we yearn for and cannot recreate.
The background in which that spirit was engendered has
changed beyond recovery. The bleak wind of oblivion had
swept over Opoa. Foreign weeds grew over the untended
courtyard, and stones had fallen from the sacred altar of

Taputapu-atea. The gods had long ago departed. To keep down the rising tide of feeling, I said bruskly in the American vernacular, 'Let's go'.

8. THE HUB OF POLYNESIA

They sailed east to Mangareva, south to the parrakeet
islands, west to Samoa, and north to burning Vaihi.

TAHITIAN LEGEND

Havai'i, the mother of lands, became the hub of the Polynesian universe. The daring mariners who had steered their
ships through the unpierced horizon into the heart of the
Pacific received the highest honour from their descendants
by being elevated to the rank of gods. The priests at Opoa
gathered the warp of myth and the weft of history together
and wove them into the textile of theology. The male parents
of the gods were Atea (Space) or Te Tumu (Source), and
their mothers were Papa (Earth foundations) or Fa'ahotu
(To-cause-to-take-form). Their children were given rule over
special departments: Tane, forestry and craftsmanship; Tu,
war; Ro'o, peace and agriculture; Ta'aroa, marine affairs
and fishing; and Ra'a, meteorology. However, there is evidence that Tane had the greatest sphere of influence. He was
given the special function of forming the first female out of
earth and procreating the first human beings. In the course
of time, various islands of the Society group tended to pay
deference to different gods. The general pattern of a Sky-
father and an Earth-mother with their deified children ruling

over various departments of life was carried abroad by adventurers who navigated their ships over new horizons to reach the remote bounds of Polynesia. The marginal areas have retained the main principles of the early theology and so enabled the descendants of a later age to envisage the early pattern.

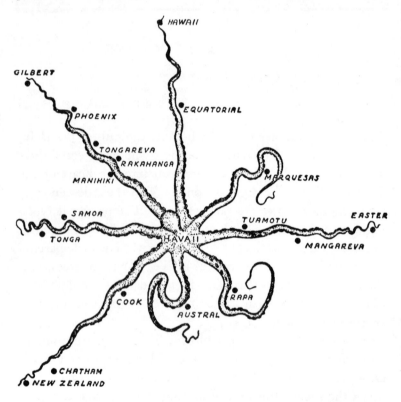

After the pattern had been carried to distant islands, the priests at Opoa elevated Ta'aroa above his brothers and made him creator of all things, not only of his brother gods and men, but of natural phenomena that had existed before he came into being. I cannot help thinking that the highest ranking chief and his priestly advisors belonged to a lineage tracing descent directly from Ta'aroa, and hence their selection of this particular god for promotion. The rising power of Ta'aroa permeated to some of the near-by islands of the Cook group and the Tuamotu and, perhaps, Mangareva, but no farther. In the far lands of New Zealand and Hawai'i he remained in his original place.

The priests at Opoa elaborated their theology still further when they created 'Oro as the son of Ta'aroa. This new god was established as the supreme deity in the great temple named Taputapu-atea. Ta'aroa was then retired and ceased to take an active part in the mundane affairs of men. In order to spread their new cult in Tahiti, the astute priests of Opoa organized the 'Arioi Society of strolling players, who took 'Oro as their tutelary deity. This unique organization has been regarded as a secret society having a possible affinity with Melanesian secret societies. However, there was nothing secret about the 'Arioi; they performed in the open and in public halls to which both men and women were admitted. It has been assumed that the 'Arioi was an institution for birth control because the female members were not supposed to have children and were forced to kill those they had. European actresses cannot afford to have children if they are to fulfil their engagements. Similarly, the Tahitian actresses were frowned upon if they were unable to appear on the stage, and, when their methods of prevention failed, they destroyed their infants.

That the 'Arioi Society was a powerful means of spreading propaganda and winning support for the new cult may be seen by analogy with the methods of certain Maori sects usually associated with some form of faith healing or herbal treatment. At the back of all these sects was the idea of *mana* (power) possessed by the leader through being the medium of a defunct ancestor. The leader and a band of followers, including good singers and dancers, travelled from village to village, not only to cure and win supporters, but to receive entertainment and rewards. The performances sponsored by members of the sect brought people into the fold more readily than would any other form of propaganda. The 'Arioi Society, like these, was founded on an appreciation of Polynesian psychology.

However, the people of Tahiti were not to be easily proselytized again. They persisted in adhering to their own god Tane, and a violent war broke out between 'Oro and Tane. In the end, 'Oro conquered Tane and ultimately became the principal god of all the Society Islands. A new temple, named Taputapu-atea after the temple at Opoa, was built in Tahiti as the centre of the new theology. That 'Oro was a late creation is amply proved by the fact that he is unknown in the marginal areas of Polynesia, even as a son of Ta'aroa. The Rarotongans, however, had some faint knowledge of what had been happening in Opoa for, when the missionary John Williams arrived in Rarotonga from Ra'iatea in 1823, he was asked if Koro ('Oro) was in power. Some of the faithful followers of Tane, who refused to accept 'Oro, left Tahiti and settled in the outer fringe of the Cook Islands. Thus in the Pacific, as well as in the Atlantic, religious intolerance played its part in causing the settlement of new lands.

Let us leave the priests and their intrigues on land and get back to the smack of the salt sea spray. The deified ancestors were succeeded by demigods, among whom are Maui and Ru. Maui we have met before and shall meet again on the various sea trails that radiate out from the centre. Ru as a navigator may be Ru who assisted in propping up the sky. He appears in Tahitian legends and chants as a deep-sea mariner who guided his ship *Te Apori* to the leeward islands of the Society group. His sister Hina, perched in the swing-bow above the foaming waves, peered into the lifting horizon. Ru, feeling that land was near, sang to his ship:

> I am guiding thee,
> I am drawing thee to land,
> O my ship, Te Apori.

Hina, the lookout, called, 'O Ru, what land is this rising upon the horizon?' Ru replied, 'It is Maurua, which will be great forever.' Maurua (Maupiti) is a small island to the west of Vavau (Porapora).

Soon Hina sighted another island, and Ru sang:

> It is Porapora; let its watchword be—
> Porapora the great, the first-born,
> Porapora with the fleet that strikes both ways,
> Porapora of the silent, muffled paddles,
> Porapora of the pink leaf,
> Porapora, the destroyer of fleets.

Porapora was the first large volcanic island sighted on a southeast course from the Gilberts and hence earned the name of 'the first-born'. In later times, its inhabitants raided the neighbouring islands in silent night attacks with their paddles muffled with bark cloth. In the period of Ru, the island bore the ancient name of Vavau, and it is evident that the poet has grouped later happenings around an earlier hero to enrich his composition.

Again Hina called and Ru, the deep-sea poet, sang:

> It is Havai'i; let its watchword be—
> Havai'i that rises in exceeding glory,
> Havai'i, ever ready to defend its honour.

Let us leave Ru and Havai'i and pass from the demigods to the heroes. The heroes belong to the period when central Polynesia was definitely settled and the priests at Opoa were weaving the first pattern of Polynesian theology. They are more human because they belong to a later period and, though miraculous elements still enshroud them, they were not deified. The heroes were deep-sea mariners who began to explore the horizons beyond central Polynesia. The great explorers of the heroic period are included in the cycle of the four generations of Hema, Tafa'i, Vahieroa, and Rata. Space does not permit of our dealing with more than one and, as Rata has already been mentioned in connection with canoe building, let us take the Tahitian account of his great voyage and the incidents that led up to it.

In north Tahiti there lived King Tumu-nui, whose sister Mamae-a-rohi married Vahieroa and gave birth to a son named Rata. Tumu-nui had a daughter who married Tu-i-hiti, a chief who came from the distant land of Hiti-au-rereva, away to the east. In due course, Tu-i-hiti fitted up his ship *Kare-roa* and, with his wife, returned to his own land. Tumu-nui felt the loss of his daughter deeply and decided to visit her in order to persuade her to return to Tahiti with her husband. He built a voyaging ship named *Matie-roa* and a canoe named *Matie-poto*. After appointing his brother 'Iore-roa regent, he sailed for the east with picked crews.

It is but natural that the deep-sea mariners of the time should have recounted to wondering audiences the many difficulties encountered on their voyages and that native story tellers should have personified them into monsters imbued with magic power. The monsters encountered on the distant seas to the east were eight in number:

1. Puʻa-tu-tahi   Isolated-coral-rock.
2. Ahifa-tu-moana   Sea-monster.
3. ʻAre-mata-roroa   Long-wave.
4. ʻAre-mata-popoto   Short-wave.
5. ʻAnae-moe-oho   Fish-shoal.
6. Tupe-ʻiʻo-ahu   Animal-with-burning-flesh.
7. ʻOtuʻu-haʻamana-a-Taʻaroa   Crane-empowered-by-Taʻaroa.
8. Pahua-nui-api-taʻa-i-te-raʻi   Giant-tridacna-opening-on-the-horizon.

Tumu-nui, having performed his religious duties correctly as a protection against the various dangers, had supreme confidence in himself. He encountered Coral-rock, Sea-monster, Long-wave, and Short-wave successively in the daytime, and his gods, in answer to his appeals, rendered each of these enemies inert. On a cloudy night, however, he sailed into the open valves of the Giant-tridacna, and both ship and canoe were swallowed by the monster. Their fate was made known to the people of Tahiti by the gods.

The regent ʻIore-roa decided to recover the bones of his brother and built a ship *Tumu-nui-mate* and a canoe *Meiʻa-roa* for the voyage. Accompanied by Vahieroa, father of Rata, and a picked crew of brave men, he sailed forth. He had sacrificed a pig to his god and, as he was challenged successively by Coral-rock, Sea-monster, Long-wave, Short-wave, Fish-shoal, and Crane-of-Taʻaroa, he told them that their inimical powers, both above and below, had been overcome by his sacrifice of a pig. Coral-rock and Sea-monster let the ships pass safely, Long-wave and Short-wave subsided beneath their bows, Fish-shoal turned aside, and Crane-of-Taʻaroa flew out of sight. The Giant-tridacna was next encountered and the ship was drawn by suction toward its gaping valves. ʻIore-roa defied the Giant-tridacna too late to stay the way on his ship, and the vessel disappeared into the interior. The canoe *Meiʻa-roa* had fallen behind and so escaped to tell the tale of disaster in Tahiti.

The three remaining brothers, 'Iore-poto, 'Iore-mumu, and 'Iore-vava successively built ships and sailed forth to avenge the deaths of the king, the regent, and their crews, but all were swallowed by the Giant-tridacna. Rata thus became king of Tahiti but his mother, Maemae-a-rohi, served as regent and issued the edict, 'Tread the earth, cultivate food, let people grow fat, and take care of your offspring that they may replace those who sleep on the pathways of the sea.'

The people prospered and Rata grew to giant stature. The Queen Regent decided that the time had arrived for her to retire in favour of her son. A feast was held and a wild boar hunt was organized to celebrate the assumption of power by the young king. The regent urged upon her son the necessity of remaining strictly neutral during the competition between the two parties, each composed of two of the four districts that comprised his kingdom. Rata, however, became excited and, dashing into the hunt on the side of one party, struck down competitors of the other side who got in his way. His strength was so great that some were killed and others badly injured. The sport ended on a tragic note. His mother bitterly upbraided Rata for killing his own subjects and, in spite of his shame and tears, she decided to go with her sister to the far land of Hiti-au-rereve to visit her sister's daughter. The great double canoe *Tahiri-a-varovaro-i-te-ra'i* was launched and set sail through the long chain of atolls of the Tuamotu Archipelago. The crew evidently steered a course that avoided the monsters of the sea, for the canoe arrived safely at Hiti-au-rereva.

Rata, by his deep contrition, regained the favour of his people. He determined to recover the bones of the dead from the bowels of the Giant-tridacna. His artisans told him that the finest trees in the lowlands had been used for the previous ships and that he must seek suitable timber in the uplands. It was this scarcity that led Rata to trespass on the territory of the elves of the upper woodlands, the cliffs, and the mountain mists. Certain details of the adventures which befell him have been described in Chapter 4.

The fairy artisans who directed the building of Rata's ship were Tuoi-papapapa and Feufeu. On the completion of the ship, they made an offering of sennit braid to Ta'aroa, and the god responded by sending a shower of rain for the ceremony of making the new ship drink water. The ship was named *Va'a-i-ama* and, with the elves aboard, it was wafted by the mountain breeze into the air and deposited gently on the surface of the sea. Rata, early awakened by dreams of the promised ship, went down to the seashore. The rising sun threw a magnificent rainbow on the clouds facing him, and his magic ship under full sail appeared below the middle of the arch. Manned by its invisible crew, it sailed proudly into the waiting lagoon, furled its matting sails, and dropped anchor to await its human owner.

With such a ship, success was assured. Rata manned it with picked warriors and, before he sailed, made the necessary offerings of fish and coral rock on the altar of the gods of the land. Long strips of bark cloth were cast on the ocean billows to placate the gods of the sea, and large sharks immediately appeared to convey marine approbation. A skilled pilot took the steering paddle. He was termed the *hoa pahi*, friend of the ship, an apt term, for it was through his knowledge that the ship successfully avoided treacherous reefs and surmounted towering seas. The voyage went well until the pilot called, 'Behold! There is the Giant-tridacna'. It was a fearsome sight. The upper valve arched high over the horizon and, above the submerged lower valve, the purple fringe of the huge mollusc waved up and down on the surface of the rippling sea in dreadful expectancy. Nothing daunted, Rata and his armed warriors stood erect on the bow, for the sea trail had led them to the end of their quest.

As the ship glided over the edge of the lower valve, the purple fringe, like monster tentacles, undulated forward and lapped against the sides of the vessel. The shining inner surface of the upper valve, with its indented edge like huge teeth, loomed above them, poised for the downward plunge. Before it could fall, however, Rata and his men with one accord drove their spears below the purple fringe and along the inner surface of the lower valve toward the hinge; they completely severed the great muscle that held together the upper and the lower valves. The huge upper valve that towered above the mast of the ship remained poised on its locked hinge, motionless and impotent.

The body of the Giant-tridacna was cut open and in the interior were found the undigested bones of Tumu-nui and those who had followed after him. In addition, there were found the bodies of Rata's mother and her crew who, returning to Tahiti from Hiti-au-rereva, had been swallowed by the Giant-tridacna but a few hours before. Their bodies were still warm, and the priests with the aid of the god Ta'aroa restored them to life. Thus the living and the dead met between the now impotent valves of the Giant-tridacna. The bones of the dead and the bodies of the living were transferred to Rata's ship, which stood off while the warriors with their spears pried the base of the great bivavle from its coral pedestal. With a gurgling sound, the lifeless Giant-tridacna sank to the bottom of the ocean, nevermore to menace the voyagers who sailed the eastern seas.

Rata returned to Tahiti, where he restored his mother to

her people and the bones of the dead to their weeping relatives. He then set out to rid the seas of the remaining enemies of deep-sea mariners. He slew the Sea-monster that had its base at the Coral-rock, and the Coral-rock, robbed of its mate, became innocuous. Next he killed the Animal-with-burning-flesh and the Fish-shoal. When the Crane-empowered-by-Ta'aroa, which was inimical only to evil people, flew over Rata's ship, it greeted him kindly and flew to a quiet lagoon to be seen no more. The Long-wave and the Short-wave are essential dangers of the great ocean, and they remain alive today to test seamanship.

Coming back to land, we must mention the development that had been taking place in social organization. In Polynesian society the family was ruled by the senior male, who was succeeded by his eldest son. As the family extended into a wider group of kinsmen, the senior family head became a chief of increasing power according to the number of men he could control in peace or war. The extended family groups developed into tribes which claimed descent from early ancestors. History, prestige, and social ceremony developed around chiefs descended from the tribal ancestors. The ruling family at Opoa claimed seniority above all others in the Society Islands, and their claim was admitted. Ritual was built around them as around the gods. Human sacrifices were offered to the god 'Oro, and human sacrifices were demanded for the chiefs on birth and through the varying periods of youth until they were invested with the famous red feather belt at the temple of Taputapu-atea. The red feathers of the parrakeet became the symbol of high chiefs and of the gods. Wooden images that represented the gods were abandoned in the course of time to sorcerers and were replaced by wood beautifully encased in twined coconut fibre. These were decorated with hanging cords of coconut fibre to the ends of which were attached red feathers. The symbol of the great 'Oro rests unrespected in the British Museum. It is a beautiful example of technique but it is dead spiritually, for the red feathers which symbolized the divinity of 'Oro have long since disappeared. The royal family of Porapora wore girdles of yellow feathers to denote that their line was junior to the royal house of Ra'iatea. Through intermarriage both forms of girdle spread to the chiefly houses of Tahiti. With greater fertile lands and a greater population, Tahiti became increasingly powerful. It acquired prestige, and the poets changed its name from Plebeian Tahiti to Tahiti-nui-mare-'are'a, Great-Tahiti-of-the-golden-haze.

Coincident with the development and progress in theology and social organization, the arts and crafts expanded. The development of shipbuilding has been described in Chapter 4. The voyagers who succeeded Rata made explorations and returned to the homeland, not only with tales of their discoveries, but with the sailing directions by which the new lands might be reached. The explorers followed a star over a new horizon, but ever they looked back at the stars over the homeland and, when winds were favourable, returned to the centre from which they had set forth.

Among the voyagers of the later period were Hono'ura and Hiro. Hiro was born in Havai'i but was brought up in Tahiti, whither he was sent to be educated by his maternal grandfather, Ana. He was too young to be admitted immediately to the school, but his thirst for knowledge was so great that he climbed on the roof of the schoolhouse and learned all that his grandfather taught below. Apart from his adventures at sea, Hiro was said to be the first to make a ship constructed of planks instead of the usual dug-out hull.

The tales of discovery led to the peopling of the nearer

islands and for a time communication was maintained between the new colonies and Havai'i. Teuira Henry states that the various colonies were grouped into two divisions termed the Ao-tea (Light-world) and Ao-uri (Dark-world), and each division had a high priest termed respectively Pa'oa-tea and Pa'oa-uri. The two divisions formed the Friendly Alliance, and representatives from the different islands came to Opoa with offerings to the gods on the temple of Taputapu-atea. The great drum used in the temple ritual was named Ta'i-moana (Sound-at-sea). During a convention, an altercation arose in which both the high priests were killed. The people returned home in disorder and the connection of the outlying colonies with the homeland ended. A memory of the Friendly Alliance is retained in Rarotonga for, when John Williams visited that island from Ra'iatea, he was asked why the Ra'iateans had killed the high priest, Pa'oa-tea, and what had become of the great drum, Tangi-moana (Ta'i-moana).

At some time following the period of discovery of lands within Polynesia, there occurred a dispersal from the central hub to permanently occupy the new lands. The dispersal was probably caused by conflict due to increasing population with the inevitable striving after power in the homeland. Organized expeditions were headed by junior members of chiefly families who saw no chance of advancement at home. Because of their social prestige they were able to have voyaging ships built and to command adventurous crews to man their vessels. They were accompanied by priests skilled not only in navigation but versed in the traditional lore that had been developed up to the time of departure. From our knowledge of the theology and traditional lore of the far-away colonies, such as Hawaii and New Zealand, we know that they left after the first pattern of theology had been evolved at

Opoa and after the tales of Hema, Tafaʻi, Vahieroa, and Rata had been incorporated in the traditions of the homeland.

The period of greatest colonizing activity probably extended from the twelfth to the fourteenth century. Settlement was by a process of infiltration by individual canoes arriving at different times and not by a migration of large numbers at one time. It is certain that the Marquesas was settled at an early period, for it became a secondary centre for distribution from which adventurers set out to the east and colonized Mangareva and Easter Island. It is probable that the Marquesas was also used as a place of call by some, at least, of the colonists who made their way north to Hawaiʻi. The emigrants who set out to the marginal areas took with them not only the myths, legends, and traditions of the central homeland but also a rich supply of food plants and domestic animals with which to stock their new homes. The later colonists found some of the islands already occupied by their kinsmen of an earlier infiltration. Though conflict ensued, time led to a blending of the two.

And so, from Havaiʻi, the hub of the Polynesian universe, a more abundant life was carried to the outer isles by those brave navigators who directed their ships on the course of a star that led to a safe haven. Others there must have been, as daring and as trusting in their star, whose course led them into empty seas. Such unlucky ones sleep beneath the barren sea roads they so vainly followed. If the sea ever gives up its dead, what a parade of Polynesian mariners will rise from the depths when the call of the shell trumpet summons them to the last muster roll! Their numbers will bear witness to the courage of those who dared but failed to reach land which was not there. For them no human songs were sung, but the sea croons their requiem in a language that they understand.

9. THE SOUTHWEST COURSE

As the rainbow spans the horizons,
So the canoe of 'Ui-te-rangiora crosses the open seas between.

SONG OF 'UI-TE-RANGIORA

AMONG those who followed a lucky spoke of fortune's wheel
was Ru. Ru lived in 'Avaiki (Havai'i) and, realizing that
overpopulation was taking place in his district, he called his
family together. He said, 'I see that the valleys are thick with
people and even the uplands are becoming crowded. I have
selected a star, and beneath that star there is a land that will
provide us with a peaceful home.' A voyaging canoe named
Te Pua-ariki was built and provisioned. Besides his own
family and near relatives, Ru selected twenty young women
of high rank to people the island of his dreams. When in
1926 I visited the island discovered by Ru, a feast in honour
of my wife and me was given by one of the villages. At its
conclusion, the presiding chief said, 'You are blood of our
blood and bone of our bone. Behold the story of our ancestor
Ru.'

To the accompaniment of drums and singing, a procession
of twenty young women, keeping time with paddles, marched
in before us. They lined up on either side of a length of
coconut leaves tied end to end to represent the voyaging

canoe. Four men taking the part of Ru's brothers were at the bow of the canoe on watch, and Ru himself with the married women of the party was at the stern. Ru, with a steering paddle, guided the canoe on the course of his star.

The canoe remained stationary before us, but the paddling movements indicated that it was speeding ahead over new seas and under new skies. Suddenly one of the lookouts dashed back and in agitated tones reported to Ru that a whirlpool lay on their course and would destroy them. The crew ceased paddling in pretended alarm, but Ru, striking a heroic attitude, cried, 'Am I not Ru who has been girdled with the scarlet belt of chieftainship and who knows the things of the air and the things of the sea? We shall not die. Paddle the canoe!' The lookout returned to his post and the reassured crew resumed paddling in time to the seafaring chant.

A rock and later a waterspout were reported, but Ru again restored confidence to his crew by repeating his oratory. The person taking the part of Ru happened to be our cook boy, but during the play I forgot his humble occupation and saw only that in spirit he was true to the blood of his seafaring ancestors. A chorus announced that a storm had arisen, the skies were clouded, and Ru could no longer see his guiding star. The storm continued for three days and three nights; it was only then that Ru sought divine assistance from Tangaroa, God of the Ocean. Standing erect in the stern of his canoe, he raised his right hand aloft and, in sonorous tones, thus invoked his deity:

> O Tangaroa in the immensity of space,
> Clear away the clouds by day,
> Clear away the clouds by night,
> That Ru may see the stars of heaven
> To guide him to the land of his desire.

The clouds parted, the stars shone through, and the good ship *Pua-ariki*, following the southwest course directed by Ru's star, made its landfall on the island of Aitutaki, the most northerly of the Cook Islands. In the time of distress, Ru had not whimpered to his god to land him in safety on the sought-for isle. All he asked for was a sight of his star, for, with the blood of sea kings running in his veins, he knew that he could do the rest. It was the confidence of leaders in themselves that inspired faith in their crews.

The opening lines of Ru's invocation in the native text ran as follows:

> Tangaroa i te titi,
> Tangaroa i te tata.

As I wrote the words down, I mentally translated them as 'Tangaroa in the *titi*, Tangaroa in the *tata*'. It seemed a mere play on sounds, so I turned to my senior host and asked, 'What is the meaning of *titi* and *tata*?' The old man stood up, swept his arm the full horizon round, and, pointing upward, said, 'That!' In answer to my puzzled look he asked, 'Can we find words? Are not *titi* and *tata* as good as anything else to represent what we cannot express?' A light dawned upon me, and I murmured in English, 'The immensity of space'. 'What?' he queried. 'Yes,' I answered, 'Tangaroa in the *titi*, Tangaroa in the *tata*. It could not be better expressed.' I thought so then, and I feel more so now.

Aitutaki, as already mentioned, was originally held in position by a knotted vine which anchored it to the bottom of the sea. The sinews of the fish Tahiti were severed to prevent it from swimming off. Rarotonga was originally named Nuku-tere (Floating-island) because it moved about until the goddess Ari went below and fixed its foundations. Such tales are echoes of the romance of finding islands in the earliest days of Pacific exploration. The elusive islands moved about on the sea of imagination until the Polynesian discoverers brought them into the world of reality and so fixed their positions.

In the wake of Ru's great canoe, other mariners steered their ships to the southwest and, diverging from their course, found the islands of Atiu, Mauke, Mitiaro, Mangaia, and Rarotonga. Centuries later these islands were rediscovered by Captain James Cook and named the Hervey Islands in honour of the First Lord of the British Admiralty. More recently the name was changed officially to Cook Islands. The group is administered by the New Zealand Government through a Resident Commissioner at Rarotonga.

The first tropical island I ever visited was Rarotonga. At the time, 1909, I represented a Maori constituency in the New Zealand Parliament. To eke out a meagre stipend, I managed to get myself sent to Rarotonga during the recess to relieve the local medical officer in his fight against an epidemic of dengue fever. I shall never forget the first odour of tropical plants, the first sight of the lush foliage and vivid scenery, the strangeness of outrigger canoes and of houses thatched with pandanus, and, above all, the kindly salutations and spontaneous hospitality of the handsome brown-skinned inhabitants who were kin to my own people. Their dialect was similar to Maori, for they retained the *k* and *ng*, and like the people of my own district they did not aspirate the *h* sound.

On the first day that I passed through the main village, two venerable chiefs barred my path and guided me to the verandah of their near-by house. The smiling family gathered with handshakings and salutations of 'Kia orana' (May good health attend you). A platter of peeled green oranges and drinking coconuts was placed before me. One of the

old men, who I later learned was a descendant of a hereditary line of high priests, handed me a drinking nut, saying,
'In New Zealand you have drunk the water of the land, but
here in the land of your fathers you will drink of the water
of trees.' Since then I have drunk the contents of many nuts
in various isles of the Pacific, but that first drink with the
old priest looking on approvingly was in the nature of a liba-
tion to the shades of my ancestors.

I had met many of the Rarotongan chiefs who had attended
an International Exhibition in New Zealand two years before.
We had lived together in a model Maori village to which I
had been assigned as medical officer. Now my old friends
and others vied with one another in feasting my wife and me.
The high chief (*ariki*) of Arorangi village sent his son for us
with a four-wheeled carriage surmounted by a canopy with a
tasseled fringe along the edges and drawn by a single horse.
The harness, however, had decayed and the leather traces
were replaced by ropes. The diminutive horse found our
triple weight embarrassing. In response to the suasion of a
long stick, the horse made a jerky effort to start, both the
rope traces parted, and we came to a standstill. The prince
leaped out and examined the parted ropes, but they were too
short to be knotted together. The Maoris of New Zealand
wonder what their kinsmen do without the flax with which all
things are tied. I wondered also what our escort would do.
Without the slightest hesitation, he took a large bush knife
from the back of the carriage and went to one of the native
hibiscus trees which grew all along the road. He slashed the
trunk high up, tore down a long, wide strip of bark, joined
the ends of his traces together with the bark, and we went
gaily on our way. Thus I learned that what the flax was to
the Maori, so the bark of the wild hibiscus was to the inhabitants of volcanic islands.

The food for the feast had been provided by the chief's family and his tenants who paid for the use of the land with part of its produce. Sweet potatoes, yams, taro, breadfruit, bananas, coconuts, fowls, pigs, and fish were assembled. The requisite quantity went into the earth ovens, and the remainder was heaped up to make a brave showing. Various puddings of pounded taro and breadfruit mixed with coconut cream were cooked beforehand in leaf wrappings. We arrived on an animated scene with the whole village population bedecked in garlands of flowers and scented leaves. Choice wreaths were put about our necks, and people crowded in with outstretched hands and smiling salutations of 'Kia orana'. In the old days, they would have pressed their noses against ours. I held my nose poised for the nasal contact to which I was accustomed in my own land, but the reciprocal movement did not come. The ancient pattern of greeting had been abandoned throughout tropical Polynesia. I was both disappointed and relieved.

The steaming mounds before us were rapidly denuded of their covering of leaves and the pigs baked whole were revealed on the hot stones beneath. Coconut and banana leaves were spread on the ground before the pile of uncooked food, and on these were placed the pigs and other cooked foods from the oven. The chief's orator standing beside the food thus addressed me, 'This is the oven of food of the high chief Tinomana and his people. Here are pigs, fowls, fish, and other foods. Here are uncooked taro, breadfruit, and other foods. This food is in honour of your visit.' As he pointed to each kind of food, he called it by name. He continued, 'We come of the same ancestry. We welcome you as a kinsman to the land through which your ancestors passed on their voyage to the South. All this food is now given into your hands.'

The Rarotongan dialect is very similar to that of New Zealand. I arose with what dignity I could assume and replied in fitting terms for the honour done me. I chanted a Maori incantation which impressed them, though they did not altogether understand it. I ended by saying, 'Divide up the food that we of the same blood may eat together.'

In a short time, the pigs were divided into individual portions. In every Polynesian community, there are experts who can divide the food into heaps so that each family gets its correct share. Then all sit down to eat, and what is left over is taken home together with the share of uncooked food. After we had eaten, listened to songs, and watched dances, our liberal share of the food was packed into the carriage that took us home. All the live fowls came into our share of the feast. We had no hen coop at the doctor's residence, so our maid tethered the fowls with strips of hibiscus bark to the shaded fence in the back yard. Our cook worked down the line of fowls as occasion required, but before he could reach the end, another invitation to a feast would arrive and the casualties in the ranks of the chickens were replaced by fresh recruits.

At one feast, I forgot the usual concluding remarks of my speech in reply. A dead stillness ensued. The air of suspended expectancy was retained. The orator came quietly to me and whispered, 'Will we load all the cooked pigs and the food into your conveyance?' With Polynesian politeness they were prepared to send the whole feast to my home unless I said a word to the contrary. I stood up as if I had never sat down and cried, 'Divide up the food that we may all eat together.'

I have digressed somewhat in the hope that these first experiences in Polynesia might convey a little of the atmosphere that eighteen years later influenced me to give up medicine to join Bishop Museum in its programme of research in Polynesia. It was not until twenty years after my visit to Rarotonga that I was given the opportunity of visiting all the islands of the Cook group.

The early settlement of the Cook Islands passes from myth and legend to the period of traditional history. Each island has its own story of the first human discoverers and those who came after. After the discovery of Aitutaki by Ru, came Te Erui and his brother, Matareka. Te Erui first set out in his ship *Viripo*, which was dismasted by a hurricane. He was sorely puzzled that a hurricane should have arisen in what he knew to be a favourable season for exploration. So after his return to 'Avaiki, he consulted a priest as to the cause of his misfortune. The wily priest asked, 'What name did you give to your ship?' '*Viripo*', repleid Te Erui. 'Ah,' said the priest, 'that was the cause of the trouble. You should have included the name of a god in some part of your vessel.' Te Erui built another ship, which he named *Te Rangi-pae-uta*, and, on the advice of the priest, he named the two masts after the gods Tangaroa and Rongo. With divinity support-ing both sails, Te Erui set forth once more and landed on the west side of Aitutaki. Here he was met by the descendants of Ru, who said, 'This is the land discovered by Ru and left to his children's children. Before you lies the purple sea of 'Iro. Go there to seek out a land for yourself.' Te Erui, however, forced a landing after slaying various opponents. With his famous adze, Haumapu, he cut a channel named Te Rua-i-kakau through the encircling reef, and thus made a passage for his ship to enter the lagoon. This passage at Aitutaki and two at Rarotonga are the only ones in the group that will admit whaleboats—a great advantage in modern times in the landing and loading of cargo. It is natural that the Aitutaki people should boast of their ancestor, Te Erui, and the boon he conferred on the island.

A third navigating ancestor who came to Aitutaki was Ruatapu, who had ventured to various islands. He changed the name of his ship during his voyages, and when it arrived at Aitutaki, it bore the name of *Tuehu-moana* (Sea-spray). He is credited with the introduction of coconuts and the gardenia known as *tiare maori* (*Gardenia tahitiensis*). The spot where he planted the flower is known to this day as Tiare (Flower). The ruling chief at the time was Taruia, and Rautapu, after establishing friendly relationship with him, began to scheme as to how he could supplant him in the rule of the island. He excited the curiosity of Taruia by telling him tales of the islands he had visited. He finally persuaded the high chief to accompany him on a sea voyage to see the beautiful women of other lands. Each fitted up a voyaging canoe, and Ruatapu purposely set sail before the other was quite ready. To Taruia's appeal that he should wait so that they might set sail in company, Ruatapu called back, 'I will go on to Rarotonga and be on the beach to welcome you in.' Ruatapu sailed off to the other side of the small islet of Ma'ina, and, when he saw Taruia set sail, he purposely capsized his canoe. Taruia shortly after appeared, and, to Ruatapu's appeal to wait until he had righted his canoe, he replied with no small satisfaction, 'No, I will go on to Rarotonga and be on the beach to welcome you in.' Ruatapu waited until Taruia was out of sight. He righted his canoe and returned to Aitutaki, where he usurped the position of Taruia. Taruia eventually arrived at the atoll of Tongareva (Penrhyn), where he settled down. His name occurs in the lineages of that region.

A comparison of lineages and traditions, both in New

Zealand and the Cook Islands, shows that Ruatapu lived about 1350 A.D., when the last voyages were being made to New Zealand. Aitutaki lineages show that Te Erui lived about three hundred years earlier, while Ru was earlier still. Though the descendants of these three ancestors have inter-married, the groups which claim direct male descent live as distinct tribes in different villages. On festive occasions, each village puts on plays illustrating incidents in the traditional history of their particular ancestor. During my stay, the descendants of Ru enacted 'The Voyage of Ru', those of Ruatapu played 'The Fishing Quarrel Between Ruatapu and his son, Kirikava', and those of Te Erui danced 'The Song of the Adze Haumapu'. No village would dream of acting a play concerning an ancestor not its own. Even a theme not based on history was respected.

At a village where I asked for information about stilts, my informant said, 'Stilts? Yes, we have stilts, but they are the property of the village of Vaipae. When you go to Vaipae, ask them. They have a stilt dance.' Later at Vaipae, I asked again about stilts. 'Yes,' they said, 'we have stilts. We have a stilt dance. Would you like to see it?' 'Certainly', I replied. A middle-aged man walked quickly over to a large drum of European pattern but native make, suspended from the roof of an open shed. He beat loudly upon it, shouting, 'Ho, the stilt dancers! Come and dance for our guest.' Four young men appeared carrying stilts. Four boxes were placed in a row. Mounting their stilts beside the boxes, the dancers went through various movements in time to the beating of the large drum and a smaller wooden gong. They hopped on one stilt, turned round, clicked stilts together, climbed onto the boxes where they performed various steps, dropped to the ground again, and carried out a regular series of movements in perfect time with the music and with each other. Stilts had been common to the whole island, but Vaipae had been the first to put on a stilt dance in public. They had therefore established a copyright which was protected by no law except that of innate courtesy.

Atiu, the nearest island to Aitutaki, was peopled from central 'Avaiki. The first colonists were led by Mariri and his younger brothers, Atiu-mua and Atiu-muri. Their father was Tangaroa, whose qualifying epithet, the Source- without-a-father (Tumu-metua-kore), implies that he and consequently his sons were of divine origin. Mariri named the island 'Enua-manu, the Land-of-insects, in order to stress the fact that there were no previous human inhabitants. According to the most reliable lineages, this first settlement took place about 1300 A.D. Though the lineages of the present inhabitants include Mariri as an ancestor, the principal descent is traced from Atiu-mua, and, in his honour the name of the island was changed to Atiu.

Mauke was settled at the same period as Atiu by an ancestor named Uke, whose daughter married a son of Atiu-mua. These ancestors came by voyaging canoes from central 'Avaiki.

The Atiuans were redoubtable warriors, and about 1820 A.D. they conquered the neighbouring islands of Mauke and Mitiaro. In their wars they wore sennit helmets of coiled work as protection against slingstones. On a field expedition in 1929, a group of Atiuans, while displaying their family war helmets, vividly described the last occasion upon which they had been used.

'A warrior from Tahiti arrived on his voyaging canoe and was peacefully received on the island of Mitiaro. He incited the people of Mitiaro to defy us, the warriors of Atiu. He instructed them to build a defence in the midst of the coral rock of the upraised inland reef known as the *makatea*. When our war canoes landed on Mitiaro to deal with the challenge, we found the villages deserted. Our scouts, however, soon located the stone fort in the midst of the *makatea*. We immediately attacked in three divisions representing the three ruling high chiefs of Atiu. The division of Rongo-ma-tane under its war leader had the place of honour in the front. The coral of the *makatea* had so many sharp points that we could not rush the fort. We laid our long clubs of ironwood down on the sharp points and crawled along them. When we got to the end of the clubs, we upended them and laid their full length in front of us for another advance. Our progress was slow, and all the time the Mitiaro people, from platforms built up above their stone walls, showered slingstones down upon us. We could not stand up to return their fire. All we could do was to keep our heads bent forward so that the stones, which would have struck our heads, were stopped by our sennit helmets. You will notice that the helmet fits close against the sides of the head, but, being high, there is an air space between the top of the head and the top of the helmet. A stone that hits the top of the helmet has its force weakened, and so the head is saved from being split open. We kept our helmets at the proper angle to stop the slingstones and kept crawling along. Some were hit on the body, but we kept crawling along to get to close quarters. The chief warrior of Rongo-ma-tane led the van. He was a tried fighter with a great war record, and we knew that once we reached the walls of the fort, the victory would be ours. Then disaster fell upon us. A Mitiaro slinger threw a large slingstone made of the white stone that is found in caves [a stalagmite]. This is the best kind of slingstone, for if it hits a rock it will burst into fragments that fly in all directions with great force. The slingstone struck the hard coral in a hollow near our leader and burst. A large piece struck him in the eye, and he rolled off his club, badly wounded. A yell of triumph rose from the fort and the attack of the Atiu people was stayed. We thought our leader was dead. In the supporting line at the back was the youngest son of the high chief, Rongo-ma-tane. He was so young that his place was among the womenfolk and not among adult warriors. We hardly knew him, yet the warrior's courage ran in his blood. He had slipped in among the supporting line without being noticed.

'The Mitiaro people had hung the figure of their god, Te Pare, from a pole in order to inspire the defence. They were still shouting and raising their hands to Te Pare for having helped them to put the attacking leader out of action. At this critical moment, when we were about to retire, the youngest son of Rongo-ma-tane stood upright on the points of the *makatea* in the supporting line behind. He had a sling in his hand, and, as he made a preparatory swing, he recited an incantation to direct his slingstone and give it power. He was young, but he had been taught as the son of a high chief should be taught. The enemy jeered—what could one youth with a sling do against so many? But again, mark the battle wisdom that runs in the blood of chiefs. In his chant he called upon his own gods to direct his slingstone against the hostile god, Te Pare. He threw with all his force and skill. His gods heard him and guided his stone straight and true so that it struck Te Pare on the head just below the pole lashing with such force that the sennit braid broke and the god tumbled to the ground. A cry of horror broke from the fort, for it was indeed an ill omen for them. But the front and supporting lines of the Atiuans, as they saw the god fall, raised a great yell of exultation. They rose in one body and, taking no heed of the sharp points of the *makatea*, dashed across the intervening space, poured over the coral walls, and captured the fort.'

The mythology of Atiu and Mauke includes the Tahitian concept of Te Tumu (Source) and Papa (Earth-stratum), who, in these islands, gave birth to Tane, god of forests, birds, and forest foods. Tane begat Rongo-ma-tane, god of peace, and Tu, god of war. Tangaroa occurs as the guardian of all things and the protector against adverse winds and rough seas. In Rarotongan mythology, Te Tumu married Papa; and, after the stages of childbirth, as personified by Te Uira (Lightning-pains), Te 'A'a (Massaging), and Te Kinakina (Amniotic fluid), Papa gave birth to the gods Tane, Rongo, Tu, Tangaroa, and Ruanuku. This seems to be the pattern that was carried out from Havai'i before the Ta-aroa elaboration took place at Opoa.

In Mangaia, Vatea, whom we recognize as the Tahitian Atea, took the place of Te Tumu. He married Papa and produced the gods Tangaroa, Rongo, Tane, Tonga'iti, and others, but, curiously enough, not Tu, the war god of other islands. When Vatea was considering the division of his inheritance among his sons, he wanted to give all the food to Tangaroa, the first-born. Papa suggested instead that Tangaroa be given only the chiefly food, signified by a reddish colour, and that Rongo, the second-born, be given the rest. Her secret reason was that a mother was not allowed to eat with her eldest son, because of the taboo of primogeniture, but the restriction did not apply to the second son. Vatea consented to Papa's wish, and, at a great feast held shortly afterward, a few reddish coconuts, taro, crustaceans, and fish were placed before Tangaroa; all the other foods were heaped in front of Rongo. Rongo's pile was so large

STONE IMAGE FROM RAIVAVAE near Papeete Museum, Tahiti; with
the author beside it

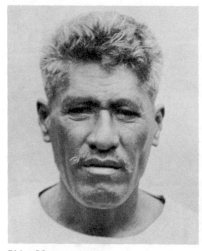

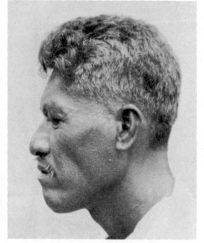

TAHITI

TOTAKOTO, TUAMOTU

TALKING CHIEF, SAMOA

RURUTU, AUSTRAL ISLANDS

HAWAII

TONGAN DOUBLE CANOE showing lateen sail with apex down at bow

TAHITIAN DOUBLE CANOE with vertical spritsail

HIGH CHIEF OF RENNELL ISLAND
ready to receive guests

A HIGH CHIEF OF RENNELL ISLAND
in Melanesia. The island is inhabited
by a tattooed people speaking a Polynesian dialect

PEOPLE OF PORAPORA (Vavau)
assembled for a dance

THE CORONATION PILLAR, named
Te Papa-ia-ruea, at Taputapu-atea,
with K. P. Emory and the author
beside it

FARETAI, at Maeva on Huahine, TEMPLE ALTAR OF
similar to Taputapu-atea

ANCIENT VAVAU (Porapora), the first high volcanic island sighted on eastward
voyages to central Polynesia

THE UNIQUE TEMPLE OF MAHAIATEA, erected in 1769, which gave rise to mistaken theories of affinity with the pyramids of Egypt

S. Savage

RAROTONGAN HIGH PRIEST ON THE TEMPLE OF ARAI-TE-TONGA with the pillar of investiture named TUAMAKEVA

CORNER PILLAR OF RAUHARA TEMPLE, IN TONGAREVA
Note the curb stones set on edge

OUTRIGGER FISHING CANOE FROM MITARO, COOK ISLANDS, showing
method of carrying

ALTAR OF TEMPLE OF TE REINGA ON PENRHYN ISLAND

MARQUESAN STONE IMAGE

PARTLY TATTOOED WARRIOR FROM THE MARQUESAS
Note hair, club, and shell trumpet

WESTERN CURVE OF HAO ATOLL

TE VAITAU FORT, RAPA

PHASE IN CEREMONY TO PROMOTE ABUNDANCE OF FOOD
AT VAHITAHI, TUAMOTU

INVESTITURE PILLARS ON THE RAMAPOHIA TEMPLE, FAGATAU ATOLL

PLANK FISHING CANOES FROM TATAKOTO, TUAMOTU
Note inner lagoon and coconut-covered islets

OUTRIGGER CANOES with mat sails on the lagoon of NAPUKA ATOLL

that some of the food rolled off and was trampled under foot
—a figure of speech indicating plenty.

Tangaroa, in a fit of jealousy, left Mangaia, and Rongo
became the principal god of the island. In giving Rongo
the greater portion of food, the Mangaians retained an early
pattern with Rongo as god of agriculture. They made him
the war god, which conflicted with his earlier position in the
Tahitian pantheon as god of peace. Human sacrifices were
made to Rongo, and, after the temple ceremony, the body
of the victim was thrown into the bushes as food for the
hungry Papa. Tu, the ancient god of war, appears in Mangaian myth as a valiant warrior from the underworld. He taught
the Mangaians the art of war, though he had been deprived
of the portfolio of war by Rongo.

The period of darkness was personified under the names
of Po-tangotango and Po-kerekere, as it was in the centre,
north, east, and south but not in the west. The myth of
the sky resting on the flattened leaves of the arrowroot is
present. The sky was raised by Ru-te-toko-rangi (Ru-who-
propped-up-the-sky).

Mangaia departs from the orthodox pattern of human
settlement by maintaining that the island emerged from the
Underworld of 'Avaiki with the first settlers upon it. These
ancestors were the sons of Rongo by his own daughter.
Thus the creation of man from earth and his arrival on the
island by voyaging canoe were discarded. Among the gods
of Mangaia are Tangiia and Motoro, who appear as human
ancestors in the genealogies of near-by Rarotonga. The
genealogies of Mangaia include seventeen generations from
1900 back to the god Rongo, but the genealogies of Rarotonga include twenty-six generations from 1900 to the navigator Tangiia, who lived in about the thirteenth century.

Mangaia was probably settled after the time of Tangiia by people from Rarotonga who omitted from their histories the accounts of discovery and settlement and, perhaps to increase their prestige, revised their mythology and linked themselves directly to the gods. The chiefly tribe, Ngariki, claimed that their ancestors were autochthonous, the direct descendants of Rongo. The Tonga'iti and Ngati-tane tribes admitted that their ancestors came later by canoe. The Mangaians were doughty warriors, and created the special spirit land of Tiaria for the souls of warriors slain in battle. All other souls descended on a *pua* tree that reached down into the Underworld, where they fell into the clutches of Miru, a female cannibal, who cooked and ate them.

The Rarotongan genealogies, with the exception of those of Hawai'i and Marquesas, are the longest in Polynesia. Percy Smith accepted them as human documents giving the movements of people from India to Indonesia and on into Polynesia. However, so much post-European information has been included in the native text accompanying the gene-alogies that I cannot accept them as accurate and ancient. Rarotongan mythology includes tales of remote ancestors who ventured forth on the seas in the dim past. Among these was 'Ui-te-rangiora, who lived in the early part of the seventh century, and in his ship *Te Ivi-o-Atea* sailed to the far south where he saw the rocks that grew up out of the sea named Tai-rua-koko, the long hair that floated on the surface, the sea covered with foam like arrowroot, the animal that dived down under the sea, a dark place where the sun was not seen, and the high white rocks without vegetation upon them. These wonders have been interpreted as the sea south of Rapa, bull kelp, the frozen sea, sea lions, the Ant-arctic night, and icebergs.

Three hundred and fifty years later Te Ara-tanga-nuku felt the call of the sea and decided to leave the land of Kuporu where he was living. His uncles shouldered their adzes, and, on their way into the mountain forest in search of a tree for the keel of Te Ara-tanga-nuku's canoe, they encountered a white heron and a sea snake that were fighting out an old-time feud. The white heron was sorely wounded and it appealed to the first two brothers, but they passed on. The third brother, who had dropped behind, went to the assistance of the heron and killed the snake with his adze. In gratitude the heron directed its rescuer, Oro-taere, to a suitable tree. Oro-taere and his party felled the tree, trimmed it, fixed the hauling rope, and went home.

After the craftsmen had left, Tangaroa-i'u-mata, the owner of the forest, arrived and found one of his trees prostrate. He sought out his keeper, Rata-of-the-forest, and others, but no one could tell him who had felled the tree. Tangaroa by a magic chant erected the tree trunk and restored the branches, chips, and leaves to their original position.

Next day, Oro-taere returned with his party to the spot. The only apparent evidence of their previous work was the hauling rope hanging from the branch of a tree. They searched through the forest and finally located the tree they had felled by a white spot on the trunk, due to their having taken a piece of bark home with them.

Oro-taere realized that it had been possible to raise the tree again because his adze, consecrated to a specific task, had been defiled by killing a sea snake. He went to the shore with his party to reconsecrate their adzes. They returned with purified adzes and again felled the tree, trimmed, and dragged it to the place where the high priest lived. During the night, the ship was built by a spirit craftsman with four assistants on either side of the vessel. Hence the ship was named *Tarai-po* (Built-at-night). Atonga, the high priest and father of Te Ara-tanga-nuku, sent a messenger to the white crane to assemble the birds to transport the ship down to the shore.

The sea birds and the land birds gathered on either side of the ship, and, lifting it on their wings in time to a chant sung by one of their number, they carried it through the air and deposited it before the boathouse that had been especially built for it. The ship was then renamed *Te Manu-ka-rere* (The Flight-of-birds).

The ship was launched before the multitude of Kuporu who had gathered for the occasion. Under the command of Te Ara-tanga-nuku, it made voyages to other lands grouped together under the name of Iva. The ship was renamed *Te Orauroa-ki-Iva* (The Long-voyage-to-Iva). Later Te Ara-tanga-nuku sailed to the south in order to verify the wonders seen by 'Ui-te-rangiora. If the details of the trips to the south are pre-European, these two voyages were wonderful feats of endurance, considering the scanty clothing of the Polynesians. However, I believe that no Polynesian voyager would continue south into grey, cold, inhospitable seas. Traditions of several islands mention a dangerous sea to the south, generically termed Tai-koko. Probably the original Rarotongan legend said that 'Ui-te-rangiora and Te Ara-tanga-nuku voyaged into the Tai-koko, and later historians embellished the tales by adding details learned from European whalers and teachers.

Rarotonga, under the name of Nuku-tere (Floating-island), was located by the god Tonga-'iti, who stamped upon it; and his wife Ari dived down to fix its foundations. The island was then named Tumu-te-varovaro. The god

Toutika arrived and deposed the other two by trickery.

The first human settlers came from Iva under Ata, and afterward another group arrived from Atu-'apai under 'Apopo. 'Apopo appears in the widespread story of Apakura, who waged war against her eight brothers to avenge the murder of her son. After the defeat of the brothers, 'Apopo, the only survivor of the eight brothers, fled to Rarotonga at about the end of the ninth century. He was killed and his party defeated in a war with the people from Iva.

The great ancestors of Rarotonga were Tangiia and Karika. Tangiia was a direct descendant of 'Ui-te-rangiora and Te Ara-tanga-nuku, and lived in Tahiti in the middle of the thirteenth century. He fought with his half brother, Tutapu, over the share of breadfruit and other perquisites associated with the position of their father, the high chief, Pou-vananga. Though Tangiia was successful in the first engagement, he was subsequently defeated and pursued to different islands by his brother, who earned the title of Tutapu-the-relentless-pursuer. During this period of flight, Tangiia sailed to the west, to Samoa, Wallis Island, and Fiji. In addition, he went to 'Avaiki-te-varinga, which Percy Smith assumes to have been in Indonesia, where a religious ceremony was being held at the temple. Tangiia interviewed the priests and the gods, and they gave him power (*mana*), goods such as drums and shell trumpets, ritual dances, and various gods. On his return, he met the celebrated Tahitian navigator, 'Iro (Hiro), and asked him for his son to be a chief over some of his people, because his own sons had been killed by Tutapu. 'Iro replied that his son was at Rapa; and the native history says that Tangiia sailed for Rapa-nui (Easter Island) where he found the youth and returned with him to Tahiti.

In this extraordinary series of voyages, Tangiia is credited with sailing from Tahiti to Indonesia and, after his return, sailing to Easter Island and returning. The total distance travelled would be well over 20,000 miles. A range from Tahiti to Samoa in the west and to Rapa in the east might be possible, but the extension to Indonesia in one direction and to Easter Island in the other would imply friendly ports of call for food and water supplies and a knowledge of such a stretch of the Pacific Ocean that no one Polynesian could possibly possess.

I believe that the 'Avaiki from which Tangiia received his gods and ritual was not a remote island in Indonesia but Ra'iatea in the central Pacific. Why go to Indonesia for gods who had been established at Opua long before Tangiia was born? It is likely that the 'Iti where he met 'Iro was not Fiji but an old form of Tahiti. Probably Tangiia played hide-and-seek with Tutapu in central Polynesia and then fled to Rarotonga.

On his voyage to Rarotonga from Tahiti, Tangiia encountered the ship of Karika, who hailed from Manu'a in eastern Samoa. Hostilities were smoothed over and both settled in Rarotonga. Tutapu-the-relentless-pursuer, true to his name, pursued Tangiia to Rarotonga where he was slain in battle. Temples (maraes) were established in the various districts and among them was Taputapu-atea, which derived its name from the mother temple at Opoa. In addition to the strictly religious temples there were courts of honour, where the highest chiefs and priests sat on stone seats that were the special privilege of high rank. The most noted of these courts was Arai-te-tonga with its tall stone pillar of investiture named Taumakeva.

The districts were peopled and tribes developed with tribal chiefs (*mataiapo*) and high chiefs (*ariki*) ruling over island divisions. The *ariki* line from Tangiia is that of Pa-ariki living at Ngatangiia and ruling over the human canoe of Takitumu. Kainuku is a supporting *ariki*. The *ariki* line from Karika is that of Makea residing at Avarua and ruling over the Au-o-Tonga. An early Makea was evicted for tyranny and fled to Arorangi, where he was accepted as *ariki* and his successors established the Tinomana title. The Makea title split and the divided authority is now held by Makea Tinirau and Makea Karika.

The distance between Rarotonga and Tahiti is about seven hundred miles so that the Cook Islands were within easy range of central 'Avaiki. Noted ancestors sailed their named ships to the various islands and erected maraes after landing to conduct a ritual of thanksgiving to their gods for their favour. They brought the various cultivable food plants to stock their new homes. The pig was introduced in Rarotonga, Atiu, Mauke, and Mitiaro, where it was used symbolically to express rank in social and religious functions.

The myths, religion, and social system of the Cook Islands link up directly with the culture of the central home in 'Avaiki. Variations, omissions, and additions have occurred, bu the main principles were never lost. In the material crafts there is much that is identical, as the shapes of wooden bowls and stone adzes with their hafts and lashing patterns. It is in weapons and the representation of gods that extreme diversity took place. Each island evolved its own form of art in carving on wood, and art motifs differ. The ceremonial adzes with hafts carved with a K-pattern that are erroneously attributed to the Cook (Hervey) Island as a whole belong exclusively to Mangaia. Though bound to a certain extent by tradition in religion and social matters, the artist's hand followed the guidance of his own spirit until he saw that his work was good.

10. THE NORTHWEST ATOLLS

The sea seethes,
The sea recedes,
It appears, the land appears
And Maui stands upon it.

RAKAHANGA CHANT

ALONG the route probably followed by the earliest voyagers in the Pacific on their long sail from the Gilbert Islands to the Society Islands are the Phœnix Islands, where ruined temples of coral limestone are the sole witness of previous occupation. Farther to the southeast are the inhabited atolls, Manihiki, Rakahanga, and Tongareva (Penrhyn). As these small islands are low-lying and unattractive for permanent settlement, they were probably occupied only temporarily by the earliest people who cherished hopes and dreams of better lands ahead. However, when increased population at the centre of Polynesia led to renewed exploration, the three atolls were repeopled from Rarotonga and Tahiti. Tongareva alone retains a legend of an early settlement that preceded the voyages from Tahiti.

In 1929, I visited Manahiki and Rakahanga with Judge Ayson, Resident Commissioner of the Cook Islands, and members of his staff. We sailed from Rarotonga by the schooner *Tiare Taporo*, under the efficient command of Captain Viggo Rasmussen. At Rakahanga, Judge Ayson conducted a Court to inquire into the genealogies of the various families and the history of their ancestors, as a basis to land claims which might subsequently arise. By courtesy of the Court, I was allowed to sit in and obtain a complete set of the local lineages.

Both Manihiki and Rakahanga are small atolls whose islets are set on a coral reef encircling an inner lagoon. Neither atoll has openings through the reef which will admit canoes. In order to land and to discharge cargo, the schooner lays off as close to the reef as is safe, and passengers and cargo are transhipped into outrigger canoes. The old type of canoe has completely disappeared and a modern form is made from imported sawn timber. Though shaped like a flat-bottomed boat with sharp bow and stern, the outrigger is retained. The natives paddle in close to the reef and wait patiently until the right wave comes surging along. They paddle vigorously, the wave lifts the canoe over the outer lip of the reef, and, if deep enough, floats it across the reef into the outer lagoon that stretches between the reef and the shore. If the wave is too shallow, the canoe grounds on the reef; the crew leap out and hold the canoe to prevent it from being drawn back by the suction of the receding wave. As the wave subsides, one may gaze fearfully down the vertical outer side of the reef and into the yawning, gurgling chasm below. The newcomer is not reassured by tales of people who have been sucked down into coral caverns from which they never reappeared.

The islands rise only ten to twenty feet above sea level and do not support the food plants, animals, and raw materials used on the volcanic islands of central Polynesia. Our respect must be great for these early settlers, coming from the verdant lands of Tahiti and Rarotonga, who accepted these unfriendly isles as home and so quickly adapted themselves to an unfertile environment. There are no breadfruit trees, no bananas, plantains, sweet potatoes, yams, arrowroot, or *cordyline*, and no domestic animals on these atolls. Coconut palms grow luxuriantly and supply the staple vegetable food. A kind of taro termed *puraka* is grown in deep trenches or in wide, excavated areas which reach the brackish subsoil water. The fruit of the pandanus, seldom eaten on volcanic islands, is an important food on atolls. The fruit of the *noni* (*Morinda citrifolia*) is also used, but it is an ill-smelling food that can be rendered palatable only by extreme hunger. The wild hibiscus and plants of the nettle family that furnish cordage elsewhere do not grow here. Lines and nets are made of coconut-husk fibre, and ordinary lashings from the skin of the midrib butts of coconut leaves.

One of my early lessons on adjustments to local conditions was obtained on watching a young man climb a coconut tree to get some drinking nuts. He cut the leaf off a young coconut tree, tore strips off the midrib, beat them against the trunk of a tree, and even chewed them to soften them. He tied the ends together with a reef knot and, looping this over his feet, speedily climbed the tree.

Large timber was scarce and, before the introduction of sawn timber, the two kinds of trees suitable for canoes were split into planks so as not to waste any material by dubbing out trunks as hulls. The tools, as already mentioned, had to be made from tridacna shells, owing to the lack of basaltic stones. Clothing had to be made from coconut leaves or plaited pandanus leaves, for the paper mulberry which provided elsewhere the raw material for bark cloth does not grow on atolls. Even firewood was scarce; coconut shells, dry coconut husks, and the dry sheaths and racemes of coconut flowers were collected for the cooking fires.

Nature, however, was kind in providing a rich and varied fish supply, both in the lagoon and in the ocean beyond. Flying fish and bonito were plentiful. In the lagoon was an inexhaustible supply of shellfish in the tridacna and also the pearl oyster, if occasion demanded. Crayfish were numerous, and land crabs and coconut crabs enriched the larder.

At Rakahanga we were given some coconut crabs, and when our hosts learned that I enjoyed the oily part of the body that most strangers find too rich, they raised the taboo on catching crabs on a particular island. We hunted them there at night with torches made of dried coconut leaves bound together. After dark the crabs come out of their holes and wander around, even climbing up the trunks of trees. They are loathsome bloated creatures of a purplish-blue colour with huge claws that will nip off a finger quite readily if it comes their way. Our hosts seized them expertly and, with a strip of coconut-leaf midrib, tied them in such a way that the claws were imprisoned and could not gape open for attack.

We also fished by torchlight in the outer lagoon. Fish that were attracted by the light were speared or struck with a piece of hoop iron. Crayfish on the shallow bottom were stepped upon, then grasped with the hand, and turned belly upward to prevent their kicking with their powerful tails. Each man carried a basket tied around his waist in which to carry the catch.

The same night, we went torch fishing by canoe in the inner lagoon. The expert fisherman stood in the bow with a long-handled scoop-net, while the torch bearer stood behind him. No matter where the fish appeared, on the surface, deep down, on the right or on the left, the net was plunged into the water and the capture was sure and unerring. It was all so easy and self-assured. One realized that a high degree of expert skill had necessarily been developed to make the most of the opportunities that nature had provided so sparingly in these less-favoured isles.

It has already been related how Maui fished up the land, and, by stamping upon it during his fight with Huku, separated Manihiki from Rakahanga. The first human settler on Rakahanga was Toa, a defeated warrior who came from Rarotonga in about the middle of the fourteenth century. He had no interest in priestly ritual and did not erect the usual temple upon his arrival to thank the gods for guiding him safely to land. Apparently he was accompanied only by his own family, for he committed incest with his daughters in order that males might be produced to ensure the continuance of the human species on the island.

About one hundred and fifty years later, Tangihoro and Ngaro-puruhi voyaged from Rakahanga to foreign lands and Ngaro-puruhi brought back two stolen gods named Puarenga and Te Uru-renga. He built a temple on Manihiki for the worship of Te Pua-renga and another on Rakahanga for Te Uru-renga. These temples were thought to be the first constructed on the atolls. Ngaro-puruhi probably obtained these gods from some lesser priest in Tahiti, for had he been admitted to Opoa he would have returned with a richer ritual and a more detailed mythology.

The major gods and heroes of the Cook Islands were unknown. Tangaroa, however, appears as the guardian of fire in the Underworld. Maui, as the grandson of Tangaroa, defeated him in a body-tossing contest and learned the secret of fire. A local embellishment to the tale tells how the two pet sea birds of Tangaroa stood on the under piece of wood to steady it while Maui worked the upper stick back and forth along the groove to make fire by friction. When Maui had finished, true to his impish nature, he ungratefully struck the two birds on the head with the charred end of the friction stick, and the family of those birds have borne black marks on their heads ever since.

After several generations the descendants of Toa developed into two groups, each with its own *ariki* chief, termed Whainga-aitu and Whaka-heo, terms which occur nowhere else. In the course of time, Manihiki was visited and planted with coconut trees, and an annual migration between the two atolls became established. Thus the coconut trees went unused, the ground lay fallow, and the crabs and fish were undisturbed during alternate years on each island. The Whaka-heo leader had power over the elements, and in a fast double canoe he commanded the fleet during the voyages between the islands. In spite of his alleged divine power, accidents sometimes occurred due to unexpected storms encountered on the twenty-five-mile voyage. After native missionaries became established in 1849, a number of lives were lost during a storm. The missionaries persuaded the people to split into two divisions and permanently occupy the two atolls by giving up the annual migrations.

In spite of the abridged mythology and limitations due to an atoll background, the culture of Manihiki and Rakahanga is essentially related to that of central Polynesia. The dialect contains the *wh* sound instead of the Tahitian *f* and more nearly resembles the dialect of New Zealand than that of the Cook or Society Islands. The lunar calendar, in which each night of the moon has a specific name, is based on the pattern used in central Polynesia. Most of the night names are identical with those of Rarotonga and Tahiti.

Just before we left Rakahanga to go to Manihiki, the people gave us a farewell dinner in which every native food that an atoll can produce was placed before us. We were loaded down with presents of baskets, fans, bonito hooks, and everything that local technique and raw material could provide. From the inner leaflets of young coconut leaves, the women make the best hats in Polynesia, which are as fine as any panama hat. They also make beautiful mats from pandanus leaves. The gift-making was climaxed when women from each division of the village came carrying large mats and crying, 'E Te Rangi Hiroa e! Teia to moenga' (O Te Rangi Hiroa! Here is a mat for you to sleep upon). No more kindly, more hospitable, and more lovable people can exist in this round world than the people of Rakahanga and Manihiki.

We sailed for Manihiki to spend the night at the principal village of Tauhunu, but as we passed along the reef opposite the nearer village of Tukao, a boat came off with a message that my services as doctor were required ashore. Judge Ayson, his two staff members, and I got into the boat, the messenger stating that we would be transported later by a sailing boat across the inner lagoon to Tauhunu.

The patient was a girl who was not ill enough to warrant the interruption of our voyage. After some refreshment, her father said, 'We had better go. The people are waiting for us.'

We were conducted to the village hall, where the entire population of Tukao had gathered. Amid smiles, greetings, and handshakes we were led to seats on the platform. An elder welcomed us to Tukao and regretted that our time was all too short for the village to entertain us in a fitting manner. I replied in our kindred dialect.

The master of ceremonies stood forward and cried, 'Where are the baskets?' Four women came forward, each with a bundle of plaited pandanus baskets made in the best style, laid them at our feet, shook hands, and stepped back with the smile of duty pleasantly accomplished.

The master of ceremonies called, 'The fans!'

Four women stepped forward, each with a bundle of fans of the typical Manihikian shape, plaited in twill from bleached young coconut leaves and fringed with the dyed bark of the *tou* tree. A handshake, a smile, and the four piles at our feet had grown.

'The fishhooks!'

Four men stepped out with bundles of the pearl-shell lures used in catching bonito. I received an extra in the form of a large wooden hook used for catching the deep-sea Ruvettus or so-called castor-oil fish.

And so, in response to the commands of the master of ceremonies, squads of four, with military precision, deposited specimens of their arts and crafts at our feet. Sennit cordage, samples of old-time plaited garments, hats, and large sleeping mats were added to the heaps. The people derived the greatest satisfaction from seeing the heaps grow, for they were vindicating the honour of their village by officially welcoming us and loading us with presents in a manner that could not be surpassed by the other villages. The whole reception had been planned beforehand, and the exaggerated case of sickness was the means of getting us ashore.

At Tauhunu, we were the guests of the Government agent, Mr. Henry Williams, who had Manihikian blood in his veins. He had set such a high standard of sanitation that the villages of the two atolls were the cleanest in the Cook Islands.

After a hearty evening meal, we went to the village hall in response to an invitation to an evening dance. Imagine our embarrassment when we found a table groaning under the weight of a banquet given in our honour. We groaned with the table as we took our places. The President of the Young People's Club made a speech of welcome, and, indicating the food on the table and the piles of husked drinking nuts underneath it, he invited us to partake of their hospitality.

At last the dancing commenced. Captain Viggo, a past master on the accordion, proved a star performer in helping with the dance music. The young men of the club were dressed in white duck suits with black edgings to their coats and wore white shoes that were speckless with pipeclay. The girls in neat white dresses with frills and furbelows were dazzling. The programme included old-fashioned European dances, such as the polka, mazurka, schottische, barn dance, and square dances, and these alternated with native dances put on for the guests. In no other island group have I seen a cleaner, more healthy-looking, and handsomer set of young people. They were courteous to a degree in the old-fashioned quadrilles and lancers, and they danced their own native dances with that perfect rhythm and grace of movement that is typically Polynesian. Here was a native people on a small atoll with limited resources, miles from the beaten highways of the world, thoroughly enjoying every moment of life. Has civilization with its heights and depths, its poverty and starvation, its aerial bombs, high explosives, submarine torpedoes, and lethal gas any greater happiness to offer than that now enjoyed by these simple people?

The next day, the Manihiki people put on some historic plays to rival those of their cousins in Rakahanga. Just before we left, the people gathered on the beach to bid us farewell. They sang hymns, and the native pastor conducted a short service in which he prayed that we might have a safe voyage to Tongareva. I glanced at the reverent congregation in their loom-woven finery, the pastor in the sombre black trousers of his calling, and then at the *Tiare Taporo* outside the reef with its modern rig and auxiliary oil engine. The scene was modern, and yet the atmosphere throbbed with the spirit of the past. I closed my eyes and saw a gathering of people with clear brown skins shining through wreaths and garlands, a high priest making ritual offerings on a coral-gravelled temple to the gods of the sea, and a great double canoe waiting to hoist its triangular matting sail to bear adventurers to some far-off isle. The picture was blurred, for it happened so long ago.

Tongareva, situated in latitude 9° S. and longitude 157° 10″ W., is the largest and northernmost of the atoll islands under the Cook Islands Administration. It is composed of a ring of islands spread along a reef 40 miles in circuit with a contained lagoon of 108 square miles. Unlike Rakahanga and Manihiki, Tongareva has three passages through the reef that admit small vessels into the lagoon. The west passage is the largest, being 40 yards wide and 21 feet deep. Because of the entrance into an inner, sheltered lagoon, Tongareva has been selected as the place where the Cook Islands' trading schooners lie up for the hurricane season, extending from about November to April.

Whatever gods there be harkened to the prayers offered on our behalf by the Manihikians. The *Tiare Taporo* made an excellent trip and sailed through the western passage of the reef at Tongareva to dock at the wharf at the main village of Omoka. The native population, which had heard of our coming, was massed in front of the wharf shed, and Pa, the oldest inhabitant, stood in front of them. As we stepped ashore, Pa held up his hand in a gesture that bade us halt. He recited an incantation to placate the unseen forces of the land and to remove the taboo of strangers. He then advanced toward me, saying, 'According to the ancient custom of Tongareva, I could not come near you nor could you come near me until that was done.'

We shook hands and exchanged greetings in our respective dialects, and, though we may not have understood every word the other was saying, we knew that he was expressing the correct sentiments. The people came forward and shook hands all round. We had been admitted over the threshold of Tongarevan society.

Judge Ayson held a meeting of the Court the day after our arrival to inquire into the local genealogies, and again I was allowed to sit in. It is customary, before commencing the recital of a lineage, to chant an introduction. Tupou Isaia, one of the leading chiefs of Omoka, was the first to give evidence, and the following is an extract from his introductory chant:

> The lineage goes back,
> Back to the period of the parent sky.
> The descent traces back,
> Back indeed to the line of Atea.
> Bind the knowledge securely,
> Let the tying be firm,
> Let the knotting be fast,
> That it hold.
> The lineage descends
>   from a far-off age,
> From the family of Iki,
> From the children of Atea and Hakahotu.

Though the mythology of Tongareva has lost its details, the chant established the important fact that the primary creation parents were Atea and Hakahotu. Hakahotu is the local form of the Tahitian Fa'ahotu, who shares with Papa the functions of the primary female element. Hakahotu, which conveys the idea of development from a coral up-growth, has naturally been preferred to Papa, which conveys the meaning of a large earth foundation or stratum. Haka-hotu belongs to coral atolls, and Papa to volcanic islands.

The union of Atea and Hakahotu resulted in eleven off-spring, among whom were Tane, Tangaroa, and Rongonui, major gods of the Society and Cook Islands. The pattern thus definitely belongs to the theology that was dispersed from central Polynesia. The other children have a local significance, chief among them being Te Porourangi, from whom the human line is traced.

An important ancestor was the voyager, Mahuta. He is stated to have lived in Rakahanga but, owing to domestic troubles, went to Tahiti, where he married the daughter of a local chief named Tu-te-koropanga. Another voyaging ancestor, named Taruia, came to Tongareva, and he was held to be the same person as the Aitutaki chief who was tricked by Ruatapu. Taruia landed on the islet of Tokerau, where he built a marae and left a son, Titia, with some attendants to occupy the land. Taruia sailed to Tahiti, where he met Mahuta and gave him the sailing directions to Tonga-reva. Mahuta sailed for Tongareva in his voyaging canoe *Waimea*, which was so large that on sailing through the western passage, which is forty yards wide, the outrigger float struck against a large rock that stood on the side of the passage. Very likely the wind or current caused the mishap. Mahuta was descended from Iki mentioned in the chant, and he is credited with introducing coconuts and pandanus.

The earliest human beings, descended from Atea and

Hakahotu, had lived so long on the eastern islets of the atoll
that they were held to have grown up with the islands from
the time of Atea. Mahuta met these people on friendly terms
and married his daughter Pokiroa to their chief, Purua. From
Mahuta and Taruia to the year 1900 A.D. there are eighteen
generations, thus placing the period of resettlement from
Tahiti in the middle of the fifteenth century. In Cook Islands
genealogies, Ruatapu, the contemporary of Taruia, lived a
hundred years earlier. Probably the Tongarevan lineages
have been shortened through defective memorizing. Short
lineages indicate that genealogies are not important until the
growth of population forces the recognition of social distinc-
tions and chiefs feel the need of long lineages to stress their
position and descent from the gods.

The descendants of Atea and those of the two voyagers,
Mahuta and Taruia, occupied different islands in the atoll
group and thus formed three distinct centres for development
and subsequent distribution. As the population increased,
all the habitable islands were occupied. The large island
upon which Omoka is situated was settled at either end by
two independent groups who spread toward each other until
they met in the middle, where a boundary line was established between the two districts of Omoka and Motu-kohiti.
Each district had its own chief and often fought the other.
In sailing on the lagoon, I noticed a wide gap in the coconut
trees and was told that it marked the land boundary between
Omoka and Motu-kohiti. It seemed unnecessarily wide and
a waste of land, but I was told that this wide strip had been
established generations ago and that if either side planted any
coconuts to diminish the waste of land they were immediately
torn up by the other side. A further attempt was regarded as
an act of war, and hostilities ensued. Neither district had

completely conquered the other, and so there is no general name for the island. What was the need for a general name to include two districts that had never combined?

In order to protect their coconut groves from theft, the people lived on their land-holdings situated throughout the various islets. After the introduction of Christianity in 1854, the people concentrated in villages built around the churches that were established on four of the islets. In 1864, the inhuman Peruvian slavers descended upon the atoll. Lured by lying promises of good pay and a safe return, the native pastors influenced the people to go abroad to earn money to erect better churches for the worship of God. At least 1000 people left their homes and died in exile. The population was so diminished that two of the villages were abandoned and the remnants of the people dwelt in the remaining two villages of Omoka and Tautua.

At the time of my visit, the village of Omoka was an architectural disappointment. All the houses were made of sawn timber, erected on piles and roofed with corrugated iron. My information of the building of houses was entirely oral. When I inquired about canoes, I found that they had been entirely supplanted by large sailing boats made from imported timber.

'Is there no old hull or part of a canoe that I may examine?' I asked.

'No,' replied Pa, 'the old canoes, after the sailing boats came in, were cut up to form piles for the new houses. The piles of this house were cut from an old canoe.'

A little comfort crept into my soul, and Pa and I spent the rest of the afternoon under that house. Pa lectured on each pile as he diagnosed it as part of a keel, hull plank, or wash-strake, and I, with a measuring tape and a notebook, was glad of the crumbs that the gods had vouchsafed. Except for a picture drawn by Choris, the artist with the Kotzebue expedition in 1815, these house piles form the only material record of the old-time Tongarevan canoe.

Much of my time on Tongareva was devoted to an archeological survey of the marae temples. Twenty-four maraes were known on the various islands, and their names were remembered. Mr. Wilson, Resident Government Agent, Phillip Woonton, local trader, Tupou Isaia, and two young men with tools, accompanied me in the survey. From Omoka, our base, we sailed to the different islands until we made a complete circuit of the atoll.

The maraes were rectangular spaces, roughly 70 to 110 feet long by 60 to 100 feet wide. Rectangular pillars of coral limestone were erected at intervals along the four sides, and a curb of low coral rocks, about ten inches above ground, filled in the spaces between the pillars, defining the rectangular court. Most of the maraes were near the coast on the sea side of the island, with the back, marked by the highest pillars, toward the sea. Within the court and near the back line was a raised platform composed of limestone slabs set on edge in the earth to form a rectangular enclosure about two feet high and filled in with coral rock. The floor of the court was spread with coral gravel.

Besides the maraes, we saw numerous house sites on the different islands. The ground plan of the houses was defined by a low curb of coral limestone blocks set on edge to prevent the fine coral gravel used to carpet the floor from being scattered. The coral limestone used for the house curbs and the marae pillars has the appearance of a composition made artificially and hence has given rise to theories of an extinct civilization that used cement. If the authors of such erroneous beliefs had looked on the beaches of islands surrounded by coral reefs, they would have seen the natural strata of coral limestone from which the Polynesians cut their slabs.

During the course of our explorations we came to the little islet of Te Kasi, which is shaped like a cone with a hollow in the centre. This hollow is intersected by tracks of large flat stones, some of which extend over the rim and down to the water's edge. Beside the paths are small rectangular spaces covered with coral gravel in marked contrast to the sharp, branching coral which has been washed over the islet by storms. A trader named Lamont, who was wrecked on Tongareva in 1853, saw the hollow with its radiating paths and wrote later that it must have been used for some peculiar ceremonies of an unknown nature.

Sitting on a smooth area within the hollow, Tupou Isaia said to me, 'Te Kasi was a great camping place for fishermen. You may see from its position that you may fish in the sea, in the passage, or in the lagoon. The fishermen brought coconut leaves with them to make shelters against the sun, and they covered the floor with coral gravel so that they could lie down to rest without being disturbed by the sharp points of the branching coral. Even the thick-soled Tonga-revans could not walk with comfort over the sharp points, so they made paths with flat coral slabs. You see the paths pass over the rim to the sea, to the north-west passage, and to the lagoon so that they could go comfortably to wherever the fishing was good according to the wind and the tide. Paths also extend on the fourth side toward the neighbouring islet in order that the fishermen could make their way to their shelters which were out of the wind within this hollow.'

'Thank you,' I said. 'It is all very simple and real. There is no room left for mystery or peculiar ceremonies.'

I found here also that some of the people remembered me as a doctor, for they had been at Rarotonga during my first visit there, when I had relieved the regular doctor; so I held a sick parade in the mornings before starting my routine of ethnological inquiries. Husbands usually accompanied their sick wives to explain the patient's symptoms. One day a woman explained that she had a pain in her back.

'No,' said her husband, 'it is in her chest.' A heated argument followed as to the anatomical situation of the pain.

'How long have you had it?' I asked in order to create a diversion.

'It started yesterday,' she answered.

'It started two days ago', asserted her husband with warmth.

A violent altercation took place until at last the husband cried with an apologetic look at me, 'Oh, what a woman! What a woman!'

I remained neutral and produced a stethoscope to create a further diversion. I applied it to her back to the patient's evident satisfaction and then to her chest to the husband's grunted approval of 'Yes, that's the place'.

Finding nothing wrong, I prescribed some cathartic pills, the most appropriate remedy that the limited medical supplies contained. To reward the husband for sharing so vehemently in his wife's symptoms, I gave him some pills also. At the next morning's parade, he reported that they had both recovered, but he asked for some more medicine in case of a relapse.

The day for departure approached all too quickly. The village of Tautua, across the lagoon, invited me to visit them before I left. The population gathered in front of the chief's house. A tin plate was placed on a table on the veranda. The chief, holding his hand aloft, cried that all might hear, 'Here are two pearls of perfect shape and colour. One of them is worth at least five pounds.' He placed them on the dish and rolled them around with an expression of admiration that was not entirely simulated.

'Now,' he cried, 'show your respect for your kinsman and your gratitude to your doctor by filling this dish with pearls that roll true.'

The people filed forward, unknotting the corners of handkerchiefs or opening match boxes, and deposited their contributions in the tin place to the accompaniment of the running criticism of the chief. Some apologized for the poorness of their offerings but explained that they had had no luck. I felt mean, but I was bound hand and foot by the conventions of Tongarevan hospitality.

At Omoka, the people came to me individually with their contributions to the pearl fund.

Pa said, 'These are not so good as I would have liked to have given you, but I am too old to dive now.'

I pressed his hand in thanks as I replied, 'You have given me pearls from the depths of your wisdom that far exceed any pearls that could come from the depths of the sea.'

In farewell, I rubbed noses with Pa and Ma whose wrinkled, kindly faces were but a transient link with the old order giving place to new. A boatload of green coconuts accompanied us to the ship.

'To drink on the voyage', they said.

As we steamed out through the western passage, I waved in farewell to a large rock sitting on the reef, a rock like a sentinel of the land, the rock that had caught the outrigger float of the voyaging canoe of the ancestor Mahuta.

Although the Tongarevans are not as skilful in craft work as their southern neighbours, they are as honest and kindly within. The pearl necklace my wife wears I prize as a token of affection from kinsmen on a remote atoll set on the ancient sea road that led into the heart of Polynesia.

11. THE NORTHERN EQUATORIAL ISLANDS

Sail out and sail whither?
Sail north beneath Orion's Belt.

TAHITIAN SAGA

BETWEEN the centre and the northern angle of the Polynesian triangle there is a stretch of 2400 miles. On this
northern radial, the modern chart shows a number of small
islands that would have formed useful ports of call had the
Polynesian voyagers been able to sail directly north. Bruce
Cartwright suggests that the Polynesians, who were practical
naturalists, may have followed the flight of the golden plover,
land birds that migrate south from Alaska in winter and
return in summer, to lands which they knew awaited their
coming in the northern seas. Whether or not the prevailing
winds would have allowed sailing canoes to follow the direct
route of the birds, I do not know, but certain it is that
explorers reached the Hawaiian islands of the northern angle
and made permanent settlements upon them. It is also certain that the Polynesians discovered the intervening islands
and, though they passed on, they planted coconut palms and
left enduring monuments composed of coral rock to bear
witness to their discovery and temporary occupation.

The islands on the northern radial are Christmas, Fanning, Washington, and Palmyra, lying just north of the Equator on a southeast to northwest line, covering a stretch of about 400 nautical miles, with Palmyra, the most northerly, about 1000 nautical miles from Hawai'i. Fanning is important today as a cable station, and Christmas, with an area of 300,000 acres is said to be the largest of all atolls. South of the Equator and 250 miles southwest of Christmas is Jarvis Island which, though not an atoll, has a desert climate. Farther south are Malden and Starbuck. Not so very far southwest from Starbuck is Tongareva, already referred to as the most northerly atoll on the northwest radial.

These islands situated north and south of the Equator have been termed collectively the Line Islands, but of late years, they have been referred to as the Equatorial Islands. Howland and Baker Islands, lying farther to the west, are included in the term. Howland has *kou* trees and a depression which may have been excavated by Polynesians to grow taro. Though the two islands were probably not touched by the Polynesians travelling to the northwest, they are now of practical importance to the United States as bases for air service across the Pacific. Among the colonists sent down recently by the United States to take possession of Howland and Baker were young Hawaiians from the Kamehameha Boys' School in Honolulu. It is interesting that today Polynesians should become pioneers in reoccupying Pacific atolls undoubtedly discovered by their remote ancestors.

When first visited by European ships, the Equatorial Islands were uninhabited. There are no myths or legends which might connect them with other phases of the great Polynesian adventure. So their brief history must be reconstructed from material traces of human occupancy. On lone islands the outstanding signs of previous habitation are the presence of coconut trees and coral temples erected to their gods by Polynesian navigators after landing. One or both of these traces have been found on all the Equatorial Islands except Howland, Baker, and Jarvis.

Coconut trees were seen by Captain Fanning on Washington and Fanning Islands in 1798 and by Captain Cook on Christmas Island in 1777. Both captains remained ashore for so brief a time that they did not see the archaeological remains and concluded that these islands had never been inhabited. Botanists now hold that coconuts are not endemic to atoll islands and must have been transported and planted by early Polynesian mariners. Those who remained for any length of time on these northern atolls adjusted themselves to the changed environment and made use of local materials much as do the present Tongarevans.

How these atolls were discovered we shall never know. They may have been touched during the course of longer expeditions to the north, following the flight of the golden plover, or winds and currents may have blown ships upon them during storms. They may have been visited during short voyages between neighbouring atoll groups, or by turtle-catching and fishing expeditions. Even today uninhabited islands of the Tuamotus are visited to catch turtle, a great delicacy, which may be found in abundance near atolls not permanently settled.

The early visitors to the atolls made themselves as comfortable as circumstances permitted. Their primary needs, apart from food that teemed in the sea and lagoon, were water and shelter. The need for water was not so pressing to the Polynesian as it is to a present-day European. Western civilization with its improvement of sanitary conditions and refinements of living has required more and more water. A

European uses water to wash his food, his clothing, and himself. He needs water to cook his food and to drink either by itself or in combination with other beverages. He requires it to water his garden and his crops, to flush out his water closets, to wash down streets, to use in various manufactures, and in a host of ways unknown to his own ancestors. On seeing an atoll without rivers or streams, he is likely to assume that life would be untenable owing to lack of water supplies.

After being on an atoll and entering into the everyday life of its inhabitants, I was amazed to find that under the old conditions water was not so vitally important as I imagined. The coral islander cleaned his fish and shellfish in sea water and did not need to wash coconuts and pandanus fruit. He replaced his simple garments with new ones when they became soiled, and washed his body daily in the sea. In volcanic islands, where streams or springs abound, the inhabitants washed themselves in fresh water after swimming in the sea. One of the perquisites of a high chief was a fresh-water pool reserved to his own use and named in the recital of his chiefly possessions. It is said that the fresh water removes the itchy feeling left by salt water. On atolls, however, the people spent so much of their time in salt water that their skins became inured to what was unpleasant to others. When rains occurred, they availed themselves of a natural shower bath and, at times, a scooped-out excavation in a fresh-water seepage on the beach with a coconut-shell dipper provided all the necessities for bodily ablution.

The earth oven, with its heated coral or shells, did not require water for cooking purposes. The beverage required by man was supplied by the coconut. During the time we spent on the atolls of Rakahanga and Tongareva, we were provided with a constant supply of drinking nuts which, for drinking purposes, were much superior to tepid water. When a person called for 'vai' (water), he was brought a coconut.

However, on atolls without a luxuriant growth of coconuts, water was a necessity. It was obtained by digging shallow wells. Even though the water on the lower rock stratum was brackish, it was not unpalatable to those who had become accustomed to it. In post-European times, Polynesian labourers on Malden Island preferred the well water to rain water caught in tanks because they attributed medicinal properties to it. On this island, there are a number of shallow wells lined with coral limestone slabs. At the bottom of the wells, shells were found that had been used as dippers.

The inhabitants of these atolls built houses with poles procured from local plants and roofed them over with pandanus leaves or coconut leaves when coconuts had been planted. In order to have a smooth surface upon which to sleep, the floor was carpeted with a layer of coral gravel, which the ceaseless wash of the waves had smoothed on the beach. To prevent the gravel from being scattered, a low curb was constructed of flat slabs of coral or of low blocks of coral limestone. The curb was rectangular, conforming to the dimensions of the house and about six or ten inches high. When the temporary settlers sailed away, the framework and roofs of their houses crumbled to decay, but the rectangular curbs, having been embedded on edge in the ground, remained as permanent witnesses of previous occupation.

On Washington Island, a coral enclosure was reported of indefinite shape, but on Fanning, Christmas, and Malden Islands, they were of the characteristic rectangular form. In Fanning, the coral limestone curbstones were worked with an inner step and a few were shaped with an upper ornamental projection which rose a few inches above the general level of the curb. Two corner stones were L-shaped, a form described only in Tonga. Emory, in his study of the archeology of these atolls, rightly, I think, pictures the builders of the Fanning Island structure as having come from Tonga. As the structure in Tonga is dated by the Tongan lineages as having been built in the sixteenth century, it is apparent that the Fanning Island structure cannot antedate that. The Tongan origin of the structure is further supported by the discovery of some bonito hooks in an old grave. Polynesian hooks for bonito trolling are made in two parts: a shank of pearl shell which resembles a small fish when trolled and a curved piece which forms the point to hook the fish. The point pieces differ in the various groups, and the Fanning hooks, which are now in Bishop Museum, resemble more closely those of Tonga than any other group. Also, some basaltic adzes have been discovered which are shaped like those of Tonga. Porpoise teeth with holes drilled through them have been found in a grave, but though our present knowledge would attribute these to the Marquesas, we cannot be dogmatic about them.

In both Christmas and Malden Islands, there are raised rectangular platforms with walls defined by coral slabs 2 to 3.5 feet high and with the interior filled with coral rocks. The platforms of Malden Island are definitely associated with curbed rectangular courts. These platforms resemble the maraes described for Tongareva and were used for religious purposes.

On Fanning, Christmas, and Malden Islands, there are small rectangular enclosures about six feet long by three feet wide or larger, defined by coral limestone slabs from one to two feet high and covered in the interior with a layer of coral gravel. Similar structures were made in Tongareva and other atolls for the burial of the dead. Instead of digging a hole down into crumbling coral with inadequate tools, the atoll dwellers found it easier to build upwards with the easily accessible limestone slabs and then to cover the dead with a layer of coral gravel. This technique shows a perfect adjustment to local conditions.

Other signs of Polynesian occupation are given by the discovery of tools or implements. The basaltic adze found on Fanning and one on Christmas indicate that the early settlers came from a volcanic island. When they moved on again, they generally took their stone tools with them, but an occasional one may have been mislaid or purposely left as a funeral offering. Those who remained on atolls for any appreciable time were forced to use tridacna-shell tools; the number of these found on Christmas and Malden indicates a settled occupation for some time. Starbuck Island has no archaeological remains.

In the twentieth century, Malden Island was worked by a guano company with labour recruited from the Cook Islands and Niue. I was acting medical officer in Niue in 1912, when a recruiting ship called for labourers. The Island Government, which is under New Zealand, allowed a certain quota to sign on for two years, but half the wages in gold had to be deposited with the Resident Commissioner to be paid to the men on their return. In this way, the wives and families of the labourers were assured of sharing in the benefits of the temporary exile. As medical officer, I had to make a physical examination of each recruit and stamp his passcard with the Administration rubber stamp. There was great excitement with the recruits and their wives and sweethearts clamouring about the dispensary door.

When I stamped the first man's card, he held his face over the table.

'Here', he said, pointing to his forehead.

'What?' I asked in surprise.

'The stamp,' he replied: 'stamp it here.'

Being affable and quite content to let things explain themselves, I imprinted the Government's ink stamp upon his ample forehead. Immediately he dashed through the doorway and ran, leaping and yelling, among the crowd that had gathered outside.

The examination went on and each man asked to be rubber-stamped. The older married men had it on the back of a hand, but the young, unmarried men preferred a cheek or the forehead. The ship was sailing the next day and, in the festivities of farewell, the young men with stamped faces lorded it over their fellows in the competition for the favours of the opposite sex. I never reached Malden myself but my rubber stamps did, for no man would attempt to wash off his badge of honour.

Malden Island was first seen by Europeans in 1825, At that time H.M.S. *Blonde*, commanded by Lord Byron, was returning to England from the Hawaiian islands after taking back the bodies of the King and Queen of Hawai'i who had died of measles in London. The atoll was named after Lieutenant Malden who, with the naturalist, Mr. Bloxam, went ashore to explore.

Mr. Bloxam described the archaeological remains fairly accurately, but the drawing of a temple by Dampier, based on this material, represents it falsely as a truncated pyramid. The late Professor Macmillan Brown used the evidence of Bloxam and the drawings of Dampier as a basis for his theory of drowned archipelagoes. He saw an affinity between the simple Malden structures and the pyramids of the sun and moon on the coasts of Peru, the *teocallis* of Mexico, and the

Metalanim structures of Ponape. He concluded that an army of men would be required to build these temples and that men could not possibly live on Malden; hence Malden must have been a sacred island of a people who lived on a fertile archipelago near-by which has now sunk below the sea, perhaps carrying with it the entire population.

Accurate knowledge of the Equatorial Islands was obtained by the *Whippoorwill* and *Kaimiloa* expeditions directed by Bishop Museum in 1925. On Malden, K. P. Emory measured the structures seen by Bloxam. The limestone slabs were no larger than those in the temples of Tongareva. Any structure on Malden could easily be built by a working party of fifty men. 'Paved roads' to the sea, mentioned by Brown, are simply paths for fishermen, similar to those in Tongareva, and have no sacred significance. I have already pointed out that the requirements for living on an atoll island were extremely simple. Emory states that Captain Stenbeck and fifty labourers lived on Malden for six months in 1914 after their imported supplies of food were completely exhausted. They lived on fish, birds' eggs, and imported goats and pigs. Atoll islanders could have subsisted on fish and eggs, purslane (*Portulaca lutea*), their only vegetable food plant, and perhaps also seaweed. Thus there is no necessity for assuming the existence of a sunken fertile archipelago from which people came to worship at temples constructed on an uninhabitable atoll. In all Polynesia, worship was conducted on temples built close to inhabited villages. Even the great international temple of Taputapu-atea, to which people from surrounding islands came at the height of its fame, was built in a thickly populated district.

The story of Malden Island is as simple as that of any atoll. Some Polynesians settled upon it, made temples for the worship of their gods, buried their dead, made paths to the sea, dug wells, and made implements of tridacna shell. They lived on the native plants and animals. It was a hard life and, perhaps after a drought or a bad storm, they migrated elsewhere.

Tempting as it may be to weave mysteries about extinct civilizations that existed on sunken fertile lands, imagination along such lines conflicts with common sense. Geologists have found no evidence to support the theory of extensive lands that have sunk within the Polynesian triangle during the period of man's existence. The material evidences of previous human occupation on uninhabited atolls have nothing mysterious about them and can all be accounted for by temporary Polynesian occupation. Hardy Polynesian ancestors paid their visits, stayed their span, and passed on to return to or to seek more attractive isles. If they were lost on the sea paths of the Ocean Maid, they went down gallantly on their foundered ships and not on a sinking archipelago. Hawaiki, the common fatherland of us all, is not sunk deep beneath the waters of the Pacific, but Havai'i, the mother of lands, rests serene in the centre of Polynesia and will live on forever though we, her sons, may pass into oblivion.

12. THE NORTHEASTERN RADIAL

Over the sea the Tăkĕ spread,
Spread to a world of light;
Spread did the Tăkĕ, spread, yes, spread,
The Tăkĕ spread.

MARQUESAN CHANT

A BRANCH of the Polynesians, who termed themselves the
Tăkĕ, spread from the central nucleus in a northeasterly
direction. Their ships passed through the darkness of the
unknown to emerge where the sun shone on a group of
volcanic islands which they hailed as a world of light. The
islands discovered were grouped together under the name
of Hiva, but centuries later they were renamed by another
people, the Marquesas.

The westernmost island of the group is about a thousand
miles from Ra'iatea. The archipelago is divided into a southern and a northern group. The inhabited islands of the
southern group are Fatuhiva, Tahuata, and Hivaoa; those
of the northern group are 'Uapou, Nukuhiva, and Uahuka.
A number of smaller islands were inhabited until western
man arrived with the host of deadly microbes that seem to
accompany him wherever he goes. The ancient population
of the islands went into tens of thousands. Captain Porter in
1813 calculated that there were 19,200 warriors in Nuku-

hiva, and he estimated the total population of the group at 80,000. This was perhaps an overestimate, but, in 1904, the population had diminished to 4000; and the census of 1911 gave it as 2890. Venereal diseases, tuberculosis, and epidemics were introduced by ships into what had been a world of light so far as disease was concerned. No branch of the Polynesians has suffered more for its kindness and hospitality to Europeans than have the Marquesans.

The Marquesas are rugged islands with an abundance of basaltic stone which provided tools for the early settlers. From a backbone of mountainous ridges reaching an elevation of 4000 feet on 'Uapou, the streams have cut deep valleys with almost no level land beside their beds. The ridges between the valleys form precipitous walls which isolate the valleys from each other and slope steeply to the sea, leaving little level land along the coast. The ends of the valleys form bays, but there are no protecting coral reefs. A little coral, found in some of the bays, is of no significance in the plan of the Great Architect of the Universe.

Legends refer to the first comers as the Tăkĕ, for *tăkĕ* means the cause, the root. They were the cause of life that spread from the centre of Polynesia to take root in the deep isolated valleys of the rugged isles of Hiva. They took root so long ago that the legends which have filtered down through the generations have left the names of the first discoverers and their voyaging ships behind with a bygone age. The sacred chants, which correspond to abridged forms of the log books of deep-sea mariners, record the names of various lands through which they passed in the seas to the southwest. Among these are Havai'i, Upo'u, Vevau, and Fiti-nui which we may recognize as the ancient forms of Ra'iatea, Taha'a, Porapora, and Great-Tahiti. These ancient names were given to localities in the new home and, just as the name New England in the eastern part of the United States bears witness to origin in England, so do the names in the Marquesan chants and those of local districts point definitely to the Society Islands as the last place whence the people came.

At the centre of settlement in each island group there should be a monument to the leader of the first settlers or a simple shrine to the unknown discoverer. There are many of Polynesian blood today who would thrill to lay a fragrant wreath at the foot of some plain stone pillar in honour of their own unknown. Perhaps some faint vibration from the dim past might stir our dry bones or gently touch our heart strings to a better appreciation of our bygone ancestors e'en though their names be forgotten.

One of the regrets of my life is that Fate and Bishop Museum did not give me the opportunity of absorbing some of the atmosphere of the Marquesas. I joined the staff of Bishop Museum after the field work had been done in the Marquesas by the Bayard Dominick Expedition. Let me tell you about Bayard Dominick, for, though he may not realize it, he materially helped toward the initiation of an intensive survey of the culture of the Polynesian people. Bayard Dominick is a graduate of Yale University, and he gave a liberal sum of money to his Alma Mater for research work in the Pacific area. Yale, through its affiliation, passed the donation on to Bishop Museum to spend on field work in Polynesia. As a result of this financial assistance, university graduates in anthropology were sent out to various island groups to make regional surveys. An expedition was sent to the Marquesas in 1920-21, consisting of Dr. E. S. Craighill Handy, his wife Willowdean Handy, and Dr. Ralph Linton to study the culture of the people, and Dr. and Mrs.

Forest Brown to study botany. Failing personal knowledge, I have compiled much in this chapter from the reports of the expedition published by Bishop Museum.

In order to understand the apparent differences between Marquesan words and those of central Polynesia, it is necessary to say a little about the consonant changes that have taken place. The southern islands of the Marquesas have evidently been affected by the later changes in Tahitian speech. The *k* has been dropped, as in Tahiti, Samoa, and Hawai'i, and the Tahitian *f* is used where *h* is used in the northern islands. In both the north and south, the *ng* is represented by *n*, though some regions substitute *k* for *ng* as in the South Island of New Zealand. The most curious change, however, is the dropping of the *r* in both groups, though it is retained in a few words. Dropped consonants are represented in speech by a catch in the voice and in writing by an inverted comma. Thus we may recognize the Marquesan '*a* as the *ra* (sun) of the basic language, '*una* as *runga* (above), and '*a'o* as *raro* (below).

Marquesan myths had evidently been partially forgotten when they were first recorded in writing long after European contact. The creation myths lack many details that the old priests must have known. However, some of the general themes have been transmitted in a confused form that may yet be translated by those who can interpret the displaced sequence of events.

Creation begins with Papa-'una (Upper-stratum) and Papa-'a'o (Lower-stratum) as primary parents. Their offspring were numerous, and among them were Atea, Tane, Tu, 'Ono-tapu (Rongo-tapu), Tonofiti, Tiki, and Aumia, whom we have met in other islands. The Upper-stratum and the Lower-stratum were very close together, and their children were born in darkness. The children rebelled and decided to force their parents apart and so let light into their world. Ru, who propped up the Sky-father in Tahiti and the Cook Islands, is absent in Marquesan myth, but his place is taken by Tonofiti who pushed the Upper-stratum on high. Thus the gods, born of the two primary parents, assumed their functions in a world of light.

The Marquesan myth departs from the pattern previously observed in that one Papa married another Papa and produced Atea. In other islands, Atea married Papa, but since Papa was already given in marriage, the Marquesan school created the new personage, Atanua, as wife for Atea. Te Tumu and Fa'ahotu, who played an important role at this period in other myths, are conspicuously absent. It seems to me that the Tăkĕ (Source), as applied to the early people who spread to Hiva, has been substituted for Te Tumu (Source). Fa'ahotu had either not been invented in the central area before the Tăkĕ left or had been forgotten, else the Marquesan school had surely mated Atea with Fa'ahotu and so saved themselves the trouble of inventing Atanua.

Atea retained importance by being made the direct ancestor of man. Atea also married various personified females and produced mountains, rocks, earth; various food plants such as coconuts, breadfruit, chestnuts, other non-edible plants; and the pig. He was also the father of the months of the lunar cycle. Thus Atea was given the procreating function attributed to Tiki in the myths of Tuamotu, Mangareva, New Zealand, and Easter Island.

Of the other progeny of the Upper-stratum and the Lower-stratum, Tu functioned in his normal capacity as god of war, and those who took particular part in his ritual were alluded to as the Ati-tu (the Tribe-of-Tu). 'Ono or 'Ono-tapu, who appears as Rongo, god of peace and agriculture, in other islands, is merely a legendary character without divine attributes. It may be that the Marquesans were so warlike that they had no use for a god of peace and that their cultivable lands were so limited that they had little for which to thank a god of agriculture. That Rongo had power at one time is indicated by the legendary account of his defeat of the god Tohetika who, as Toutika, finds a place in the Cook Islands' pantheon.

Tane is another of the important gods of Opoa who lost his divinity in the Marquesas. His association with craftsmen, however, is dimly remembered in local legends associating him with a sacred adze. He is also associated with people of light skin and hair and thus, in historical times, was held to be the ancestor of the white race.

The local gods, Manatu meaning thought and Pupuke meaning the source or welling-up of knowledge, were the patrons of the sacred chants; and Pupuke was the god of one of the houses of the inspirational priests. In New Zealand, Rua-i-te-pupuke occurs as a mythical character who is a source of wisdom, I mention Pupuke in order to show that certain abstract concepts were widespread throughout Polynesia, expressed either as part of educated speech or as divine personifications.

One of the most striking features of Marquesan myth is the absence of Tana'oa (Tangaroa) among the progeny of Papa'una and Papa'a'o. He functions, however, as the god of the winds, the sea, and fishing. As Tangaroa occurs as the god of the sea and of fishing in New Zealand, it would appear that these were his true departments when the ancestors of the Marquesans and the New Zealanders left central Polynesia and that his elevation as creator belongs to a later stage of development in central Polynesia.

Some myths elevate Tiki as the primary ancestor of man. He is stated to have lived in Havaiki without a wife. He made a mound of sand into the form of a child. Returning three days later, he found that the mound had developed into a living woman. He named her Hina-tu-na-one (Maid-standing-on-the-sands) and took her to wife. From this couple were born the Upper-stratum and the Lower-stratum who, in turn, gave birth to Atea and Atanua. Tiki created the island of Nukuhiva by invocation and placed Atea and Atanua upon it. The Nukuhiva people made images in stone of Tiki and used them in their worship. I believe that this version has been compounded by the later Marquesans out of dislocated fragments to satisfy the inquiries of modern seekers after ancient lore. I do not believe that any old-time priest or historian would have departed so greatly from the pattern that exists in other islands. Another Tiki myth states that the woman he made out of sand or earth was named Hina-mata-one (Earth-maid). By this wife he had a daughter for whom he built a separate house in order that he might visit her secretly to commit incest with her. This is the version that is held in the Tuamotus and Mangareva, and it conforms to a more general pattern. It is evident that the Marquesan school had the original myth in which Tiki is credited with being the direct ancestor of man, but modern historians blundered in substituting Atea for Tiki.

In a genealogy recorded by Handy, there are one hundred and fifty-nine generations commencing with 'Ani-motua (Rangi-matua), the Sky-father. Vatea (Atea) and his wife Atanua occur on the fiftieth generation from the Sky-father. Tiki occurs on the seventy-first generation, so that the order in sequence of Vatea and Tiki is orthodox. If assessed at twenty-five years a generation, this genealogy goes back to

2000 B.C. which, of course, is impossible. It includes natural phenomena, concepts of creation, the growth from roots, material objects in the sea and on land, the winds, and various lands, which in the form of males are mated to females. It is a confused list of evolutionary processes—confused because there is no living person who can interpret the teachings of the ancient Marquesan school of learning. We can but admire the effort of memory that handed on such a lengthy list after its significance and meaning had been irrevocably lost.

The genealogies were learned and taught by experts termed *o'ono* (*orongo*). They used a device of twined coconut fibre termed a *ta'o mata* to which were attached long cords with knots to represent the various generations of the gene-alogy. A resemblance has been seen to the *quipus* by which the Peruvians, with knotted cords, kept or calculated their business accounts. The Marquesans are held to have used their device as an aid to memorizing their genealogies, but, even though fresh knots may have been added as children were born to a lineage, the knots in themselves could not give the cue to the individual names. The knotted cords, like the carved knobs of the wooden genealogical sticks of New Zealand, were used for spectacular effect. The number of knots on a cord or the knobs on a stick might indicate the number of generations in a lineage, and it was a fitting climax when the reciter ended the last generation on the final knot or knob.

Among the legendary characters we have already met are the Maui brethren, of whom there are seven in the Marquesas. The eldest was Maui-mua and the youngest Maui-tikitiki. Between were Maui-mu'i, Maui-pae, and Maui-taha. If we substitute Maui-roto for Maui-mu'i, we have exactly the same names as in the New Zealand family of five. The two extras are Maui-vaveka and Maui-hakatata-mai; there were probably alternative names for two of an original family of five but, in the course of time, they came to be regarded as distinct individuals, so raising the number of the family to seven.

In the Marquesas, as in other islands, Maui-tikitiki, the youngest, fished up various islands, obtained fire from his grandfather Mahuike in the lower regions, and snared the sun with a noose of human hair to delay his passage across the sky in order that Maui's laundry might have time to dry. He converted himself into a pigeon (*'upe*) to recover his wife. In New Zealand, he changed himself into a pigeon (*rupe*) in order to discover his sister.

Coming down to the period of legendary human ancestors, we find a number of names recorded as early settlers of the six inhabited islands. These ancestors are held to have arrived in Hiva between the tenth and the twelfth centuries, but there is no record of the names of their ships. Of these, Mahuta occurs in the genealogies, and it is interesting to note that an ancestor Mahuta occurs in the legends of Rakahanga and Tongareva.

Handy's informants believed that the first settlement in the land of light was on Hivaoa in the ancient district of Vevau, now comprising the valleys of Atuona, Te Hutu, Ta'aoa, and Tahauka. Here in the most fertile section of the most attractive island, the Tăkě settled themselves; here they established a cultural centre, where they gathered together and consolidated their mythology and traditional lore into a definite pattern.

In the narrow valleys of Vevau the people increased and formed themselves into tribes. Some of them migrated to near-by islands and founded new tribes. In the north, Taipivai on the island of Nukuhiva became a second culture centre. Yet Vevau retained its pre-eminence as the first settlement.

The departing place of spirits, a western promontory named Kiukiu, was near Vevau. The souls of the dead from outer islands had to return first to Kiukiu before setting out on their long journey to the westward. The people of Vevau called themselves Na-iki, a contracted form of Na-'iki which, translated into the basic language, is Nga-ariki (the High-chiefs). Thus, like the descendants of the first settlers of Mangaia who called themselves Ngariki, the Marquesan Na-iki, by their very name, claimed priority and superiority over all other tribes. They might be defeated in war by other less ancient tribes, but they could not be robbed of their illustrious name and the achievement for which it stood.

In the isles of Hiva the Marquesans developed their own civilization, built upon the basic culture brought from central Polynesia. Hivaoa became the centre for carving in wood and stone and Nukuhiva became the centre for stone masonry. However, the crafts spread in an even pattern throughout the group. Expeditions penetrated to the Tuamotus and Cook Islands and farther to the east where they influenced the culture of Mangareva and Easter Island. It is probable that some of the voyages north to Hawai'i passed through the Marquesas. Thus the Marquesas became a centre for the development and dissemination of culture in the east, corresponding to Havai'i in the centre of Polynesia.

From Havai'i the Marquesans brought the pig and the fowl, but the dog was either left behind or died out. They also brought the paper mulberry and various food plants, among which the breadfruit was given preference. The surplus of each crop was stored in pits lined with banana leaves, where the fruit fermented and kept indefinitely. Besides being a reserve food, the breadfruit trees were so prolific that fermented breadfruit became the staple article of food.

The preserved breadfruit (*ma*) was kneaded with the hands, wrapped in leaves, cooked in the earth oven, and then pounded with stone pounders and thinned with water to form a paste (*popoi*). This treatment led to the use of a stone pounder with a flared circular base running up into a rounded neck for grasping with the hand and surmounted by a knob to prevent the hand from slipping upward. These pounders were so sought after by curio hunters that they became scarce in the islands. The Germans with their keen commercial instinct imported rock from the Marquesas to Germany and manufactured a large number of pounders to sell back to the Marquesans. The Marquesans of modern times quickly adopted the commercial methods of western civilization and sold the imported articles to tourists and traders as old, original specimens. We have several in Bishop Museum that serve to illustrate western progress in Polynesia.

Next to the New Zealanders, the Marquesans were the best carvers in Polynesia. They carved their wooden utensils and weapons with a richness of intricate designs that commands our respect. But they were not content with wood and bone as media for artistic expression, and they transferred some of their best designs to the human body in the form of tattooing. The body was completely tattooed from the upper limits of the hair to the toenails. It seems as if the early artists could not bear to waste any portion of the human canvas. In carving and tattooing, original motifs, including the curve and the single spiral, were developed.

In their houses as well as in their art the Marquesans developed an original form. The roof descended in a continuous oblique line to the ground at the back, whereas the front raised wall was normal. The horizontal poles to brace the rafters were placed on the inside of the rafters instead of on the outside as in Tahiti. The houses were built on level stone platforms extending out from the slopes of the deeply cut valleys. The house was built on a raised site at the back of the platform with an open court on a slightly lower level before it. On the court, some large flat stones were erected on an inclined plane to form backrests. Thus the father of the family and any distinguished guests could sit at ease on the stone pavement and recline against the stone backrest while they gossiped or watched the evening life of the valley pass before them.

In ornaments the Marquesan craftsmen displayed great initiative. They made ear ornaments of exquisite design and workmanship from the teeth of the sperm whale. Their breast ornaments and headdresses were unique. Armlets, anklets, and even kilts were fashioned from locks of human hair skilfully attached to braided bands of coconut fibre. The black hair of such ornaments was curled in a permanent wave by rolling the hair tightly around a wooden rod, wrapping it in green leaves, and subjecting it to heat in an earth oven.

The hair of the face was also used for ornaments but here a grey colour was preferred. Tahitians used grey hair from the tails of dogs to form tasseled fringes for breast ornaments, and the New Zealanders used similar tassels to ornament cloaks and weapons. The Marquesans had no dogs, so they used old men as a source of raw material. When a grandfather received news of a prospective grandchild, he allowed his beard to grow to provide material for making ornaments for his child. On examining museum specimens with tufts of wavy grey hair neatly seized with single coconut-husk fibres, I could not help thinking of the affection with which the grower must have combed his beard and the joy he experienced when it was of sufficient length to reap the crop.

One of the peculiar head ornaments of the Marquesans is a forehead circlet consisting of alternate plaques of carved turtle shell and curved marine shell. These were fastened to a twined band of coconut fibre with circular pieces of pearl shell fixed to it. Such headdresses came into great demand after European contact. However turtle shell was scarce and difficult to carve, and pearl-shell discs were hard to shape and drill with holes. So Europeans provided the Marquesans with carved vulcanite plaques and shirt buttons with which they made many of the headdresses that today repose unsuspected in the world's museums.

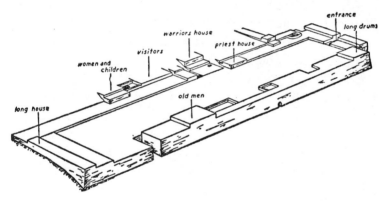

THE MARQUESAN STADIUM OF NANAUHI

The Marquesans built stone terraces termed *me'ae* for their religious ceremonies. Here human sacrifices were offered the gods, and images in wood and stone were displayed, representing those gods who had been created in the image of man. For these sculptures a conventional form was developed locally. The flexed lower limbs and hands clasped on the abdomen are shared by other regions. The large eyes defined by a low, circular flange like spectacles, the nose with wide nostrils, the wide straight mouth defined by parallel lines evenly curved at the ends, the ear with the lobe enhanced by single spirals, and the hands with the five fingers curved in to meet each other in pairs on either side of the middle finger are all elements of a local technique. Some authors have interpreted the conventionalized images of gods as a crude attempt to represent the human form. However no Polynesian artists, with the possible exceptions of the Mangarevans, tried to carve the human figure in a realistic manner. They created symbolic forms, subjectively interpreted, in which anatomical exactness was not desired.

After studying Linton's plan of the assembly place of Nanauhi, in the Hatiheu Valley of Nukuhiva, I dreamed a dream compounded of what I had read and what I felt. I imagined myself on the visitors' terrace about four feet above the middle of the great dance floor with the sloping hill rising behind me. The level rectangular dance floor was over 300 feet long and 60 feet wide and was bounded on all sides by wide terraces one to two feet high which were crowded with people. Here and there were higher platforms built behind the terraces and reserved for various social groups. To our left was a long terrace seven feet above the dance floor, with a long house for accommodation of warriors of the tribe. Here they sat, row on row, with their beautifully polished and carved clubs of ironwood within easy reach. No woman dared to approach this house, for it was taboo. Beyond the warriors and on the edge of the dance floor was a stone platform three feet high with the peculiar tall house that marked the residence of the inspirational priest. The left end of the dance floor was bounded by open terraces with house terraces behind them, and in the middle was the gap formed by the ascending steps by which we had entered.

The low terrace stretched away to our right, but next to us was a platform over seven feet high which carried a house and an open space in front of it. This was the ladies' stand, and it was crowded with women and children.

At the right end was an open terrace a foot high and behind it another terrace three feet higher on which was the great long house of the high chief of the tribe. He sat on the open platform, leaning against a slanting stone backrest with his supporting chiefs and relatives beside him.

On the opposite side, facing us, was a low platform with a terrace, a foot higher behind, and both were crowded with people. On the right, a platform four feet high was occupied entirely by old men. On the left-hand corner was another platform four feet high occupied by the great wooden drums. They were so high that the young men who beat them had to stand on supports to reach the drum heads with their hands.

I gazed in admiration at the people around me. Their bodies had been annointed with scented coconut oil. The intricate patterns of tattooing covered their bodies from hair to toes, leaving undecorated enough of their skins to show off the lines of the blue designs. All the men wore a bark cloth band passed between the legs and around the waist, with the ends hanging down in front and behind. Many wore a kilt of human hair over this inner garment. Some had a shoulder cape of human hair like the kilt, and others wore a cape of bark cloth tied in a large knot in front. They wore human-hair ornaments both as wristlets and anklets. On their breasts were hung polished pearl shells attached to a neck cord. Others bore crescents of wood covered with red seeds, and others again wore necklaces of the teeth of the sperm whale. In their ears, the men wore discs of sections of whale teeth, which covered the ear in front but were fixed by collar-stud projections which passed through holes in their ear lobes. The women wore more delicate ornaments carved in miniature human form from whale ivory.

It was the headdress, however, that commanded most attention. Those of the priests were made of pandanus leaf and so shaped that from the front they resembled a bishop's mitre. The young men wore sennit bands around the forehead with alternating curved plaques of white shell and carved turtle shell. The most magnificent were composed of the long, black tail feathers of roosters, waving vertically above the head and fixed to a sennit band, with the ends tied beneath the chin. Over the forehead of some men was a crescentic wide band covered with the iridescent feathers of the pigeon and tied at the back of the head. Others again wore wide sennit bands, carrying a whole pearl shell in the middle with carved turtle shell forming an arabesque in front of the shell. Forehead ornaments of white hair obtained from old men's beards added variety to the gala attire.

The treatment of the hair added further variety. The older men had shaved the sides of the head with a shark's tooth, and the central tuft of hair was tied in a bunch on top of the head with a strip of white bark cloth. The younger men had two tufts in front wrapped with white bark cloth, which looked like horns.

Each man of any importance carried in his right hand a long staff with a decoration of waved human hair at the top, and in his left hand a well-made fan of plaited pandanus leaf with a beautifully carved wooden handle.

The drums beat without ceasing, for, as soon as one man became tired and stepped down from the platform, another took his place. Below the drums was a group of chanters who kept vocal time to the rhythm of the drums.

On the right corner of the dance platform was a long, open shed with the great cooking ovens, from which the food had just been removed. Great wooden bowls filled with cooked fermented breadfruit were brought forward, placed in a row on the dance floor, and covered over with banana leaves. Pigs, baked whole, were placed upon banana leaves beside them. Uncooked breadfruit was piled in pyramids, and yams, bananas, and all the foods of the country were heaped up in lavish hospitality. Men stepped forward with bamboo knives, and quickly cut up the pigs. Assistants laid out the portions of pork and other foods into appropriate heaps. The official distributor then called a name and pointed to a heap. The person named stepped down from his terrace or platform with his friends and took up his share of food. So it went on until all were served.

In my dream, I fancied I heard the distributor call, 'To ha'afiti ia Te 'Ani Hi'oa' (This share for Te Rangi Hiroa). I would it had been real. All having been served, the assembly feasted. The drums, the chants, the hum of conversation, and the gaiety of laughter created a continuous din that made life happy.

Suddenly the drums beat a different rhythm, and the blast of a shell trumpet silenced the murmur of sound. Into the central dance floor wove a procession of girls, graceful and beautiful, and bedecked with fragrant leaves and flowers. Attached to the second finger of each hand by ring bands were the long red feathers of the bosun bird. Their lissome bodies swayed in perfect time to the music of the drums and the chants, their feet kept rhythm, and the quivering feathers on their slender fingers seemed to make the air vibrate.

They were followed by the young men known as the *ka'ioi*. Clad in yellow loin cloths with their tattooed bodies gleaming with coconut oil and saffron-coloured turmeric, they formed a golden galaxy of youth and virile beauty. The beat of the drums and the stamping of feet entered into one's pulse beat. Was there ever such a perfect scene as the great dance floor occupied by swaying forms, and the surrounding terraces filled by a silent, tense audence that gazed down approvingly? The stonework, the buildings, the costumes, the ornaments, the ceremonial, and the dances were all expressions of the culture of one of the most virile branches of the Polynesians.

Can we ever see the throbbing past except in dreams? I do not wish to awake, for when I do, I will see but a line drawing in a book that conjures up a lone terrace overgrown with exotic weeds, and sad stone walls crumbling to decay.

13. SOUTH AND SOUTHEAST

How can you and I know what the heathen thought about?

POLYNESIAN INFORMANT

I ASKED an old man with grey hair and a wrinkled face, a question about the Polynesian idea of creation. He gave me a modern version based on Genesis. I tried to lift him over the intervening years by saying, 'Yes, that is what you and I think now, but what did your ancestors think before the Bible was introduced?' With a deprecatory shrug of his shoulders, he replied, 'How can you and I know what the heathen thought about?'

The early missionaries laboured to destroy belief in the Polynesian concepts of the world and the origin and power of the local gods. In this they were helped by the natives themselves who, eager to accept and adopt new ideas, broke almost completely with their old religion. Frequently when a chief accepted Christianity those who had opposed his temporal rule remained with their old faith. Bitter wars were waged for political as much as for religious reasons, and the converts took keen delight in destroying the temples and gods of their enemies. Priests and scholars who had accepted the new teaching refused to pass on the concepts and the legends of their old cult. Thus the continuity of oral transmission was broken. When questions were asked in after years, only scattered, dislocated fragments could be recalled.

Many European missionaries recorded the principles of the old religion, perhaps to show the church at home from what they were rescuing the heathen. Wherever white missionaries were stationed, a certain amount of information has been saved from the wreck. Ellis and Orsmond in Tahiti, Gill in Mangaia, and Laval in Mangareva are notable examples of missionaries who recorded invaluable information that would otherwise have been lost forever. However, native converts and pastors had no outside world to which to report and ruthlessly destroyed material objects and suppressed teachings which to them had no intrinsic interest. Hence it is that little information concerning the past has been preserved on islands which were converted by native missionaries and teachers. Extremely little is known of the myths and early traditional history of the Austral Islands, presumably because of the complete break in continuity that followed early proselytizing.

The Austral Islands—Rimatara, Rurutu, Tupua'i (Tubuai), and Raivavae—lie about 400 miles south of Tahiti. These islands are volcanic and continue the chain of the Cook Islands toward the southeast. Between Mangaia, the most easterly of the Cook Islands, and Rimatara is the small uninhabited atoll of Maria (Hull Island) which may have served as a landmark and resting place on voyages between the Austral and Cook groups. These volcanic islands with fairly high mountain ranges and fertile valleys were fit lands upon which the early settlers could develop the culture they brought with them. All the cultivable food plants, including the breadfruit and coconut, were introduced. From what little we know, it appears that the westerly islands, Rimatara and Rurutu, were influenced from the Cook Islands and that the easterly islands, Tupua'i and Raivavae, had more contact with Tahiti in the north.

The European navigators who first visited these islands toward the end of the eighteenth century reported a large and healthy population. They saw large double canoes, as well as outrigger canoes, made of split planks sewn together, with raised sterns well carved and with the gunwale tier also carved. The canoes were decorated with sea-birds' feathers held under the lashings of the topstrake in apparently the same technique as in New Zealand war canoes. They also had streamers of feathers hanging from the stern and bow pieces.

The weapons were well made and better carved than those of Tahiti. The carved paddles, the polished clubs with lozenge-shaped blades, and the stone pounders of Raivavae were eagerly sought after by sailors as South Seas curios. Many of these have found their way into museums and are usually attributed to Raivavae (High Island). It is exasperating that we know nothing definite about the clubs and paddles of the other three islands.

The Raivavae paddles are often erroneously attributed to Mangaia in the Cook Islands because they have some decorative motifs that are similar to those on Mangaian ceremonial adzes. However, the Mangaian paddles are of quite different shape. Circles, curves, and female figures which occur on the Raivavae paddles were never used in Mangaian art.

Another extraordinary 'curio' that is common in museums is the fully carved object labelled as a food scoop. It is made from a single piece of wood with the body shaped like an elongated bowl and the long handle shaped and carved like a paddle shaft. The manufacture of these scoops is probably post-European, for in the old Polynesian culture there was no use for a food scoop and such objects are found nowhere

else in Polynesia. The method of cooking in the earth oven
did not permit of the making of soup or stews. A friend has
suggested that the natives got the idea for a ladle from visiting foreign ships, and, by combining a bowl and a paddle
handle, produced an article which was popular in the European market.

There is less recorded information about the Austral
Islands than about any other inhabited group in Polynesia.
In order to supply a serious want, the Bishop Museum's
Bayard Dominick Expedition of 1920-22 included the Austral Islands and Rapa in its scope of investigation. Owing to
irregularities of schooner service, the two western islands
could not be visited but Robert T. Aitken was landed at
Tupua'i and J. F. G. Stokes at Raivavae. Though valuable
information was obtained by both field workers, the material
relating to myths of creation and early settlement was found
to be meagre.

In Tupua'i, Hiro, the navigator so well known in Tahiti,
the Cook Islands, and New Zealand, is mentioned as a visitor
and an ancestor. In Raivavae, Hiro is an ancestor called
Hiro-mata-atua (Hiro-of-the-divine-face) who married a
woman named Evari'i, the daughter of the god Tane, by
whom he had a son named Maui.

In order to trace the relationship of Austral Islands gods
and heroes to those in other parts of Polynesia, it is necessary
to digress for a moment to mention the changes in the language and the local use of glottals. In the Australs the *k* and *ng*
are dropped as in Tahiti. In Rurutu the *h* also is dropped as
in the Cook Islands. Evari'i, through fusing two vowels and
dropping a *k*, is really Eva-ariki (Eva-the-high-chiefess). Eva
is the Austral Islands form of Eve, and I suspect that the
name has been borrowed from Genesis to replace a Poly-

nesian lady whose name had been forgotten. When the great demigod Maui can be given such a unique parentage, anything may have happened in the period of mental aphasia that followed the desertion of the Polynesian gods.

Maui, in spite of his new lineage, was credited with several deeds belonging to his full list of accomplishments. In Tupua'i a fragment refers to Maui's building a temple, to his fishing up of various islands, and to his introduction of fire. He likewise snared the sun, but the tale is quaintly distorted.

Maui and his mother had no means of cooking their food so they put out their ration of taro for the sun to cook. The sun, however, travelled so quickly across the sky that when evening came the food was still uncooked. Maui and his mother ate it raw with the result that their mouths and throats were irritated. Chemists tell us now that taro contains crystals of oxalic acid which irritate the mucous membrane but which are broken down by cooking. Maui, irritated both mentally and physically, proposed to snare the sun with a strong rope and tether it until their food was cooked. His mother advised him to consult her father Tane, who lived somewhere in the upper spaces.

Maui visited his grandfather and retailed his grievance and his scheme of snaring the sun whereby their food might be cooked. It will be noted that in many myths the story has been composed backwards. We naturally wonder how Maui knew that their food would be rendered more palatable by cooking. Perhaps the food had been cooked by the sun in the long days of summer and had not been in the short days of winter. The 'perhaps' is mine, for the myth does not offer this suggestion.

Tane, who had usurped the invidious position of Mahuika, god of fire, said, 'Your scheme is altogether impracticable because the sun cannot be snared. The solution to your problem may be solved by a way other than that of attempting the impossible. I will show you.'

He took a piece of dry wood and broke it into two pieces. Leaving one piece stationary on the ground as the 'aunoti, he rubbed the sharp point of the other piece, termed 'aurima, backwards and forwards on the lower piece until a long groove was worn by the pressure. As the groove deepened, the fine particles of wood were collected in a little heap at the forward end of the groove. The movements increased in rapidity and the heat caused by the friction made the heap of wood dust smoulder and smoke. Tane quickly turned the lighted dust onto a bunch of dry fibre that he had in readiness and, by waving the bunch to and fro, the fibre caught alight and blazed into flame. The lighted kindling was laid on the ground, small pieces of wood were deftly placed over it, and then larger pieces were added. Before Maui's startled eyes, the first fire he had ever seen blazed merrily. Tane took hold of his grandson's hand and placed it briefly over the flame to instruct him in the properties of the new element that had been stored in the growing trees by the sun. Thus by the ritual of 'Burnt fingers' Maui was instructed in the method of producing fire by means of the Polynesian fire plough.

Tane proceeded with his instructions. He dug a shallow hole in the ground, built a fire within it, and placed stones as large as a closed fist above the wood. By the time the wood had burned down, the heat had been relayed on to the stones which became red hot. The stones were levelled to form a bed for the uncooked food which was placed upon them, and the whole was covered over with leaves. After some time, the leaves were removed and the food was found to be cooked.

Thus was demonstrated the simple form of cooking oven that spread throughout Polynesia. Maui's problem was solved.

Tane said, 'Return to the lower world and tell your mother how fire may be made and how food may be cooked.'

Tane took pity upon Maui because of the long journey before him, so he placed Maui in a sacred coconut which he threw down from the upper sphere. The coconut sped swiftly through space and alighted at Te Mahara on the island of Raivavae. It split open, and Maui emerged safely and returned to his mother, to whom he imparted the knowledge he had gained. Somebody is bound to ask why Maui's mother had not learned how to make fire from her father, Tane. The answer is simply that in the disruption of the ancient culture, the names of certain legendary characters have been displaced. By analogy with other Maui legends, it is clear that Maui's mother was not the daughter of Tane and that Maui could not learn the secret of fire from the great god Tane.

Another fragment from Raivavae states that Tihauone married Hinahuone, the daughter of Toareva, a king of the Underworld. Tihauone is a confused form of Ti'i-ahu-one (Tiki-ahu-one) and is a distorted memory of Tiki, who is associated in the richer myths with the creation of the first woman from earth. The first woman made from earth was Hina, and her name is usually qualified with the words *ahu* (to heap up) and *one* (earth). The Raivavaean name of the wife of Tiki is Hina-ahu-one, which is proof positive that the old myth of human creation was once known in a fuller and richer form than is indicated by the abbreviated records. The names of Ta'aroa, Tane, and Ro'o occur at the beginning of genealogy lists but Tu is curiously absent.

The temples of Raivavae, as described by Stokes, are numerous and unique in structure. They had the orthodox rectangular court, but the boundaries were marked by single lines of high basaltic slabs set close together. The middle slabs at the ends were ten to twelve feet high. On the outer side of the slab walls was a neat low curb formed usually of a red tuff. Between the curb and the wall, images of red tuff were set in the ground facing outward. Smaller subsidiary courts were built at the back of the main court. In the most elaborate temples, there was a long paved avenue, flanked on either side by basaltic pillars set at regular intervals, which led to the middle entrance at the front of the main court of the temple. When the temples were being used, they must have been an impressive sight, but unfortunately we have no information as to the form of ritual observed or even as to the names of the gods who were in residence.

In all the temples examined by Stokes there was no evidence of any raised platform altar such as we have come to regard as a necessary part of the Polynesian structures. There is one exception, however, at the reputed earliest temple of Te Mahara, the place which served as a landing field for Maui in his mythical flight. It may be that this oldest temple retains an element of an early technique which, in the course of time, was abandoned for what became a local pattern. If people could evolve a local form of paddle design and carvings, why shouldn't they change the architecture of their temples?

In the other three islands, the temples are not only fewer but they do not seem to have reached the standard attained at Raivavae. There are no stone images definitely recorded from the other islands, but on Raivavae several images of red tuff have been found. These are female forms, similar in technique to those carved on the paddles, and may have been more ornamental than religious. Macmillan Brown, in his work already quoted, figures two large images, one 11 to 12 feet and the other 8 to 9 feet high, standing on their original site. The French warship *Zélée* tried to remove them but failed. Later the images were carried to Tahiti and erected on either side of the path leading to the Papeete Museum. There, in 1935, I was studying them on the morning that the round-the-world tourist ship *Stella Polaris* berthed at the Papeete wharf. Two American women who had been to the Museum paused to look at the images.

One said, 'They are similar to the Easter Island images.'

The other remarked, 'I wonder where they are from?'

I volunteered the information though we had not been introduced.

The first lady transferred her attention from the images to me. With that admirable unconvention acquired by travel, she said, 'You are a New Zealander'.

'Guilty', I replied.

With growing conviction, she paused, 'You are a Maori'.

'Guilty again', I admitted.

She continued, 'I heard a lecture in New York that was given by a New Zealander and he was a Maori.'

I ventured a guess and said, 'At the English Speaking Union'.

'Yes,' she answered. 'He was a doctor and his name was Doctor Buck.'

'It still is', I apologized.

And so New York and the Antipodes were introduced to each other in Tahiti by a stone image that came from Raivavae.

The lack of images from Rimatara, Rurutu, and Tupua'i does not mean that they never existed. In 1826, a mission boat from the London Missionary Society's headquarters in

Ra'iatea returned from Rurutu laden with 'the gods of the heathen'. They were publicly exhibited from the pulpit. One, named Aa (Ha), was the chief god of Rurutu. It was carved from wood in human form, four feet high, and the body and head were hollowed out and provided with a lid at the back. The cavity was found to be full of small gods. The missionary, John Williams, stated that no less than twenty-four were taken out, one after another and exhibited to public view. What happened to these works of art may be readily guessed; the souls of the wicked were burned in the Underworld, and the wooden gods of the Polynesians were burned in the upper world. So far as I know, the large image of Aa was the only one saved, and it has now sanctuary in the British Museum under the name of Tangaroa-upao-vahu. The image is ornamented with small human figures cut in the solid on its face, body, limbs, and lid. Some of the figures have been carved with the head downward and present a somewhat ludicrous appearance. They remind me of the two tall panels in stone on either side of the entrance to Bath Abbey in England, which represent Jacob's ladder with the angels ascending and descending. The descending angels are upside-down like the inverted figures on Aa.

Rapa, on the southeast radial from the centre, is the most southerly island in tropical Polynesia and is sometimes included in the Austral Islands. Like the Austral Islands, Rapa had been so neglected that Stokes, who went there from Raivavae, found the myths and traditions scanty and confused. The few fragments that were gathered are interesting as remnants of a richer oral literature that was not committed to writing by the early native missionaries who were preoccupied with spreading the new theology.

The Reverend Davies, who visited the island in 1826,

stated that the religion of Rapa was the same as that of Tahiti but without the parade and show. There were no regular religious structures, but a few stones were regarded as sacred shrines with magic power. No images in stone or wood were found, but the gods Paparua and Poere were represented by material objects. Paparua, neatly made of coconut fibre in the form of a miniature cask two to three inches long, was consulted in war and sickness and was appealed to for turtle. Poere, a stone about one foot long planted in the ground, promoted the fertility of food and the maintenance of spring-water supply. He was evidently the god of artisans, for he was invoked at the launching of canoes and the building of houses. Offerings of fish were made to him to promote recovery of the sick.

It may be that Paparua was reminiscent of Papa, the great Earth-mother, and that the Rapa people combined two Papas into the single god, Papa-rua (Papa-the-two). The Rapa dialect differs from that of the other Austral Islands in retaining the *k* and *ng* sounds but dropping the *h*. It has been so affected by late Tahitian contact that one wonders whether or not the god Poere should be Po-kere and thus mean 'Dark-night'. If so, the name may be a memory of the Cosmic Night that occurs in the creation myths of other islands. Certain it is that Te Tumu, Atea, Fa'ahotu, and the great major gods —Tane, Rongo, and Tangaroa—are missing in Rapa.

There were a number of minor family gods, and the expression of their wishes or, perhaps, of the wishes of their human mediums conforms to the regular Polynesian pattern. There was apparently no organized priesthood, which may account for the meagre mythology. The widely spread terms *tohunga* and *taura*, as applied to priests, are lacking in the dialect, and the local term of *tangata-kai-pure* (man-who-ate-prayers) seems an apology.

Human origin, though abbreviated, is interesting. The first man to appear on Rapa was Tiki, who came from 'Avaiki. He married a woman of Rapa, who gave birth to two daughters. In the Biblical story of human creation, we learn that the primary couple had two sons, Cain and Abel. When Cain slew his brother, Abel, it seemed that the end had come, but Cain took unto himself a wife from the land of Nod, whereby the human species was continued. I have no explanation for the presence of a woman on uninhabited Rapa, unless Rapa may be a Polynesian form for the land of Nod.

Tiki's two daughters, while stooping to gather clams, were touched by the burrowing organ of a clam, which represented the phallus of Tiki. They both became pregnant, and one gave birth to a son, the other to a daughter. The son, named Tama-tiki (Son-of-Tiki), married his cousin, and from them the people of Rapa were descended. In any creation myth that stops short at a single male and a single female, incest must occur. The Polynesians recognized this biological fact and, in the creation myths of most island groups, Tiki commits incest directly with a daughter. Rapa departs from the pattern in that the incest is cloaked through the medium of a clam.

On Rapa, as in Rarotonga and the Austral Islands, we might expect to find a mention of the great navigator, Hiro. Although the local form 'Iro occurs, it is without clear detail. There seems little doubt, however, that Hiro was one of the outstanding navigators of the thirteenth century and that from the Society Islands he sailed to the various islands lying to the east, southeast, south, and southwest. Though he never reached New Zealand, his fame was carried to that far-off land by his descendants who emigrated from central Polynesia in the fourteenth century.

Though the myths and traditions of Rapa have been so poorly transmitted, it is comforting to find that Vancouver, who rediscovered Rapa in 1791, has a word of praise about material things. He was greatly struck with the canoes of that island, which carried crews of twenty-five to thirty men. They have carved stern pieces which were raised, and Vancouver wrote, 'The mind is filled with admiration at their ingenuity and persevering industry'—rare words of praise to fall from the lips of a non-Polynesian.

Rapa is too cold for the breadfruit, coconut, and plantain to grow. The pig, dog, and fowl were somehow left behind by the early discoverers, but the ubiquitous rat managed to stow away in some early ship. The food plants present include the taro, banana, sweet potato, yam, and mountain apple. Taro, fermented in pits in a manner similar to that used for breadfruit in the Marquesas, is the staple food. The fermented taro is cooked in wrapped-leaf packages in the earth oven and then pounded into a paste with stone pounders. The smooth paste is wrapped in *ti* leaves in bundles that look very like Christmas puddings. The bundles are hung up in the native trees and are a familiar sight in the village landscape.

The women outnumber the men and do most of the hard work, tending the cultivations, carrying home the supplies of food, and cooking. They even wait on the men at meal times and put the food into their mouths. Macmillan Brown, on seeing this usage, came to the conclusion that the men were taboo and could not touch the food with their own hands. This interpretation was evidently influenced by his acquaintance with a New Zealand custom in which individuals, owing to religious sanctions, might place themselves under taboo for a certain time. During this time, the taboo person could not touch food with his hands, as food was common (*noa*).

He, therefore, had to be hand-fed by a male or female attendant until the taboo period expired. In Rapa, however, the men were not taboo, as Brown stated, but were simply waited upon by their womenfolk, according to a usage that had been established locally. A similar usage existed in Mangareva.

Rapa has suffered as much, if possible, from European contact as have the Marquesas. The island is small, being but 5.7 miles from north to south and 5 miles from east to west. It is indented by fifteen bays, of which Tairirau Harbour, on the east, penetrates beyond the middle of the island. Vancouver, in 1791, estimated the population at 1500, and missionary Davies, in 1826, estimated it at 2000. But the ship that bore the gospel to Rapa in 1826 also carried the germs of epidemic diseases. Mœrenhout, who visited Rapa in 1834, stated that the population had been reduced to 300, as the result of introduced venereal and epidemic diseases. As if their cup was not full to overflowing, in 1863 smallpox and cholera broke out aboard a ship that had been chartered to return people taken from Tonga, Tokelau, and Manihiki by a Peruvian slaver. The captain, to save his own worthless life and that of his equally valueless crew, dumped his sick freight on Rapa. The Rapa people died like flies, and when Hall visited the island a year later, the surviving people of Rapa numbered only 130.

In the halcyon days before European contact, the people of Rapa had adjusted themselves successfully to their peculiar environment. The cultivable lands were fully utilized in the growing of taro, and by the system of preserving the taro in pits the people were enabled to provide reserve supplies. The early families had developed into groups which became tribes and subsequently divided into subtribes. The tribes were named after specific ancestors with the prefix Ngate (Ngati) and Ngai, on the same pattern as prevailed in New Zealand. As the population increased, conflicts occurred, as has happened the world over. The people built fortified villages on commanding ridges and mountain peaks, not only for defence but in order that they could overlook their cultivations and watch the neighbouring tribes. The razor-backed mountain ridges with steep subsidiary ridges leading up to them were ideal positions for defence, because they prevented a massed attack on a wide front. A ridge with a peak was selected and the summit was levelled off to form the topmost terrace. The sides were cut down with digging implements of pointed wood and rude adzes of dyke basalt, until a second terrace could be formed of sufficient width to accommodate houses. The military architects of the day continued the plan of successive terraces which necessitated high walls at the back. The razorback on the ridge leading to the peak was levelled off and the sides were cut to increase the steepness against assault. Deep ditches were cut across the main ridge on either side of the citadel to improve the defences. On the secondary ridges leading up to the main fort, further terraces were dug to provide house accommodation and outposts for defence. The back walls of the terraces, particularly near the citadel, were further reinforced with stone slabs carefully built in to protect the earth face against the detrition of wind and rain. Projecting stones formed footholds by which the defenders could retreat from terrace to terrace. Within the fort itself were hollows to catch rain as reserve water supply in event of attack. Each fort, however, had some near-by spring on the lower slopes, which were guarded.

On the topmost terrace of the citadel peak, the high chief resided. In war he was the commanding officer. An attacking party could advance by one ridge only, and from his vantage ground the chief could call up his forces to concentrate on the section attacked. Fighting was hand-to-hand, and thus the citadel which commanded all points of the compass was the ideal position for the commander of the defences.

The hill forts of Rapa, termed *pare* or *pa*, were qualified by *maunga* (mountain) or *tamaki* (war). It may be that the peculiar geographical formation of Rapa suggested this unique development of fortification. In principle the Rapan forts resemble the *pa* forts of New Zealand. Had it been my fortune to visit Rapa, I might, perchance, have sensed an affinity that personal contact may convey with more subtlety than the written words of others.

The hill forts of Rapa were the material expression of a warlike people. The highest fort of Karere was at an elevation of 1460 feet. A perfect model of defensive engineering was Te Vaitau at the height of 840 feet. I dreamed a dream about a stone stadium in the Marquesas, but I dare not dream again. Look at the picture of Te Vaitau, people its terraces with armed warriors, harken to the shell trumpets calling defiance, and dream of Rapa for yourselves.

14. THE EASTERN ATOLLS

Grew up the land Havaiki
With its king Rongonui;
Then grew up the land Vavau
With its king Toi-ane.
Then appeared the land Hiti-nui
With its king Tangaroa-manahune.

TUAMOTUAN CHANT

I WAS born in the south of Polynesia, lived in the north, worked in the west and centre, but had never visited islands east of Tahiti. In 1934, after I had spent two years at Yale University as Bishop Museum Visiting Professor of Anthropology, Bishop Museum sent me to join its Mangarevan Expedition. A high-powered sampan, *The Islander*, and a small schooner *Tiare Tahiti* (Tahitian Gardenia), had been chartered to visit various island groups east of Tahiti. The sampan party, under the leadership of Dr. C. M. Cooke, Jr., Malacologist at Bishop Museum, made collections of plants, insects, and land shells from islands not hitherto explored scientifically, and gathered an amazing amount of material new to science.

The *Tiare Tahiti* for the use of the ethnologists, J. F. Stimson, K. P. Emory, and myself, met me in Tahiti in August, but, as it had to go into dry dock for repairs, I took passage on the trading schooner *Moana* to join my colleagues in the eastern Tuamotu.

On the second afternoon out from Papeete we passed Kaukura, the first atoll of the Tuamotu group. Over the near horizon peeped the tops of coconut trees. As we approached, the trees seemed gradually to stand up, until finally they came to rest with their bases wrapped round by the dazzling white coral beach. Other islets appeared over the horizon, curving off to follow the round of the great reef on which they are set. On the far side of the nearer islands lay the still, green waters of the lagoon, contrasting sharply with the deep purple of the outer sea. Beyond the green waters were indistinct specks, clumps, and lines of coconut trees, indicating other islands which complete the ring of an atoll.

On the next afternoon, our captain pointed to some clouds to the southeast and said, 'Anaa'. I gazed at the clouds and at the surface of the sea, but there was no trace of land. I did not understand how an island could be seen in the sky when not visible on the sea, nor how clouds could be tethered like a captive balloon to mark the site of an atoll.

'How do you know?' I asked.

'See that green tinge on the clouds,' he replied. 'That is the reflection of the green waters of the lagoon of Anaa. The lagoon is shallower than those of other islands, and the water is greener. Anaa can always be picked by the green clouds so long as the sun is shining on the lagoon and a cloud is above.'

I looked at the cloud. It had a green tinge. Perhaps the keen-eyed Polynesian navigators could distinguish the fainter reflection of other lagoons—perhaps even when there were no clouds. Unfortunately they have not handed on to us these finer observations that guided them to success in their early explorations.

We sailed alongside Anaa five hours later and went ashore in the schooner's boats, for there is no reef opening by which the schooner may enter the lagoon. A few native men and two Chinamen gave us a tepid welcome. While the captain attended to business, a companion and I walked along a cleared road connecting the outer shore to the lagoon shore half a mile away. On either side of the road were the houses that constituted the small village of Tukuhora. Nearly all the houses were made of scraps of boards taken from boxes and roofed over with rusty corrugated iron. A few houses were thatched with plaited coconut leaves which were attached to a single set of rafters by nails driven through the midribs of the leaves. I put my notebook back into my pocket with a sigh.

On the lagoon shore, my eyes brightened at the sight of some outrigger canoes, but my hopes were quickly extinguished. The canoes had a straight fore boom fastened to the float with connecting stanchions and a slender, curved after boom which bent directly down to the float. The technique had been borrowed from Tahiti, and even the pattern of the lashing of the fore boom was identical with that I had drawn in Tahiti four years before. The native technique of Anaa had completely disappeared.

The people, while not exactly morose, showed none of the cordiality so characteristic of the Polynesian people. I found out afterwards that their lack of vocal expression was regarded by the rest of the Tuamotu as being peculiar to Anaa.

One of the crew said, 'The *torea* bird makes a noise in the mornings and evenings when anybody goes near it.'

'What about it?' I asked.

'Well,' he replied, 'there are no *torea* on Anaa.'

On the way to Hikueru, we called in at the uninhabited atoll of Reitoru. The atoll belongs to Hikueru, and the chief of that island, who was a passenger, gave the captain permission to get firewood for the engine. Not only did we acquire firewood, but also fish, which teemed in the lagoon, and many fledgling sea-birds from their nests in the low shrubs. In the old economic system of the Tuamotus, an atoll was allowed to lie fallow periodically, while the people migrated elsewhere, in order that the food supplies might increase on both land and sea.

When we landed at Hikueru, the people lined up to greet us with the customary 'Ia orana' and to shake our hands. They were clean, athletic, and good-looking. There were evidently plenty of *torea* birds on Hikueru. However, the houses and canoes at Hikueru were as disappointing to an ethnologist as were those at Anaa. Even the speech had been replaced by the Tahitian dialect, largely through trade and the universal use of the Tahitian Bible. The *k* and *ng*, present in the old speech, have been dropped. I created a certain amount of interest by using the Maori dialect in conversation, which was recognized as being like that of the old people who had passed away.

The chief's compound was a model of a complex household. The front wall was made of concrete surmounted at intervals with pairs of pearl shells for ornament. The side and back walls were neat picket fences. The enclosed buildings were small and simple, made of sawn timber and roofed with corrugated iron, all neatly kept and very clean. Besides the dwelling house, there were separate dining room, kitchen, bathroom, and latrines. No less than ten canoes were drawn up within the compound and carefully protected from the sun by coverings of coconut leaves and sheets of corrugated iron.

The bathhouse was made entirely of corrugated iron with a spacious wooden floor. A capacious cylindrical can, open at the top and with a shower rosette attached by a short pipe to the lower end, was suspended near the floor by ropes attached to a pulley fixed to the roof. The handmaidens of the chief carried buckets of fresh water from the town cistern close at hand and filled the can. They then hauled the can upward to the requisite height, announced that the bath was ready, and departed. As a guest of the chief, I was privileged to use the shower, supplying my own towel and soap. I turned on the tap above the rosette and enjoyed one of the finest shower baths I have ever had. The towel was afterwards washed by command of the hostess. She expressed a wish to wash the clothes I had on, but as no suggestion was made as to what I should do in the interim of drying, I declined by saying I wished to watch the process of loading the boats with copra.

The copra, consisting of the dried chunks of coconut meat cut out of the mature nuts, was stored loose in various sheds. The trading schooner supplied the sacks, which were filled by the local workers and weighed in the presence of the ship's supercargo. The weighed sacks were thrown outside in a heap and were carried down to the landing, about half a mile away, by natives of both sexes. The men carried a sack over their shoulder, but the women used two fairly large handcarts that carried several sacks. Two women pulled on the pole at the front of the cart and three pushed from behind. The carts rattled speedily along to the sound of laughter. It was fun and did not last long enough to become a labour. From the landing, men carried the sacks down to the boats, which were brought as close to shore as the depth of water would allow. When a boat was filled, her crew pushed off and rowed to the schooner, which tacked up and down just outside the reef.

We called at Maro-kau and landed a Chinese trader with his stock of goods at a temporarily deserted village, whose inhabitants were probably at some other islet preparing copra. The trader's goods were widely assorted, including bars of soap from New Zealand and pots of ginger labelled 'The Product of China'.

At Tauere, the houses and canoes still followed the modern pattern. A young man took me to the marae of Rangihoa where the god Tahiri was once worshipped. A few stones marked the site, but my guide dug into the sand and produced a skull. From the ease with which he found the skull, I suspect that the temple was a show place for chance tourists.

At Hao is a deep passage into the lagoon. The passage was named Kaki (Neck), and the current was so strong that the *Moana* had difficulty in making way against it. This was a great fishing ground for sea-birds, and the frigate hawks, like enemy aeroplanes, waited high above them. When the sea-birds obtained their catch and started for home, the pirates of the air swooped down on them. The frightened birds regurgitated the fish, and the swift frigate hawks caught the falling fish before they touched water. An old man, Te Uira, gave me the chant which the Kaki channel sings:

> Kaki! Yes, I am Kaki,
> The Neck with a narrow gullet,
> Irregularly distended by the urge of hunger.
> The interior of our ancestress Tiaki is empty.
> My breath comes in short gasps,
> So little time have I for rest—ah me!
> My bowels churn as the troubled tides
> Raise the surging waves along my channel.
> My fish, swaying gently to the wavelets
> On either side the current,
> With hungry, upturned gaze,

Await the flotsam from the lagoon,
That seaward floats
Upon the surface of the stippled waters.
But what bird is that
Also waiting expectantly above?
Beware! 'tis the frigate hawk,
The bird of prey with the gleaming breast.

The Hao lagoon is one of the largest in the Tuamotu, and the islets of the far edge were but dimly seen as we sailed in to the main village of Otepa. From a distance the red-roofed houses of the village gave the appearance of a seaside resort, but on closer inspection the red colour proved to be not tiles but the rust of corrugated iron. The people of Hao were friendly and communicative, and they evinced an interest in my dialect which retained the sounds *k* and *ng* which they had dropped.

At Tatakoto, we picked up Emory and Stimson, and on the way to Reao to do field work, we landed at Pukerua. The the houses were made of native material. The canoes were built on a local pattern out of small pieces of plank sewn together with sennit braid. They were deep and narrow and were provided with a plank for an outrigger float instead of the usual thick timber in the round. The Pukerua and Reao people have a close affinity with each other, and in physical form they differ from the other Tuamotuans. They are shorter with short, broad faces and wide noses. It looks as if some other mixture of blood was present, but the analysis must be left to the physical anthropologists.

Before reaching Reao, I received a wireless from Tahiti stating that the *Tiare Tahiti* would be some considerable time in dock. If we waited at Reao, the field work at Mangareva would not be done adequately, because of the lateness of the season. We changed our plans and went on to Mangareva.

Although the atolls I visited were disappointing in material things, Emory and Stimson had been able to gather what is probably the largest collection of myths, songs, and legends yet made in Polynesia. The Tuamotuans, like other coral islanders, lacked the variety of food and textile plants grown only in the fertile soil of volcanic islands. Due to the lack of economic appeal to white traders, they remained more isolated than their kinsmen on volcanic islands and retained many of the so-called 'heathen customs' until a much later period. Finally missionaries and traders after copra and pearl shell invaded even these poor atolls, forcing the natives to share in the general change that has affected the whole of Polynesia. However, some of the old men interviewed by Emory and Stimson had taken part in the ancient ceremonies on the temples and could give first-hand information about many things.

Apparently the Tuamotuans, whose material culture was necessarily poor due to a lack of raw materials, developed a particular feeling for poetry and an ability to express themselves in beautiful words. Living on coral islands and watching the constant movement of the waves, they set their thoughts to the music of the surf beating against the outer reef. The age-long music was personified as Orovaru, the Gushing-murmur-of-the-waters.

Throughout Polynesia one of the most popular amusements was community singing, not only at public functions but at ordinary family gatherings in the evening. Once started, a group of singers would run through their entire repertoire, the adults refreshing their memories and the young people learning new songs by a process of absorption and the desire to be able to join in the chanting. As they grew older, obscure passages were explained by their elders. Thus the transmission of ancient lore was continuous from one generation to the next. European contact and conversion to Christianity generally broke this continuity, but the music-loving Tuamotuans continued to sing their ancient chants. Although temple ritual and prose teachings were abandoned, the old *fagu* chants still known today give a fairly adequate picture of the myths and concepts of creation that existed in the Tuamotu Islands before European contact. In addition to the major gods possessed in common with all Polynesia, each atoll had its own local gods who were deified ancestors.

The myths go back to the Kore (*Void*), and the period of Cosmic Night finds expression in the familiar term Potangotango. The Great Source, Tumu-nui, brought up the sand from Hawaiki, the land below the sea, and caused it to reach the surface. It became a reef and, subsequently, an island. English prose cannot adequately convey the lilt of the Tuamotuan chant as it sings of 'the growing sand, the rising sand, the lifting sand, the spreading sand, the sand that expands into land'.

The great nature gods of Opoa are richly represented in Tuamotuan myths. Many of the creation chants commence with Te Tumu-nui, the Great Source, and recite a number of forms of Te Tumu. He occurs as Tumu-po (Source-of-darkness) contrasted with Tumu-ao (Source-of-light). Papa (Earth-foundation) is associated with Te Tumu. Atea (Space) appears in the form of Atea-rangi (Sky-space), who is above; and Fakahotu (Fructifier-of-the-soil) is below. In one myth, Atea-rangi mates with Atea to produce the gods Tane (ruler of things above), Tangaroa (lord of the ocean), and Rongo (patron of oratory and eloquence). This arrangement follows the early pattern that emanated from Opoa, except that by some confusion Atea takes the place of Papa or Fakahotu in being mated to Atea-rangi. The compound name of Atea-rangi connects in thought the Atea of central Polynesia with the Rangi of New Zealand, who are the husbands of Papa, the Earth-mother.

The gods in the period of darkness called in labourers to push up the sky sphere, Atea-rangi, and to uphold him in position. The people employed were the Ngati-Ru, the family of Ru, who are alluded to as Long-Ru, Short-Ru, and Humpbacked-Ru. We have seen that Ru himself performed a similar task in the Society Islands, but desisted when he became humpbacked. In the Cook Islands, Ru was successful without any bodily ill effect.

Some of the *fagu* chants tell in detail of a conflict between Atea and Tane in which Atea gave in. This struggle occurs in the Society Islands myths, and the story is reminiscent of the New Zealand myth in which Tane took an active part in forcing Rangi (the Sky) up into his present position.

Stimson has collected information from various sources on an attempt to establish a supreme creator in the person of Kiho-tumu. The struggle for supremacy has been seen in the Tahitian elevation of Ta'aro and will be met in New Zealand in a similar treatment by some theological schools of Io.

The widespread Tiki myth is known in the Tuamotu. The Hao version records that Ahu-roa, an ordinary man, married One-rua and that they had a male child, Tiki. Tiki married One-kura, the daughter of a human couple named Mati and One-ura. In other island groups, Tiki's wife was made from earth, and her name was usually Hinia-ahu-one or some variant. Traces of the more general myth are seen in the inclusion of Ahu (to heap up) and One (Earth) in the names of

Tiki's parents and also in the name of his wife One-kura (Red-earth). The later part of the story follows the general pattern in that Tiki seduces his own daughter by trickery and commits incest with her. Though they had children who doubtless became ancestors, the Tuamotuan story is unique in making Tiki merely a legendary character who is not credited as the father of mankind.

The Maui myth is recorded with much detail and local variations. Ataranga married Hava and produced Maui-mua, Maui-roto, Maui-muri, and Maui-taha. He then married Huahenga and had a son named Maui-tikitiki-a-Ataranga, the mischievous culture hero of Polynesia. This last Maui snared the sun, bested Mahuika, the god of fire, killed Tuna (Eel from whose head grew the coconut) to retake the woman Hina, and created the first dog.

The dog story is interesting, for it indicates that though the Tuamotuans did not have the pig and the fowl, they had some knowledge of the dog. Briefly stated, Maui was married to Hina, who proved faithless by conducting a love affair with a handsome stranger named Ri. Maui found out, and one lazy afternoon he beguiled Ri into delousing each other's heads. As Ri lay comfortably stretched out on the ground with his head on Maui's knees, he fell asleep. Maui then applied digital traction to Ri's nose, ears, and spine. When Ri awoke he was not only anatomically transformed into a quadruped but he was evidently mentally transformed as well, for he became the ancestor of dogs. The myth naively continues that many people came to see the wonder Maui had performed. Maui and his four older brothers set out on a fishing expedition in an outrigger canoe named *Taitai-arohia*. Maui baited his hook with the crimson feathers that are usually associated with high chiefs and gods. It is little wonder that he hooked a marvellous fish. As he hauled in his line, he sang a vaunting song describing each item in his fishing tackle and the canoe equipment, which are given proper names. With the last haul, he chanted the final verse:

> My fish is hooked,
> It ascends to the World-of-light.
> At last my fish
> Breaks into view above the waves.
> It is Tahiti.

The Tuamotuan Maui myth has affinity with the New Zealand myth in that Maui, moved by the sight of his wife's grey hairs, sought to gain immortality for man. He was told that he could prevent death if he exchanged the stomach of Rori, the Sea-slug, for his own. He sought out Sea-slug in the shallow waters near the shore, but that obdurate individual refused to make the exchange. Maui thereupon seized him and, by squeezing his body, he made Sea-slug's stomach protrude. He vomited up his own stomach and commenced to swallow that of Sea-slug. The esophageal end of the stomach was just about to disappear when Maui's brothers, who had secretly followed him, called out, 'Look at what Maui is doing'. Sea-slug's stomach was ejected, and Maui replaced his own. The quest had failed. This was the last adventure of Maui-of-the-thousand-exploits.

The most noted lineages of the chiefly families commence with a chant termed *nanao ariki* (to grope for the chiefly source). One of them runs as follows:

> O my king!
> I will grope down
> Into the recesses of
> My ancient learning and teachings,

> Down to the Great Source, Tumu-nui,
> The Lesser Source, all other Sources.
> Let the south turn toward me,
> Let the north incline toward me.
> Papa, the Foundation, was battered,
> The Foundation was cleared,
> From the Foundation sprang the lineage,
> The lineage of Whom?
>
> The lineage of my noble ancestor,
> My ancestor Hiro.

Hiro, the great navigator of the thirteenth century, is a well-known ancestor. From him, twenty-six generations ago, the lineage is easily carried down to the present day.

Some of the old chants are composed about individual atolls and indicate the affection of the inhabitants for their homes. The following poem collected by K. P. Emory is about the atoll of Raroia:

> What is that canoe that hither sails,
> Overarched by the rainbow,
> Encompassed about by white tern?
> The land of Raroia is encircled.
> This is Raroia, land of soft breezes,
> From which sounds the lament of Marere-nui.
> Softly sound the rustling coconut leaves.
>
> Oh, how my land
> Inspires love!

Many chants have been poetically translated by Stimson, but space forbids further quotations.

In the wealth of myths and chants, there are a number of different versions of the same story and different explanations of obscure points. Even in ancient times, the learned people realized that the version of the ancient lore (*vanaga*) and the given explanation (*korero*) might not coincide. This doubt found expression in the following verse:

> Correct is the explanation, wrong is the lore,
> Correct is the lore, wrong the explanation.
> Correct, correct is the lore,
> Ah no!
> It is wrong, it is wrong—alas!

The chant at the head of this chapter shows that the Tuamotuans were acquainted with the islands of Havaiki, Vavau, and Hiti-nui. The fact that Hiti-nui is associated with the king Tangaroa-mahahune, whom we have already met in Tahiti under the name of Ta'aroa-manahune, indicates clearly enough that Hiti-nui is Great Tahiti in the Society Islands and not a name for Fiji.

Religious rituals were conducted on open courts with a raised stone platform at one end behind which was a row of spaced limestone slabs, somewhat similar to the religious structures of Tongareva. On the court itself were other erect limestone slabs that formed backrests for the principal chief and priest. The side and front boundaries of the court were not defined by any curb, as they were in Tongareva.

The principal ceremony conducted on the courts was in connection with turtle feasts. When a turtle was caught at sea, a piece of the breast bone was immediately detached and offered with an incantation to the god Tangaroa. It is thus seen that Tangaroa maintained his position as god of the sea and of fishermen, as he did in the Marquesas and New Zealand. The turtle was taken onto the court and a ritual conducted during which the throat of the turtle was cut. A piece of raw flesh from the side was hung on a forked stick erected in front of the platform. Then the whole turtle received a first cooking in an oven near the court, after which it was returned to the court. It was cut up, and the principal chief and priest ate the heart and a flipper of the turtle on the marae. The cut-up turtle then received a second cooking after which the male population feasted near the court. Women were not allowed a share, as turtle meat was prohibited to them. As it was taboo and could not be taken back to the dwelling houses, any meat left over after the feast was placed upon a wooden platform near the cooking fire. If turtle were plentiful and much was left over, the men returned the next day and feasted on the surplus.

After completing my field study in Mangareva, I returned to Tahiti by the steamer *Toia*, which fortunately went through the Tuamotu by a northern route, introducing me to new islands. The Tuamotuan archipelago is extensive, stretching a thousand miles from Rangiroa in the west to the atolls near Mangareva in the east. In fact, the Mangareva group is usually included in the Tuamotu Islands, although they are of volcanic origin with a culture distinct from that of the Taumotuan atolls.

At Fagatau I had an experience which, though inconsequential, may serve to illustrate the genuine friendship of the Polynesians for all men, but particularly for those of their own race. We landed on the beach, and I shook hands with the usual group of people watching our landing. Among them were some old men, but I did not venture any speech beyond the Tahitian greeting of 'Ia orana''. The supercargo set off for the village a few hundred yards away, and I followed in his wake. A tall, handsome Tuamotuan of middle age fell into step beside me. As we walked along, he kept glancing sideways at me with a puzzled look. He was trying to diagnose what stock I belonged to, but he dared not ask a direct question in case I should happen to be Polynesian. No Polynesian of any birth can ask the question, 'Who are you?' The person questioned might be a high chief, and the questioner would be overcome by shame for his own ignorance. In the Tuamotu, the old people might quote the following, which would have necessitated a genealogical recital in the old days:

> Manuka is where questions are asked.
> Visitors are journeying to Matahoa-a-Tane.
> I ask a question of you,
> O my high chief.
> From whom are we two descended?

In order to break the suspense, I pointed to a tree and asked, 'He aha te ingoa o tera rakau?' (What is the name of that tree?). The effect upon my companion was more striking than I had hoped it would be. He fairly jumped. His mouth opened, the name of the tree came forth, but his mouth remained open and his eyes bulged. Why? No matter how well a foreigner may learn a Polynesian dialect, he generally misuses a vowel or misplaces the emphasis on consonants. My companion knew that I came from the same stock as he did, but the problem was: Where from and who? After enjoying his surprise sufficiently, I said, 'I am Te Rangi Hiroa'. I knew that both Emory and Stimson had told some of their Tuamotuan informants about me and that possibly this man might know the name. He seized my hand with a crushing grip and then dashed back toward the old men on the beach, shouting, 'Fariua, O Fariua, here is Te Rangi Hiroa'.

An intelligent-looking old man detached himself from his

fellows and hurried toward us. He shook hands very heartily and said, 'Why did you not tell us you were coming?' I did not tell him that I had forgotten the particular atoll upon which he lived, though I did remember that he had given a wealth of information to Emory and Stimson on their previous visits. We went to Fariua's house and sat on his veranda talking. His daughter, who had also been an invaluable informant to my colleagues, sat with us. When the time approached for leaving, Fariua issued an order. A small boy disappeared and then reappeared with two live fowls. They were Fariua's gift to a kinsman from a distant land. We marched down to the boat landing with the boy carrying the fowls behind us.

I said to Fariua, 'Come out to the ship for a trip'.

I knew that the ship had brought cases of bananas and mangoes from Mangareva that were sold at the various atolls, where fruit, other than the coconut, did not grow. When the last boat left the ship, Fariua was accompanied by a case of mangoes and a case of bananas, which were my reciprocal recognition of his hospitality. We do not usually talk about these things, and I hope that Fariua will never see this book. Yet it seems to me that such minor personal incidents indicate clearly the spirit of Polynesian hospitality. Give and receive, receive and give, not for the material benefit but for the sake of one's honour.

15. ON THE TRAIL OF THE RISING SUN

Hoist up the sails with the two crossed sprits,
The two-sprit sails that will bear us afar.
Steer the course of the ship to a far distant land,
Sail down the tide with the wind astern.

MANGAREVAN CHANT OF FAREWELL

ON the third day out from Reao, the Tahitian captain of the
Moana pointed toward the east and shouted, 'Mangareva'.
We had been sailing through the atolls of the Tuamotu
which, though interesting, were monotonous in their similarity. Watching a mountain peak rising higher and higher
above the horizon, we felt the excitement of change. The
peak was Mount Duff, named by Captain Wilson in 1797
after his ship, which carried the London Missionary Society's
first group of workers to Tahiti. The mountain seemed to
float up out of the sea, and one could share the feelings of
the Polynesian discoverers when they named it Mangareva,
the Floating Mountain.

We sailed through the western passage in the encircling
reef, and the individual islands of the group unfolded before
us. We passed Taravai on our left with little Angakau-i-ita
nestling beside it. A group of small rocky islets, of which
Kamaka was the largest, lay to the south. Akamaru and
Aukena separated as we approached. We sailed along the
south coast of the largest island, Mangareva, with Mount

202

Duff towering above. The islands are the remains of crater rims, and the hillsides are steep and bare except for a kind of cane. From the main middle ridge of Mangareva, secondary ridges run down to the sea and form boundaries for small bays. Tiny pockets of flat fertile land extend back from the bays as far as the mountain slopes. The coconut groves are thus small and scattered. A plateau on the south of Mount Duff is the site of a modern cemetery in which stands a building that was pointed out to us as the tomb of Te Ma-puteoa, the last king of Mangareva. We rounded the cemetery point, and the chief village of Rikitea lay before us, with the two towers of its large stone cathedral rising above the trees.

The schooner dropped anchor near the wharf, and Captain Emile Brisson, Deputy Administrator of the Gambier Islands, came aboard with his wife and family. We received a cordial welcome and a hearty assurance of assistance in our work. Emory stayed in the Brisson residence and I lodged in the detached library of M. Tondon, the Administrator, who was absent in Tahiti. The library contained a fine collection of works on Polynesia, and the back veranda had a closed-in shower bath. It was the most comfortable quarters that an ethnologist could find in the South Seas. Stimson went on by the *Moana* to continue his linguistic work in another of the Tuamotu atolls.

On landing, the native inhabitants came forward with outstretched hands and greetings of 'Ena koe' (There you are), corresponding to 'Hello', and the exact equivalent of the New Zealand greeting, 'Tena koe'. The correct response is 'A koe noti' (You indeed). The Mangarevan dialect sounded pleasant, for it resembles a blending of Maori and Rarotongan dialects. The *h* is absent and is represented by a catch in the voice; the *k* and *ng* sounds are both present.

Unfortunately, the French priests who committed the language to writing used the system that prevails throughout French Oceania and Samoa of using the letter *g* to represent the *ng* sound. With a knowledge of both Maori and Rarotongan, I took a short cut to learning Mangarevan.

The person who says that he can immediately understand all that is said in one Polynesian group because he knows the language of another group lays claim to extraordinary insight. Maori is my mother tongue but I freely admit that I could never understand all that I heard in the Polynesian islands which I visited for the first time. A trader needs only a small vocabulary to carry on his business transactions, and a journalist can pick up a sufficient knowledge of a dialect by 'absorption'. But an ethnologist must have a thorough understanding of grammar, idiom, and variant meaning. The meanings of many words are constant throughout Polynesia, but there are notable exceptions. I have met many that sapped my confidence—but let me tell you part of a folktale as an illustration.

The folktales of Mangareva are peculiar for the ease with which the characters pass to and fro between this world and the Underworld or Po. A child named Tonga from the Po was adopted by his uncle in this world and was reared in seclusion, according to the Mangarevan custom of treating a favourite child. The adoptive father cooked the food and waited on the child in the house of seclusion without letting even his own wife see the child. Tonga was fattened with the best of foods so as to make a spectacular appearance when he was ready to be exhibited at adolescence at some public festival. When the time drew near, the adoptive father said to his wife Irutea, 'I am going to a distant fishing ground for some choice fish. If I am delayed, prepare the food and feed the boy.'

Irutea could hardly wait for her husband to get out of sight before she began preparing the food. She was very curious to get a glimpse of Tonga before he was released. She hurriedly tore away the leaves covering the fermented breadfruit pit, kneaded the breadfruit cakes quickly, barely allowing them time to cook, and pounded the food in the wooden trough with hurried blows of the stone pounder. Tonga, within the house, heard the hurried preparations outside, so different from the slow, deliberate method of his father and (as my informant said), 'He was *koa*'. In Maori and most other dialects that I know, *koa* means glad, happy. I naturally inferred that Tonga was happy on hearing the rapid preparations because he was hungry.

Irutea brought in the prepared food, and Tonga was *koa*. When Tonga had finished eating, Irutea closely appraised his handsome figure and said, 'Young man, if you and I were to recline together on a couch of fragrant leaves, what would be the harm?'

On hearing her words, Tonga became very *koa* and Irutea, observing his outward manifestations of *koa*, said, 'When your father returns and asks why you are *koa*, tell him that you yearn for your people in the Underworld.'

When his father returned, Tonga gave him the dictated answer. The father said, 'If your yearning is so great that it makes you *koa*, I will conduct you to the entrance of the Underworld tomorrow morning.'

Next morning, the two set out. They crossed three ridges and, when they rested at the top of each, the old man asked, 'My son, why were you *koa*?' The boy replied, 'I yearn for my people in the Underworld.'

At the top of the fourth and last ridge, the father said, 'My son, we are about to part. Tell me truthfully why you were so *koa* on my return yesterday.'

Tonga, at last, told the truth. He said, 'Yesterday I heard Irutea preparing the food in a hasty manner so unlike your way of doing things. She came into the house which no one but you had entered. She placed the food in a spot different to where you place it. The food was not properly cooked and tasted differently from yours. She subjected me to a trying scrutiny and then proposed that we should lie down together. For all these things I was *koa*.'

The father looked up with relief and said, 'My son, had you told me this on the first ridge, we would have returned home. But now it is too late. We are near the boundary to the Underworld and it is fated that you should go on. Your adoptive mother is no blood kin to you. All she wanted to do was to instruct you in one of the greatest lessons in life. The time will come soon when you will bitterly regret the lack of that knowledge which was offered to you.'

And so it came to pass, but that is another story.

While the story was proceeding, I began to realize that my meaning of *koa* did not fit the tale. I asked at the end, 'What is the meaning of *koa?*'

My informant replied, 'Uneasiness, fear, alarm, grief'.

'Oh,' I said, 'in New Zealand and other places, *koa* means joy and gladness.'

'Maybe,' he replied, 'but in Mangareva it means just the opposite. The word for joy in Mangareva is *koakoa*, which is quite different.'

'Quite', I acquiesced.

I had hoped that in volcanic islands so far east as Mangareva, the people had been conserving enough to preserve their native culture. Alas! the change was even greater than in the Tuamotu. The old type of house had been completely displaced by structures of sawn timber and corrugated iron;

even the oldest inhabitant had not seen the original native pattern. The rafts that were so plentiful on Beechey's visit in 1824 had been discarded for small outrigger canoes of the Tahitian model. Nets and fish traps that were abundant in the old culture had long since disappeared, and the only hand nets seen were in the houses of settlers from the Tuamotu. Our hopes were shattered, for we had come to a barren land.

The change in culture was inaugurated by the French-Catholic missionaries, Père Laval and Père Caret, who came to Mangareva in 1834. At first they met with opposition, but after King Te Ma-puteoa and his chiefs became converted, the whole population followed suit. Père Laval acquired an extraordinary influence over the people. The open temples were dismantled and the wooden images of their gods were burnt, except a few that were sent back to Europe. On the site of the great community house in Rikitea, a huge cathedral was constructed in stone, and the cut coral blocks that had formed the bench along the front of the community house were included. The people became expert stone masons, and the chiefs had stone houses built for themselves. Stone is a fitting material for temples and churches but not for dwelling houses in Polynesia. The cathedral still functions, but today the stone palace of Te Ma-puteoa and the stone houses of the chiefs in the various villages are roofless and deserted.

Laval has been blamed, perhaps unjustly, for accelerating the mortality that followed in the wake of civilization. All students of Polynesia, however, must be grateful for the record he left us of Mangarevan traditions and early history. After teaching the natives to write, he induced them to record in their own language their traditional history, mythology, rituals, and customs. The story was told by converted native priests and chiefs who had taken part in what they described. Laval translated the native text into French, adding his own personal observations. This valuable manuscript has lain for years in the archives of the Order of the Sacred Heart (Picpus) at their headquarters at Braine-le-Comte, Belgium. Through co-operation between the Order and Bishop Museum, Laval's manuscript on Mangareva has been published, making known a wealth of material that would otherwise have been lost to the world.

When at Yale, I learned that in the United States the Indians had to be paid for imparting information to field workers. In New Zealand, I was taught by old people of tribes other than my own, because they were proud of their record and they freely imparted information to those who evinced interest. When I went to islands where I was not well known, I called a meeting of the people and publicly explained the object of my visit. They responded willingly; if I had offered to pay my informants, they would have been insulted. To receive money for giving traditional history was equivalent to selling one's ancestors like ordinary merchandise. In Mangareva, people talked freely enough within their limited knowledge, but when I asked for details of ancient history, people said, 'I don't know. Ask Karara. That woman knows.'

I accordingly interviewed Karara, an intelligent woman about sixty years old, but when I went to seek her again, she was away attending to other duties. She had no obligation to remain at home. Karara was a *pou-kapa*, a leader of song, and she had a rich repertoire. I also found out that in ancient times, the leaders were paid by the chiefs who commanded their services.

I called on Karara and said, 'I want you to tell me

the songs you know. How much a day do you want?'

She replied, 'When she was here, Mrs. Routledge gave me five dollars a day.'

I was aghast until I found that a dollar in Mangareva meant five francs and, as the exchange was fifteen francs to the American dollar, we came to a financial arrangement in accordance with the world depression then prevailing. Karara and I had a session every day except Sundays. She was always sitting on the veranda of her house waiting for me, and took pleasure in displaying her learning. I copied down over one hundred and thirty songs that she recited from memory. She had another old lady with her, who acted as prompter at times when a line escaped her memory. Most of the songs were included in legends and folktales, and the prose text was given in detail.

On the morning the boat left, I went to settle up. Somewhat crudely, I asked, 'What do I owe you?'

She glanced at me sadly and, lowering her head, she whispered, 'Anything you like to give me'. She was genuinely sorry that her school of instruction had ended, and so was her pupil.

Mangarevan mythology is weak as regards the creation. At the head of the royal genealogy are the gods Atu-motua (Father-lord), Atu-moana (Ocean-lord), Atea (Space), and Tangaroa. The first two are local, but in Atea we have the widely spread concept of Space which occurs in the mythologies already quoted. Atea married Atanua and, as this mating occurs elsewhere only in the Marquesas, we have a significant affinity between the Marquesas and Mangareva. Tangaroa, important because of his wide distribution in Polynesia, is the father of eight sons, among them being Tu, Rongo, and Te Pari, the youngest, who was the father of

Tiki. Tane occurs as a fisherman, whose daughter became the second wife of Tangaroa. Tangaroa is said to have been the creator of all things, but this statement is probably a late borrowing from Tahiti, for there is nothing in the native text to support it. The functioning god who was worshipped in the temples was Tu, responsible for the fertility of the bread-fruit trees. Rongo sent rain for the crops and, appropriately enough, his symbol was the rainbow. A host of deified ancestors were worshipped by various groups of people.

Nothing remains of the principal temples on Mangareva beyond an odd stone or two. On the atoll of Temoe (Crescent Island), thirty miles to the east, there are temples that have been but little disturbed by treasure seekers. These were built by fugitives from Mangareva and thus reveal the Manga-revan pattern. Those that Emory saw consist of an open court with a raised stone platform, stepped in front, and with a chamber at each end. The people of Temoe were taken back to Mangareva after the conversion to Christianity. When the Mangarevans revisited Temoe in after years to plant coco-nuts, the zeal for temple destruction had subsided and so the stone temples of Temoe have survived to the present day.

The Tiki myth is present in orthodox form, for Tiki moulded a woman out of the earth and named her Hina-one (Earth-maid). He married her and later committed incest with his own daughter. He deceived her by building another house for himself at a distance and visiting her at night under the pretence that he was someone else. This story resembles the Marquesan version.

Maui appears in Mangareva as the youngest of a family of eight with the name, Maui-matavaru (Maui-the-eighth). Probably the variant names of the Maui brethren were treated as distinct individuals, a fresh one was added, and the tale was confused with that in which Maui had eight heads. Maui-the-eighth snared the sun and fished up an island, using his ear for bait. The fire episode has been shifted to a local folktale.

The Tahaki cycle is present with variations. Tahaki was famous for his ruddy skin. At a diving competition off the inner reef, his enemies made Tahaki dive last. As each person dived down, he was converted temporarily into a fish and waited below. When at last Tahaki dived, all the waiting fish swarmed in on him and bit off his wonderful skin. Tahaki emerged nude. He was fortunate, however, in having a fairy grandmother who attended the gathering. As fast as a fish removed a piece of skin, just so fast did the old lady remove it from the fish's mouth and place it in her magic basket. Then she returned to the Underworld with Tahaki's complete skin in her possession. Later, the naked Tahaki and his cousin Karihi went to the Underworld, where his grandmother reclothed him, fitting each piece of skin into its proper position. The stick insects in a neighbouring coconut tree had stolen some of the skin, which they used to decorate their armpits. They refused to return the part they had, and Tahaki's grandmother comforted him by saying, 'It does not matter. They have the piece from under your soles, and the loss will not show.' Thus, the stick insects of Mangareva still have red under their armpits.

Rata, the great canoe builder, was also born in Mangareva, and his adventures, though detailed, are local, taking place around the coast of Mangareva. His father and mother were captured in his youth by Matuku-takotako of Rikitea, who made his mother a menial in his cooking house and made his father an attendant at the beach latrines. Rata, in an approved local setting, slew Matuku-takotako and freed his parents.

The story of Apakura, which is found in Samoa and New Zealand, undergoes a marked local variation. Apakura lived in Mangareva and her son Tinaku-te-maku, a handsome youth, sailed to Rangitea to pay court to a woman of rank. He was successful with the lady but was killed by the unsuccessful suitors. Two frigate hawks bore the tidings back to Mangareva, where they remained stationary in the air above Apakura's home. Apakura called up to the birds, asking if they had seen her son alive. The birds gave no response. She then asked if they had seen her son dead. The birds dropped their legs, hung their heads, and drooped their wings in affirmation. Among the many chants in the story is the lament of Apakura for her dead son, the last verse of which refers to the myth that the moon dies every month but, falling into the Living-waters-of-Tane, comes to life again.

> Thou art a moon that ne'er shall rise again
> O son of mine!
> The chill dawn breaks without thee
> O son, O son of mine, O son!

The words are simple, but perhaps only the Polynesians and the Irish can feel the depth of poignant grief expressed in simple words.

The native history states that the first people to settle in Mangareva were simple fisherfolk. Without doubt, these early settlers came in small groups from the Tuamotuan atolls, without any great chiefs and without cultivable food plants. It was not until about the thirteenth century that notable chiefs with their crews arrived from the islands to the west, referred to in general terms as Havaiki and Hiva. Though Hiva is used as a general term, I believe that it refers particularly to the Marquesas, where some of the islands are forms of Hiva, such as Hiva-oa and Nuku-hiva. Many of the songs refer to Ruapou, the Mangarevan form of the Marquesan island of 'Uapou.

One of the most noted visitors was Tupa, who built temples hitherto unknown for the worship of his god Tu, and introduced the breadfruit, coconut, and other food plants. The Mangarevan names for breadfruit and coconut are *mei* and *ere'i*, which are the same as the Marquesan names *mei* and *e'ehi*; other Polynesian islands use *kuru* (*'uru*) and *niu*. Tupa returned to his own land, and his name occurs as one of the gods in the Marquesas. We may assume, therefore, that Tupa brought the breadfruit, coconut, and other plants from the Marquesas to Mangareva and then returned to his own country, where he was deified after his death.

Among those who followed Tupa were the noted ancestors Keke, Taratahi, and Anua-motua, who came in voyaging canoes from Havaiki and Hiva. Taratahi left for an island named Mata-ki-te-rangi. His son, Anua-motua, remained in Mangareva with his large family and became king of the whole group. Anua divided the islands and districts among members of his family and, under the advice of his priestly son, Te Agiangi, set out in a double canoe to Mata-ki-te-rangi. The present inhabitants, through late contact with people from Easter Island, have come to regard Mata-ki-te-rangi as Easter Island, but it is more likely that the island was Pitcairn.

With increase of population, the people grouped into tribes who took the name of an ancestor with the prefix Ati, as in central Polynesia, Marquesas, Tuamotu, and New Zealand. In the course of time and as the result of inter-tribal fighting, various smaller districts and outer islands became combined into the two large districts of Rikitea under Ape-iti and

Taku under Tupou-eriki. In a great war, Rikitea conquered Taku, and Ape-iti became ruler over the whole group. Ape-iti was a direct descendant of the senior line from Anua-motua, and hence the line became entrenched as the royal line of Mangareva. Tupou-eriki and the survivors of his party left Mangareva to seek another home.

In the time of Te Mangi-tu-tavake, a descendant of Ape-iti, the people rose against the king, because he demanded tributes of fermented breadfruit and kept them for his own use. Te Mangi, realizing that public opinion was strong against him, went into exile and perished at sea. Mangareva was then ruled by a plebeian king named Teiti-a-tuou, but the loyalty to hereditary aristocracy was too strongly ingrained in the Polynesian mind for the plebeian rule to last long. The adherents of the royal family rose in favour of the two sons of Te Mangi-tu-tavake, and the plebeian king was slain.

The royal line was restored, and the two sons ruled jointly as Akariki-tea (White King) and Akariki-pangu (Black King). Though dissension occurred between the descendants of the two brothers, the fighting took place within one family, and finally the senior line from the White King assumed complete dominance. The last of the line was Te Ma-puteoa, who ruled when the French priests landed in 1834.

After a tempestuous rule, the White King and the Black King were laid at rest in the Cave of Tetea at the base of a high cliff facing the rising sun on the small island of Angakau-i-tai. According to ancient custom, large quantities of bark cloth were heaped beside the corpses.

Emory and I decided to visit Angakau-i-tai and were guided to the tomb of the kings by Steve, a local white settler. We found that the cave was a mere recess at the base of a majestic cliff which, in my own mind, I personified. The base was covered with fallen rock, which we cleared away in order to obtain specimens of bark cloth for the Bishop Museum. We had previously obtained the consent of the local people.

Steve said, 'When Eskridge and I were here, the stones kept falling down from the cliff above. The place is uncanny and full of spooks. Don't let us stay too long.'

I gazed upwards. It was a beautiful day and not a breath of air disturbed the face of the cliff. He gazed benevolently down at me, as if in friendly recognition.

I said, 'The spirits of the dead knew that you were aliens. Today, it is different. They know that I belong to them and that information obtained here will be used to their credit. Mark my words. During the whole time we are here, not one stone will fall from the cliff.'

We found an abundance of white tapa cloth, of which we took samples, and a skull and some bones. After measuring the skull with calipers, we wrapped it up in bark cloth and respectfully covered it over with rocks. I am a poor museum man, for I cannot bring myself to carry away Polynesian skulls from their homeland. I have a feeling—a superstition, if you will—that if I did, I would destroy the sympathetic relationship that exists between their past and me.

After we left and were clear of the cliff, I said to Steve, 'Well, what did I tell you? Did a stone fall?'

Steve looked at me with a glimmer of respect and said, 'You were right'.

I waved a grateful hand in farewell to the cliff, and I fancied that he smiled back at me. He understood.

The White King and the Black King had been placed in the cave after being sun-dried on wooden biers. This was a form of land burial used on volcanic islands, as in the Marquesas and Society Islands. Mangareva, however, also retained the deep-sea mariners' method of sea burial. Each tribe had its sea burial place where the dead, wrapped in bark cloth and with a heavy stone lashed to the feet, were lowered down from the funeral raft. The women, gathered on the nearest point of the middle mountain ridge, rent the air with wailings as the body plunged down to its final resting place.

Such a burial is recorded in an incident from the folktale of Tonga. Tonga, after many adventures in the Underworld, returned to the upper world, where he became a deep-sea fisherman. He had a cherished daughter whom he named the Princess-who-plaited-beautiful-things. She accompanied him on one of his expeditions and became seriously ill. Tonga turned his canoe toward land, but a violent storm impeded him. His daughter died and was buried at sea. In his grief, Tonga composed a lament with the recurring refrain, 'I lowered thee down'. The last verse is as follows:

> A deep-sea fisherman, I,
> Storm-bound in the open sea.
> And the way was too long
> For my gods to hear,
> So thy body, my dear one,
> I lowered thee down.

In the social system of Mangareva, the hereditary aristocracy (*togo'iti*) owned the cultivable lands, and the commoners (*'urumanu*) worked them. In the numerous wars, the defeated lost their lands, which were divided among the victorious leaders. Valiant warriors not of chiefly stock sometimes received a grant of land for their services and came to form a wealthy middle class termed *pakaora*. The staple foods were preserved breadfruit and fish. Besides the breadfruit obtained from the royal estates, the nobles and wealthy middle class contributed breadfruit to the royal pits which served as granaries for the public feasts held in connection with religious ritual, funerals, and social events. Some of these festivals were very elaborate and lasted from three to five days. The priests (*taura*) conducted the religious ceremonies and were assisted by *rongorongo* chanters who were of noble birth and versed in ancient history. The *rongorongo* chants were usually accompanied by the beating of drums of hollowed tree trunks covered at the upper end with a membrane of shark skin. In addition, there were trained groups of singers under a leader (*pou-kapa*) who contributed songs termed *kapa* and other varieties with specific names according to the theme of the composition. Skilled carpenters (*taura rakau*) also took a prominent share in the festivals for which houses, biers, or tables had to be provided. The priests, chanters, singers, and craftsmen received distributions of preserved breadfruit wrapped in leaves. In the more important festivals, the entire populace received shares of food from the royal 'granary', and even children and the unborn babies of pregnant women received their shares. A wise king kept his people contented by frequent festivals with liberal distributions of food. The king, nobles, and middle class received honour from the commoners for their liberality.

Many of the *kapa* songs have been transmitted to recent times because the people continued to take pleasure in singing them. One of these, reminiscent of Shakespeare's 'Seven ages of man', is a poem composed by an old man who reviewed the stages of life through which he and his wife had passed. The last verse runs:

> We two indeed together, O beloved,
> When our dim eyes gaze at the misty skies,
> And vision fails to see their splendour,
> Ah, whither doth God draw us?

The Mangarevans tattooed from head to ankles. Members of the royal family were tattooed on their feet, and the more distinguished warriors had a broad band tattooed from ear to ear across the bridge of the nose. The extensive body tattooing and the face band bear affinity with the Marquesas whence much of the Mangarevan culture and food plants were evidently brought by the voyagers who came from Hiva.

Of the three domesticated animals, pig, dog, and fowl— Mangareva had the pig only, but it became extinct in the time of the plebeian king. If we assume that the animals, like the food plants and the paper mulberry, came by way of the Marquesas, the absence of the dog is accounted for because the dog also failed to reach the Marquesas. The absence of the fowl is peculiar, for it reached distant Easter Island. A sea-bird, named the *karako*, performs the functions of the rooster in Mangareva, for it calls in the morning to announce the dawn.

The history of Mangareva illustrates, perhaps better than that of any other island, the incentives that led to long voyages of exploration and the dauntless spirit in which they were undertaken. The primary motive for migration was defeat in war. After battle, the vanquished were hunted like game and consumed by the victorious warrior. A chance for life on the open sea was preferable to almost certain death on shore. Although conquered people were sometimes spared through the influence of powerful relatives on the victorious side, they remained in disgrace and servitude. No family with any pride could submit to such disgrace. In the course of time, it became established that honour was saved by migrating. There are two terms in the Mangarevan language that distinguish different forms of migrations. The term *tei* (to expel) indicates that the conquered had to leave immediately on a raft or any vessel they could obtain, because an enemy would not allow time for preparation. The exiled king, Te Mangi-tu-tavake, was forced to leave on an improvised raft because an implacable enemy was hot on his trail. The plebeian king, Teiti-a-tuou, evidently regretted this action of his party, for he allowed a member of the royal family, named Te ma-haka-hema, to make full preparations before leaving. This was termed *tuku* (to allow to go) and corresponded to the old European custom of allowing a garrison to leave with the honours of war. Te Ma-hakahema fitted up his double voy-aging canoe on the island of Akamaru, provisioned it, and gathered his family and adherents together for the voyage.

The plebeian king was in love with the wife of one of the departing chiefs. He asked her to desert her husband and become his wife. She replied disdainfully, 'I would sooner die in the open sea with my husband of chiefly blood than live in safety with a commoner.' It says much for Teiti-a-tuou that he allowed her to depart in peace. There was honour among commoners also.

The day of leaving was announced and the victors, includ-ing the plebeian king, assembled at Akamaru to see the departure. All the crew and passengers were clothed in their best bark cloth, bedecked with precious ornaments, and wreathed in flowers and fragrant leaves. Long cloth stream-ers, termed *marokura*, floated from the mast of the canoe. The drums on the ship beat time for the chants, songs, and dances of the departing exiles, and so, with gay faces and stout hearts, the ship pushed off to 'sail down the tide with the wind astern'.

The vessel eventually made the atoll of Hao, where Te Ma-hakahema settled in peace and honour. Years after

European contact, the descendants from Hao revisited the homeland of Mangareva, and their story was recognized.

When Captain Beechey visited Mangareva in 1824, he saw rafts only, and the lack of canoes has led to various theories about the degradation of Mangarevan culture. Many European writers have assumed that the Mangarevans made their long sea voyages on rafts, although the native history and Laval's manuscript show clearly that the Mangarevans made voyages outside the group on double canoes, like other Polynesians. Within the group itself, however, they used rafts both for transport and for fishing. They were quite convenient and were easier to make. The double canoes were owned only by the chiefs who could command the timber from their estates and could employ skilled craftsmen. In the early wars between the local islands, the warriors were transported on double canoes. The pregnant daughters of chiefs also went on double canoes to the different islands to undergo the ceremony of having a lock of hair cut on each of the temples of the god Tu. The last double canoes were destroyed early in the nineteenth century in war between Mataira and Te Ma-teoa, the grandfather of the last king, Te Ma-puteoa. Te Ma-teoa acquired supreme power and, as the construction of a double canoe was looked upon as a preliminary to war, he forbade the building of any new canoe. Hence the use of canoes for war or voyages ceased, and inter-island transport and fishing were conducted on rafts. The building of rafts is probably responsible for the large number of stone axes found on Mangareva. The cutting edges of the axes are evenly bevelled from both sides in contrast to the adzes bevelled from one side only, and they form a unique local feature. Years afterwards, the influx of people from Tahiti and the Tuamotu led to the building of fishing canoes on the Tahitian model and to the abandonment of rafts.

When Tupou-eriki was decisively defeated by Ape-iti, he asked to be allowed to leave with his remnant of people. For some reason or other he left with seven rafts; but one of his chiefs, who had a double canoe, remained behind with his mother and followers. He delayed so long that his mother became alarmed that he might forfeit his honour by not embarking for the open sea. She composed a lament for her exiled king, and her dilatory son heard her sadly wailing:

> O Tupou, my king!
> The breakers roar on the outer reef,
> And fierce winds wail in company.
> They weep and wail for thee,
> O Tupou, my king.
>
> You sought the open sea
> With your seven rafts,
> O Tupou, my king,
> But the double canoe of my son delays.
> What will he do,
> O Tupou, my king?

The son, shamed at his mother's words, speedily fitted up his ship, hoisted his sail, and, with pennant bravely flying, he sailed to death in the wake of Tupou, his king.

16. THE MYSTERY OF PITCAIRN

These people have become extinct like the Moa.

MAORI PROVERB

PITCAIRN ISLAND, about three hundred and fifty miles southeast of Mangareva, is a volcanic island three miles long by two wide. Its highest peak rises to just over 1000 feet. No coral reef protects its shores against the great breakers that crash against its cliff-girt coast. In the rugged shore line, there is but one landing place, and it requires skill and courage to safely negotiate the rough seas and jagged rocks which guard its entrance.

The island was rediscovered in 1767 by Phillip Carteret, commander of the British sloop *Swallow*. He named it Pitcairn after a marine officer's son who first sighted land. Owing to the rough surf, Carteret made no attempt to land, but he noted a stream pouring over a cliff and rich vegetation in the uplands. He surmised that the island was inhabited.

After the mutiny on the *Bounty*, Fletcher Christian and his followers with their Tahitian wives and servants attempted to settle on Tupuai in the Austral Islands. Conflict broke out between the newcomers and the inhabitants, and the mutineers were forced to take ship to seek some other refuge. Fate and a knowledge of Carteret's discovery directed them to Pitcairn Island. Here, in 1789, they sank the ill-fated

Bounty off the sole landing place in the bay now termed
Bounty Bay.

With the memory of the hostile treatment in Tupuai fresh
in their minds, the mutineers must have exercised great cau-
tion as they climbed the steep ascent from the landing place
to the more level slopes above. They had seen no canoes or
smoke, but in the rich vegetation they saw breadfruit trees
which warned them of human occupation. On a peak near
the edge of the cliff facing Bounty Bay they saw an arresting
sight. Rocks had been carefully placed together to form a
quadrangular platform, and on each corner a stone image
with its back to the sea gazed disapprovingly at the intruders
on their sacred domain. But the temple and the gods were
mute, for the people who had created them had mysteriously
disappeared.

The mutineers or their offspring dismantled the temple
above Bounty Bay and some others that had been erected on
other parts of the island. The helpless stone gods were rolled
over the near-by cliff and carried their secrets to the bottom
of Bounty Bay. In destroying the Bounty Bay temple, a
human skeleton was found interred in the structure with its
head pillowed on a large pearl shell. The pearl shell gave
evidence of contact with Mangareva or some atoll in the
Tuamotu archipelago.

In digging the foundations of houses and preparing cultivations, the mutineers found human bones interred below
the surface. Stone adzes and gouges have been discovered
from time to time and have found their way into various
museums. Some of the implements are well shaped and well
ground, and others are peculiar for their large size. The
implements are better made than those of neighbouring
Mangareva. Petroglyphs have been found on the cliffs in

the form of men, animals, birds, and geometrical figures including circles and stars. Shallow pits lined with stones and ashes in position bear witness to the use of the Polynesian earth oven.

The Franco-Belgian Expedition to Easter Island visited Pitcairn in 1935, and the scattered evidences of ancient occupation have been summarized by Henri Lavachery, a member of the expedition. Lavachery found that one of the images from the Bounty Bay temple had been picked up at the base of the cliff and used as a pile to support the veranda of a house. The image was extricated for examination. It was made of yellowish coloured local volcanic tuff and consisted of a trunk without legs. The head had broken off, but there were two five-fingered hands clasped on the abdomen in a characteristic Polynesian attitude. The archaeological evidence from temples, images, and stone tools shows that the vanished people of Pitcairn Island were Polynesian.

The presence of the breadfruit trees proves that the early settlers came from some volcanic island. The breadfruit is absent in Rapa, so they must have come from the Austral Islands farther to the west or from Mangareva.

Pitcairn was known to the Mangarevans as Heragi and in modern times as Petania (Britain). Heragi is mentioned in a localized form of the widespread legend of Tinirau and Hina. Hina-poutunui was told by her mother to air a bark cloth garment in the sun and to watch it lest it rain. Hina was careless, and the garment was spoiled by a shower of rain. Hina was promptly expelled from home and went down to the seashore to seek transport to some other island. No canoe being available, she asked various lagoon fishes whether they had crossed the horizon, but each replied in the negative. She asked a deep-sea turtle, and he replied,

'Yes! Get on my back and I will take you wherever you want to go.' Hina mounted the turtle and was carried to Heragi. When Hina landed, she saw both banana and plantain trees in fruit. She bent down a bunch of bananas, and the fruit of bananas have drooped down ever since, whereas the untouched fruit of the plantain remains erect. Tinirau, a chief of the island, married Hina. They had a daughter named Toa-tutea, who went to Tahiti and after various adventures returned to Mangareva. On her death she was buried on Kamaka on the side of the island facing her birth-place in Heragi.

The Mangarevan native history narrates that an arrogant chief named Taratahi was forced to leave Mangareva and sailed to an island named Mata-ki-te-rangi. His priestly grandson Te Agiagi had a vision in Mangareva that his grandfather had been killed by his people named Meriri and that the breadfruit trees had been destroyed. Te Agiagi, his father Anua-motua, and some brothers sailed to Mata-ki-te-rangi in a double canoe to verify the vision. After sighting some atolls, they arrived at Mata-ki-te-rangi which had a difficult landing place and which the native manuscript sur-mises may have been Petania (Pitcairn). Te Agiagi went ashore and found the corpse of his grandfather in a dry water-course. 'In those days the dead could converse with the living.' Te Agiagi asked the corpse for breadfruit and the body replied, 'You will find a small plant beside my ear.' A long account describes the planting of the breadfruit and the ritual used. Anua-motua gave the power over the land to his sons Puniga and Maro-kura but promised to create a new land of Momona-mua for Te Agiagi. Anua-motua died and was set adrift on the funeral raft. In a vision, Te Agiagi saw his father creating the land of Momona-mua by heaping up sand on the ocean waste with a digging stick. Later Te Agiagi sailed away with attendants to settle on his mythical land. His two brothers with their people remained in occupation of Mata-ki-te-rangi.

Toward the end of the fourteenth century, a voyager named Ragahenua arrived in Mangareva accompanied by warriors. After a short stay, he built a new canoe and sailed to Mata-ki-te-rangi. Conflict occurred in which both Puniga and Maro-kura were killed and their people defeated in a great slaughter. Four fugitives escaped and reached Mangareva. One was Ipo, a son of Anua-motua, who came in a canoe by himself and landed at Akamaru. He made his way to the Taku district of Mangareva which was ruled by his brother Hoi and told the tale of disaster in Mataki-te-rangi. After this incident there is no further reference to Mata-ki-te-rangi in Mangarevan history.

The Mangarevans, since post-European contact with Easter Islanders, have come to regard Mata-ki-te-rangi as Easter Island, but the very definite details about planting breadfruit is evidence against Easter Island, where the breadfruit did not grow. The escape of fugitives from battle, without opportunity for making provisions for a long voyage, indicates that Mata-ki-te-rangi was much nearer Mangareva than is Easter Island. The only volcanic island that fits the narrative is Pitcairn.

Ragahenua occupied Pitcairn before rafts had become popular on Mangareva; hence the characteristic Mangareva axes used in raft making have not been found on Pitcairn. Perhaps Ragahenua, who was merely a visitor on Mangareva, carried his own tools with him. He may have come to Mangareva from the Austral Islands, or there may have been a later influx from the Australs which would account for the similarity of some of the Pitcairn implements with Austral types and also for the presence of the stone images above Bounty Bay. The missing face of the salvaged image might have told us something, but the breakers of Pitcairn have concealed the evidence and helped to seal the mystery of their island.

The mystery of Pitcairn Island remains unsolved. We can readily understand why certain atolls were occupied for a time and then deserted for more attractive islands. Pitcairn, however, had all that an atoll lacked. It had basaltic rock, abundant vegetation, enough fresh water, and fertile soil which grew breadfruit, bananas, and other food plants. The forms and numbers of the stone implements discovered show that Pitcairn was inhabited by intelligent Polynesians for a long period of time. Yet when the mutineers of the *Bounty* landed in 1789, the previous settlers had become extinct like the *moa* bird of New Zealand. Did they die out from some mysterious disease, desert the island from some unknown cause, or were they exterminated by a marauding force that returned home? What happened to them, I do not know.

17. THE APEX OF THE TRIANGLE

Go to the island of my dreams and seek for a
beautiful beach upon which the king may dwell.

LEGEND OF HOTU-MATUA

KING HOTU-MATUA dwelt in the land of Marae-renga and he dreamed of an island with a beautiful beach that lay over the eastern horizon. He sent men on a canoe named *Oraora-miro* to locate a beach on his dream island. He followed in their wake in his great double canoe, ninety feet long and six feet deep. One hull bore the name *Oteka* and the other *Oua*. The king was accompanied by the master craftsman, Tu-koihu, in another canoe. After many days' sail, the two vessels sighted an island that Horu-matua knew to be the island of his dreams. As they approached the western end of the island, the two vessels separated, the king to survey the south coast and Tu-koihu the north. The king's ship sailed rapidly and paddles were plied to increase the speed. The king's ship rounded the eastern end of the island without having seen the beach for which he searched. On the north coast he saw the canoe of Tu-koihu paddling in to a beach that he recognized as the beach of his dream. It would never do for Tu-koihu to land before him, so he invoked his gods with the magic words, 'Ka hakamau te konekone' (Stay the paddling). The paddles of Tu-koihu's crew stayed motion-less in the water, and the sea seethed as the king's paddlers raced for the shore. The double prow of the king's ship ran up on the sands of Anakena, and Hotu-matua stepped ashore onto a beautiful beach fit for a king to dwell upon. And thus Hotu-matua added his name to the roll of famous navigators by discovering the eastern outpost that forms the apex of the Polynesian triangle.

Easter Island is 1500 miles from Mangareva, 1100 miles from Pitcairn, and 2030 miles from South America. Its greatest length is thirteen miles and its area is sixty-seven square miles. It is a volcanic island with a dry, arid soil, no streams, and but slight rainfall. Of a number of extinct craters, Rano Aroi rises to a height of 1600 feet.

The island was first sighted by the Dutch navigator, Roggeveen, on Easter Sunday, 1722. At that time it was occupied by a people of Polynesian stock speaking a Poly-nesian language. Later European voyagers, including Gonza-lez and Cook, stopped at Easter Island and brought with them the diseases that decimated the populations of all Pacific Islands. In 1862, Peruvians carried off large numbers of the Easter Islanders into slavery. Of a remnant of 100 sent back after representation by the British and French Govern-ments, 85 died of smallpox at sea and the 15 who were landed spread the disease throughout the island so that thousands died. A conservative estimate of the population before Eur-pean contact is from 3000 to 4000. Fifteen years after the first depredations of the slavers, the population had dwindled to 111, of whom but 26 were females. The census taken in 1934 gave the total population at 456.

A French adventurer named Dutroux Bornier established himself on the island in 1870 and became so obnoxious that the Catholic missionary and his flock fled to Mangareva. More would have left but the schooner was crowded to the limit. Those who were forced to remain behind finally disposed of the foreign tyrant in the only suitable manner. The exiled inhabitants returned after the death of Bornier, but one wonders how many of the one hundred and eleven survivors were fitted to pass on the torch of knowledge to their descendants. No native population has been subjected to such a succession of atrocities and disintegrating influences as the people of Easter Island. It is no wonder that their native culture was so wrecked that the records obtained from the survivors are the poorest in all inhabited Polynesia. Unfortunately the early missionaries to Easter Island hadn't sufficient vision or interest to teach the native scholars to write down their history, legends, and customs.

The early European voyagers collected curios and wrote down what they saw and often what they did not see. Behrens, who accompanied Roggeveen, stated that the natives were so tall that the seamen could walk upright between their legs. He also saw pottery in a land where there was no clay. Paymaster Thomson of the U.S.S. *Mohican*, wrote of the material things he saw in 1886, but even then it was too late to gather authentic information about ancient manners and customs. Mrs. Routledge made a survey in 1914 and her information about images, quarries, and platforms is valuable. Macmillan Brown visited later and his theory of a sunken archipelago has interested many. The Franco-Belgian Expedition visited the island in 1934 and later Dr. Alfred Métraux, a member of the expedition, worked up his field material at Bishop Museum. He and I had many discussions, and much of the information contained in this chapter was obtained from his manuscript which will be published by Bishop Museum.

From the fragments we can reconstruct but little of the native mythology. Atea and Papa, the primary parents, have not been recorded. Tangaroa came to Easter Island in the form of a seal with a human face and voice. The seal was killed but, though baked for the necessary time in an earth oven, the seal refused to cook. Hence the people inferred that Tangaroa must have been a chief of power. Tangaroa also appears in the king's lineage with Rongo as his son. This scanty information is significant as an echo from central Polynesia.

Tane and Tu are absent from the pantheon but Tu-koihu is an early ancestor. He was a skilled artisan, which reminds us of the early functions of the god Tu in the Tahitian tale of creation. Hiro, the famous voyager of central Polynesia, occurs in an invocation for rain. The first line runs:

> E te ua, matavai roa a Hiro e—
> (O rain, long tear drops of Hiro—)

Ruanuku, a well-known god, occurs in a genealogy. Atua-metua is present in a creation chant. This name is intriguing for it resembles Atu-motua, one of the early gods of Manga-reva. Though Atu (lord) and Atua (god) are different words, a change may have taken place in Easter Island. The qualifying words *motua* and *metua* are linguistic forms of the same word meaning father.

Atua-metua mated with Riri-tuna-rei and produced the *niu*. The word *niu* is the widely spread name for coconut but, as there were no coconuts on Easter Island, the name was applied locally to the fruit of the *miro*. The word *tuna* in the compound name of Riri-tuna-rei means eel, and it is evident that this fragment records a memory of the well-known myth of the origin of the coconut from the head of an eel.

The principal god was Makemake. The name does not occur elsewhere as the name of a powerful god, and Métraux thinks that it is a local name substitution for the important Polynesian god Tane. This theory is supported by the myth that Makemake created man on Easter Island in a way similar to that used by Tane and Tiki to form the first woman in other parts of Polynesia. Makemake procreated red flesh from a calabash of water. He mounded up some earth and from it he formed three males and one female. The process of mounding up earth is described in the local dialect as *popo i te one*, in which *one* is the general term for earth and *popo* is the local verb for heaping up, which in other dialects is *ahu*.

The Easter Island creation chant, first recorded by Thomson in 1886 and checked over by Métraux with native informants, follows the pattern of such chants in other parts of Polynesia. Various couples are mated to produce plants, insects, birds, fish, and other objects. As in the Marquesas, Mangareva, and the Tuamotu, Tiki, here called Tiki-te-hatu (Tiki-the-lord), is mated with different wives to produce numerous offspring. Among Tiki's wives was Rurua who gave birth to Ririkatea, a king and father of Hotu-matua, the first king of Easter Island. By another wife named Hinapopia (Hina-the-heaped-up), Tiki produced a daughter, Hina-kauhara. In Hina-popoia we find a possible memory of the first woman, known elsewhere as Hina-ahu-one (Earth-formed-maid). Thus, from the wreck of local mythology, there remain a few definite indications that the mythology of Easter Island contained fundamental elements that originated in central Polynesia.

Makemake was responsible for the fertility of food plants, fowls, and the paper mulberry from which cloth was produced. When crops were planted, a skull representing Makemake was placed in the ground and an incantation was offered, commencing, 'Ka to ma Haua, ma Makemake' (Plant for Haua, for Makemake). Makemake was worshipped in the form of sea-birds, which may be interpreted as his incarnation. His material symbol, a man with a bird's head, was carved on the rocks at the Orongo village. Wooden images representing him were carried at the feasts. Human sacrifices were made in his honour and the material part was consumed by the priests. These various items conform to a general Polynesian pattern, but the bird-headed man is an expression of art influenced by local developments.

Of the organized forms of religious ritual we know little. Priests presided over birth festivals, drove out disease demons, and regulated funeral ceremonies for which they composed dirges. The priests were termed *ivi-atua* (people of the god), which has an affinity with the Mangarevan term for priestly chants. Human sacrifices were termed *ika* (fish), a widespread Polynesian term which probably had its origin in an early period when religious offerings consisted principally of fish. Sorcerers and priestesses who claimed to be the medium of deceased relatives who had something to communicate functioned much as in the religious systems of other Polynesian islands.

The spirits of the dead were called *akuaku* and were represented by the carved wooden images termed *moai kavakava* with protruding ribs and sunken abdomens. The spirits were stated to have introduced tattooing, turmeric dyes, and a variety of yam, which they must have brought from the land of the dead away to the westward. The Easter Islanders shared in the general Polynesian concept of a spirit land, not as a place of reward or punishment but simply as a land beyond the grave to which the undying souls of all men may return.

The traditional history is almost as poorly transmitted as the mythology. Hotu-matua took up his residence at Ana-kena and shortly after the landing his wife Vaikai-a-hiva gave birth to a male child. Tu-koihu cut the navel cord of the child and conducted the ritual whereby the royal halo (*ata ariki*) was produced around the child's head to indicate its royal birth. He was named Tu-maheke and through him descends the line of Easter Island kings. On the basis of fragments of royal genealogies, Métraux has estimated that Hotu-matua landed on the island in about 1150 A.D.

As in other parts of Polynesia, tribes developed with increase in population, taking the names of ancestors and living in definite districts of the island. The highest ranking chief, who also had priestly functions, belonged to the senior line descended from Hotu-matua. This tribe was named Miru and ranked above the other tribes, enjoying certain special privileges.

Inter-tribal wars were frequent and the tale of the war between Long-ears and Short-ears may indicate that there were two early groups of settlers; one group, which pierced their ears and wore such heavy ornaments that their ears were considerably elongated, coming from the Marquesas where heavy ear ornaments were worn, and the other group which did not pierce their ears coming from Mangareva. The Long-ears lived on the eastern end of the island and were credited with making the stone images which have long ears and the stone temple structures. The Short-ears lived on the western part of the island and had the more fertile lands. The Marquesans carved large stone images and built stone retaining walls, whereas the Mangarevans did not. Conflict arose because the Short-ears refused to carry stones to assist the Long-ears in erecting a temple. In the war which followed, the Long-ears were said to be almost exterminated. This may account for what appears to have been a sudden cessation of work in the image quarry and the commencement of knocking down the images from their platforms.

The fowl, which was the only domestic animal known in Easter Island, may have come from the Marquesas where it was present but not from Mangareva where it was absent. Because it was the only domestic animal, the fowl received more attention and honour than in any other part of Polynesia. Fowls became the mark of wealth, and festivals were characterized by gifts and distributions of fowls. In order to protect them from thieves, fowl houses of piled stones were erected to house them at night. Stones were piled up against the entrance and the sound of stones being moved served as an alarm to the owner. Skulls with incised carvings, imbued with power by Makemake, were placed in the fowl house to promote the egg-laying capacity of the occupants.

It may seem a long call from the domestic fowl to the sooty tern, but both are birds and lay eggs. The sooty tern (*manu tara*) comes to breed in large numbers in July or August off the southwestern point formed by the crater of Rano-kao on three rocky islets, of which the only one accessible to swimmers is Motu-nui. What commenced as an ordinary food quest for eggs became an annual competition to obtain the first egg of the season. The warriors (*matatoa*) of the dominant tribe entered servants for the annual Derby, and members of defeated tribes were not allowed to take part in the competition. The selected servants swam over to Motu-nui and waited in caves for the migration of the birds. The warriors and their families assembled on the lip of Rano-kao that overlooked the course. Owing to the strong wind, they built houses of stone for shelter at the village named Orongo, the Place-of-listening. There they listened for the coming of the birds and waited for the call of the successful servant who found the first egg. While waiting they amused themselves with singing and feasting and carved on the adjacent rock figures with birds' heads and human bodies, the symbol of Makemake, god of fowls and sea-birds. In time, rules and ritual were developed about this annual competition which became the most important social event on the island. The successful servant leaped onto a rocky promontory and shouted across the water to his master, 'Shave your head. The egg is yours.'

A sentry on watch in a cave below Orongo, termed the Bird-listener (Hakaronga-manu), heard the call and relayed the message up to the waiting masters. The successful master was termed the Bird-man (Tangata-manu). On reception of the egg, the people escorted him to Mataveri, where a feast was held in his honour. After that he went into seclusion for a year in a house at Rano-raraku. The details of his functions and privileges are not known, but certain it is that he was held in high honour and provided with food by the people until the next annual Derby took place. The list of Bird-men was memorized and transmitted like a line of kings. The bird cult is not known elsewhere in Polynesia and is clearly a local development arising out of peculiar local conditions. The importance of the fowl as the sole domesticated animal, the annual migration of the sooty tern to a near-by islet to breed, the village of Orongo with its carved rocks overlooking the course, and the development of the bird cult are all in a natural sequence that could have occurred nowhere else but on Easter Island.

Easter Island has little fertile soil and no forests with large trees to provide adequate raw material for houses and canoes.

Consequently the framework of houses was made of slender arched poles, and houses were narrow, low, and long. In order not to waste valuable inches, the poles were not stuck in the ground but rested in holes carved out of stone blocks. These pitted curbstones, like the elaborate bird cult, are unique on Easter Island, evolved locally due to lack of timber.

The canoes were poor and flimsy, but ten to twelve feet long and formed of many small bits of wood sewn together. Even the paddles were made of two pieces: a short, narrow blade with a separate handle lashed to it. The two-piece paddle is unique for Polynesia, but again the form of the canoe and paddle was a local adjustment forced upon the people by the lack of material. Successive European voyagers saw fewer and fewer canoes on Easter Island, not because of degradation in the population, but because of constant decrease in the wood supply. The people swam out to ships sometimes with a supporting float formed of a conical bundle of bulrushes. Wood was as precious as gold in Europe or jade in New Zealand. The minimum quantity was used for necessities, and the surplus constituted wealth in the form of wooden breast ornaments, dance implements, and carved tablets.

Macmillan Brown in his work on 'Peoples and Problems of the Pacific' condemned the arts and crafts of Easter Island as being the most primitive in Polynesia. This is manifestly inaccurate and unfair. Apparently he did not take into consideration the vast importance of environment and its influence on all forms of material culture. The feather headdresses of Easter Island compare favourably with those of the Marquesas and Tahiti and are vastly superior to any similar work in Samoa and Tonga. The bark cloth is remarkable, for the shortcomings of the original material are overcome by quilting with threads by means of a bone needle. The carving of wooden ornaments, stone images, and the development of decorative techniques, such as the representation of eyes by means of a shell ring with a black obsidian pupil, are among the most remarkable in all Polynesia. Brown has condemned the Easter Islanders for not making greater use of bone, turtle shell, and obsidian to inlay their wood carvings, but neither did the other great branches of the Polynesians. The most unfair criticism is levelled at the implements, which are classed as childish. The adze or *toki* is stated to be a blunt round stone rarely ground to an edge or rubbed smooth. It is evident that the critic was referring to the hand implements that were used to shape the stone images in the rough. He totally disregarded the adzes that were used in woodwork, which are better made than those of Mangareva and Samoa. Some of them are well shaped but with a blunt edge and they were probably used as hand adzes to finish off the stone images after they had been taken from the quarry.

The stone statues of Easter Island have intrigued the imaginations of many, and a mystery has grown up around them. Some have believed them to be the work of some extinct race from a vanished continent. Yet the simple truth lies at the feet of the statues. Large stone images were made in the Marquesas and Raivavae and smaller ones in the Society Islands, Hawai'i, and New Zealand. The Easter Islanders carried the memory of stone carving from the Marquesas to their new home, where they developed a local pattern adapted to the soft, easily worked volcanic tuff found in the extinct crater of Rano-raraku.

The images have high faces, long bodies, and arms but no legs. They are really busts. Some were placed on stone platforms near the coast and others were dotted about the landscape. Those on the platforms had expanded bases to enable them to retain an erect position. The others had peg-shaped bases for insertion in the ground.

The process of carving these statues may be deduced by an examination of the unfinished forms still lying in the quarry workshop in the crater of Rano-raraku. The figures were roughly shaped with the face uppermost. Then the sides were undercut and rounded, leaving a narrow ridge along the back to hold the statue in position. Finally this flange was cut and the detached figure was hauled to its site of erection. There the ridge along the back was trimmed off. Near some figures in the quarry lie rough stone tools shaped from hard nodules in the tuff, apparently left by workmen when the image factory went out of business.

Macmillan Brown has proposed that the statues were made in the image of their mysterious creators from a now submerged land—strong, imperious men with shapely chins and scornful, pouting lips. At this statement a physical anthropologist stands aghast; if the Easter Island images resemble their sculptors, then the Marquesan images with round, owlish eyes, noses with expanded wings, mouths stretching the full width of the face, must represent their makers. What a nightmare the image makers of Polynesia would present if they were recalled from the spirit land and made to conform to the anatomy of their creations!

The difficulty of transporting the images has been adduced as an argument in favour of a large population coming from elsewhere with ropes and mechanical appliances to move the images. The present Easter Islanders were considered too weak and lazy to have had ancestors who could do hard work. The Tongans, Hawaiians, Tahitians, and Marquesans moved large masses of stone and set them in place with ropes, wooden levers, skids, and props, and built up inclined planes of earth and rock to accomplish their tasks. Brown's assumption that the images could be moved only by thousands of slaves coming from an imaginary archipelago is based chiefly on one image fifty feet high which was never removed from the quarry. The average height of the images is ten to fifteen feet and their weight between four and five tons. I doubt if the images were heavier than the logs that the Maoris dragged from the forest for their war canoes or for the one-piece ridgepoles of their large meeting houses. United manpower can accomplish much, especially when such public works were made the occasion for a festival, with feasting according to Polynesian custom.

Originally the stone images may have represented gods and deified ancestors but in the course of time they became more truly an expression of art. The images with pegged bases were never intended to be placed on the stone platforms of the temples but were to be erected in the ground as secular objects to ornament the landscape and mark the boundaries of districts and highways. Because the images remaining in the quarry all have pegged bases, it would appear that the orders for the platforms had been filled and that the people had embarked on a scheme of highway decoration when war or contact with white foreigners caused operations to cease for ever.

The stone temples of Easter Island were built near the shore line as in other Polynesian islands, and the theory that they were so placed to exercise a magical influence in preventing the encroachment of the sea is untenable. A stone retaining wall was built near the coast, and the inland side was filled in with rock to form a sloping surface which was defined on the inland side by a low curb, sometimes stepped.

The middle section of the retaining wall was higher than its wings and thus provided a raised platform upon which a number of images facing inland were placed on flat stone pedestals. Beyond the low inland curb a roughly paved area represented the paved court of the maraes of other groups. The entire enclosure was called *ahu*, a term used in central Polynesia to designate the raised platform at the end of the marae court. Recesses or vaults were provided in the mass of stone as tombs for the dead, a usage not confined to Easter Island. Owing to the loss of religious association and ritual, the *ahu* have come to be regarded as cemeteries, which was a secondary function of the older structures.

The wooden tablets with rows of incised characters have been the greatest problem in solving the so-called mystery of Easter Island. Legend states that King Hotu-matua brought sixty-seven tablets with him from the island of Marae-renga. If this is so, the use of such tablets must have been well established in that land. Cultural and mythical evidence seems to point to the Marquesas and possibly to Mangareva as the lands of origin of the Easter Island people, yet neither of these islands, nor indeed any Polynesian island, retains a memory of such tablets. Did they come from some land beyond Polynesia or were they evolved in Easter Island itself?

Students of Polynesia were startled to learn that characters similar to those on the tablets had been found on seals excavated at Mohenjo Daro in the Indus valley in India. A European investigator arranged in parallel columns selected characters from the seals and from Easter Island tablets that were similar or even identical. However, a careful analysis by Métraux showed that certain motifs had been rendered more similar by inaccurate drawing. In any event, the identity of characters would tend to raise suspicion rather than to confirm a common origin. It has been demonstrated time and again that figures do not remain identical during prolonged transmission. Easter Island lies over 13,000 miles from Mohenjo Daro, whose civilization is dated at 2000 B.C. How could these characters survive the dangers of flood and field during a migration of over 13,000 miles of space and through 3000 years in time to arrive unchanged in lonely Easter Island and leave no trace between, not even in Marae-ranga whence Hotu-matua was supposed to have brought the tablets?

We cannot suppose that the tablets themselves were brought from Mohenjo Daro, for the Easter Island tablets have a boustrophedon arrangement, that is, alternate rows are upside down. Such an arrangement has not been discovered in Mohenjo Daro. Also, the Easter Island tablets are made of local or drift wood, the largest one being made from the blade of an ash oar which must have drifted to Easter Island in the early eighteenth century. Hence there is little doubt that the tablets were carved in Easter Island itself long after the time of Hotu-matua, but were attributed to him to give them the increased antiquity that all Polynesians revere.

The tablets of local wood are flat, oblong pieces with rounded edges and are neatly cut in shallow parallel grooves with distinct edges bounding them. Commencing with the lowest groove on one surface, the carver worked from left to right; when he reached the right end, he turned the tablet upside down in order to carve the second row from left to right. Both surfaces of the tablet and even the side edges are completely covered with rows of figures. As it is difficult to understand how any written chants or records could so correspond to the size of the tablet as to exactly fill it in

MANGAREVA ISLAND showing Mount Duff

TEMPLE RUIN ON TEMOE ATOLL built by Mangarevan fugitives

CARVED ROCKS AT ORONGO showing bird man holding an egg

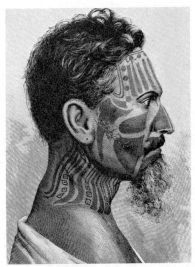

TATTOOED EASTER ISLANDER

Bishop Museum

TATTOOED MAORI, showing curvilinear
designs peculiar to New Zealand
Drawn by General G. Robley in 1865

Alexander Turnbull Library

EASTER ISLAND IMAGE on slopes of Rano Raruku

HAWAIIAN CANOES going out to meet Captain James Cook, 1777

WALLED TEMPLE (heiau) at Waimea, Kauai, Hawaiian Islands

from a lithograph of original painting by John Hayter, 1824

POKI, HAWAIIAN HIGH CHIEF, and wife Liliha in native garments

HAWAIIAN TEMPLE IMAGE
in wood

HOUSE PANEL, NEW ZEALAND,
showing excellence of carver's work

EXCAVATION FOR PLANTING TARO ON AN ATOLL

MAORI CARVER AT WORK ON A DOOR LINTEL

YOUNG MAORI WOMAN of good type

MAORI WOMAN with tattooed chin, wearing native garments

Bishop Museum

THE GREAT TRILITHON, TONGATABU

Bishop Museum

Bishop Museum

INTERIOR OF SAMOAN HOUSE, showing three central pillars and curved
rafters on either side

SAMOAN FEAST with typical houses in the background

HAWAIIAN FEATHER HEADDRESS

SAMOAN ROUND HOUSE WITH CHIEFS SITTING IN COUNCIL

IRRIGATED TARO PLANTATION ON A VOLCANIC ISLAND
Coconut leaves laid over young plants to prevent the growth of weeds

every instance, it is probable that the characters are purely pictorial and are not a form of written language.

The tablets were called *kouhau*, which, in the dialects of Easter Island, Mangareva, and Marquesas, means a rod (*kou*) of hibiscus wood (*hau*). In the Marquesas, bundles of hibiscus rods were placed vertically at the corners of religious platforms as part of the temple regalia. In Mangareva, the term *kouhau* was applied to hibiscus rods that were used to beat time for certain ritual songs and dances. From the use of the term *kouhau* in Easter Island, it would seem that the art motifs were carved originally on a staff of hibiscus and, if done along the length of the staff, it may account for the technique assuming the form of long rows. Owing perhaps to the need of lengths of wood for other purposes, the carving was transferred from staves to shorter pieces of wood in the form of tablets which retained the name *kouhau*.

The tablets were used by scholars termed *rongorongo*, who sang the old chants at various festivals. In Mangareva, the learned men who chanted at festivals and during religious ritual were also termed *rongorongo*. In the Marquesas, the inspirational priests who chanted were termed *o'ono*, the dialectical form of *orongo*. When the Easter Island *rongorongo* chanted, they held a tablet in their hands and when, in later times, a tablet was shown to an Easter Islander, he took it in his hands and commenced chanting. The connection between chant and tablet seemed so obvious that European observers never doubted but that the carved figures on the tablets definitely represented the words of the chants and were thus a form of writing. When Bishop Tepano Jaussen heard an Easter Islander chant to one of the tablets, he wrote down the words that were chanted to the various characters on the tablet. An analysis of the written native text proved to be a brief naming of the individual characters, some obvious and many doubtful. Though delivered as a chant, the whole composition had no connected meaning and was obviously made up on the spot to satisfy a white man's desire for a chanted ritual of the characters on the tablet. Any Polynesian can improvise a chant. I have improvised chants to lengthen out a recital for a European audience that did not understand the language. Neither the bishop's informant nor I had any intention of deceiving, but we were both influenced by the desire to please.

Judged from a Polynesian background, I would suggest that the *rongorongo* chanters originally carved figures representing Makemake and art motifs connected with the bird cult on staves termed *kouhau*, which they held in their hands while they exercised their duties. Later the motifs were inscribed on wooden tablets, and the natural desire not to waste any space led to the tablets being completely covered. Again to make the most of the material, the tablet was adzed or chiselled in contiguous grooves to form ordered rows for the carving. The normal technique of working from left to right and the desire to commence the first figure in a new line close to the last figure in the previous line led to the boustrophedon arrangement of successive rows. The artistic tendency to avoid monotonous repetition of a few figures led to variations of the main motifs derived from the bird cult and the addition of new figures that were regarded purely as art motifs. The tablets became works of art and, as valuable possessions, they were given individual proper names in the same manner as jade ornaments in New Zealand. The Easter Islanders, like other Polynesians, learned their chants and lineages by heart. They held the tablets in their hands as symbols replacing the orator's staff.

The Easter Islanders have been badly treated by popular writers. Erroneous assertions have been piled up one after another to make their arts and crafts appear so poor and futile that the task of making the stone images and of transporting them would appear to be beyond the capacity of the ancestors of the present people. The mystery has been deepened by regarding the art tablets as a form of script and so foreign to Polynesian culture. Because western people are now incapable of making stone images without steel tools and of transporting them without modern machinery, the very culture of the Easter Islanders has been attributed to a mythical people who never existed. Yet the fact remains that the descendants of Hotu-matua used the raw material of their little island to an extent that the western mind seems to find difficulty in realizing. The resurrection of an extinct civilization from a sunken continent to do what the Easter Islanders accomplished unaided is surely the greatest compliment ever paid to an efficient stone-age people.

18. THE NORTHERN ANGLE

Behold Hawai'i, an island, a people
The people of Hawai'i are the offspring of Tahiti.

CHANT OF THE BARD KAMA-HUA-LELE

FROM Havai'i, the mother of islands in the centre of Polynesia, courageous navigators followed the constellation of
Meremere (Orion's Belt) for 2400 miles to the north to
discover and people a new Hawai'i. The northern islands are
strung in a row from southeast to northwest and consist of
Hawai'i, Maui, Kahoolawe, Lanai, Molokai, Oahu, Kauai,
and Niihau. Beyond Niihau stretch a number of rocky islets
and reefs. When European navigators arrived on the scene,
these outer islets were unoccupied, but Nihoa and Necker
with their rocky terraces and stone gods and implements bore
silent but eloquent witness to previous Polynesian visits.

The different myths concerning the origin of the islands
indicate that conflicting theories have been composed by
various schools of thought. Though the renowned Maui
retains the credit for discovering fire and for snaring the
sun, a local fisherman has robbed him of the fishing exploits
attributed to him in other lands. The fishing-up of the
islands is thus referred to in the chant of the voyagers who

invited Lono-kaeho of Tahiti to return with them to Hawai'i:

> Come back and dwell in Hawai'i-of-the-green-back,
> A land that was formed in the ocean,
> That was drawn up from the sea,
> From the very depths of Kanaloa;
> The white coral of the ocean caves
>   that was caught on the hook of the fisherman,
> The great fisherman of Kapaahu,
> The great fisherman Kapu-he'e-ua-nui.

According to this myth, Kapu with the long name, while fishing from Kapaahu, drew up a piece of coral on his hook. He was about to cast it aside when a priest advised him to offer a pig to the gods with an appropriate prayer in order that the coral might grow into land. Kapu did so, and the coral grew into the large island of Hawai'i. Encouraged by such success, Kapu continued fishing up pieces of coral which successive pig offerings materialized into Maui, Oahu, and the other islands of the group.

A second myth carries on the idea of spontaneous emergence that has been attributed to the older Havai'i of the Society group:

> Now appeareth forth Hawai'i-nui-akea,
> Great-Hawai'i-in-the-open-space,
> Emerging out of utter darkness.
> An island, a land is born,
> The row of islands stretching away from Nu'umea.
> The group of islands beyond the horizon of Tahiti.

A unique local myth gives the primary parent, Wakea (Space), the power of producing islands by various wives. Wakea is the Hawaiian form of the Tahitian Atea and corresponds to the Cook Islands' Vatea and to the New Zealand Rangi (Sky-space). In the Hawaiian myth, as in the Cook Islands and New Zealand, Wakea married Papa who was further named Papa-hanau-moku (Papa-who-gave-birth-to-islands).

Papa gave birth to the islands of Hawai'i and Maui and to a daughter named Ho'ohoku-ka-lani. Then she went south to Tahiti to recuperate. During her absence, Wakea mated with Kaula, who gave birth to Lanai, named Lanai-of-Kaula. Wakea then mated with another female named Hina, who bore the island of Molokai. After the birth of those islands, a golden plover named Laukaula, on its annual migration south from Alaska, called in at Hawai'i and heard the gossip about Wakea's infidelity. On arriving in Tahiti, Laukaula, referred to in song as the 'teetering plover', told the tale of Wakea's new wives to Papa. Papa was greatly incensed and returned in haste to Hawai'i, where she squared the account by mating with Lua and giving birth to the island of Oahu, which bears the honorific title of Oahu-nui-a-Lua (Great-Oahu-of-Lua). Papa then forgave Wakea, returned to him, and give birth to the remaining islands of Kauai, Niihau, and Kahoolawe.

David Malo, the Hawaiian historian, thus naively sums up the position:

'In the genealogy of Wakea, it is said that Papa gave birth to these islands. Another account has it that this group of islands was not begotten but really made by the hands of Wakea. We now perceive their error. If the women in that ancient time gave birth to countries then indeed would they do so in these days; and if at that time they were made by the hands of Wakea, doubtless the same thing would be done now.

'In the genealogy of the Kumulipo, it is said that the land grew up of itself, not that it was begotten, nor that it was made by hand. Perhaps this is the true account and these Hawaiian Islands did grow up of themselves, and after that human beings appeared on them. Perhaps this is the best solution of the mistaken views held by the ancients; who knows?'

Yes, who knows? Probably the geologists will support David Malo and the Kumulipo, for the like of Wakea and Papa are not to be seen today.

The Kumulipo is a creation chant composed in honour of an ancestor of King Kalakaua. The king's sister, Liliu-o-ka-lani, while confined by her political opponents in Iolani Palace and afterwards in Washington Place, Honolulu, translated the chant which was published in Boston. The chant is divided into sixteen eras, of which the first seven cover a period of darkness, as indicated by the concluding lines of each era, ' 'Tis night'. Various terms are applied to the long period of night, such as Po-'ele'ele (Deepest darkness), Po-kanokano (Impenetrable darkness), and Po-kinikini (Myriad nights). In the Hawaiian dialect, the original Polynesian *k* was dropped as in Tahiti, but *k* was substituted for the original *t*. *N* was used instead of *ng*, *l* instead of *r*, and *w* instead of *v*. Hence the Po-'ele'ele of Hawai'i represents the Po-'ere'ere of Tahiti and the Po-kerekere of New Zealand; Po-kanokano, the Po-ta'ota'o of Tahiti and Po-tangotango of New Zealand. Po-kinikini is the Po-tinitini of other areas.

The letters of the Hawaiian alphabet were established in 1826 by a committee of missionaries who used letters to represent the sounds as they heard them. At this time, the change from *t* to *k* had begun on the island of Hawai'i but had not reached Kauai where *t* was used until comparatively recent times. Colonel Spaulding, from the reports to the American Board of Missions in Boston, prepared a paper read before the Hawaiian Historical Society in 1930 in which he showed how the alphabet was compiled. The committee of nine missionaries took various letters in turn and voted on them. The final report, facetiously headed 'Report of the Committee of Health on the state of the Hawaiian language', set forth its conclusions in terms to justify the name assumed by the committee. The greatest difficulty was experienced in choosing between *l* and *r*, *k* and *t*, and *w* and *v*. '*K* is deemed of sufficient capacity to perform its own functions and that of its counterpart *T*. *L* though two pills have been given to expel it is to remain to do its own office and that of its yoke fellow *R*. *R* though closely connected with the vitals is expelled by five or six votes or expellants, though nearly the same quantity of preservatives has been applied. *T* though claiming rights as a native member has suffered amputation by the knife and saw of the majority. *V*, a contiguous member and claiming similar rights, has suffered the same fate, and a gentle [illegible] has been applied to dry the wounds of both.' Thus the committee of health experts chose *l*, *k*, and *w*, but as *r*, *t*, and *v* are the consonants used in Tahiti, whence the Hawaiians came, I have a feeling that the purgatives and the knife were applied to the wrong patient in each pair.

A Polynesian kinswoman of mine asked, as I was leaving the Bishop Museum, 'Hele 'oe i ke kaona?' (Are you going to the kaona?). 'What is kaona?' I asked, though I knew quite well. 'Town,' she replied. 'That is how we say it in Hawaiian.' 'Why don't you say *taone*?' I asked. 'That is the way the Maoris say it and *taone* is nearer in sound to town than *kaona*.' 'How can I,' she replied, 'when there is no *t* in the Hawaiian alphabet?'

The Kumulipo chant states that during the long period of impenetrable darkness that existed for countless nights, there were born in sequence shellfish, seaweed, grasses, plants, fish, insects, birds, mice, dogs, and bats. In the eighth era, the Myriad Nights merged into the Night-receding-over-distant-waves, and Day succeeded Night. In this period were born the man Ki'i (Maori, Tiki), the woman La'ila'i, and the gods Kane (Tane), and Kanaloa (Ta'aroa or Tanga-roa). Mention is also made of the Great-octopus which figures in the myths of other islands.

The ninth and tenth eras deal mainly with Ki'i and La'ila'i, who increased the population of the world and from whom the sacred birthright of man is derived.

The following eras enumerate male and female pairs in the form of a genealogy and give long lists of various kinds of Nights. The gods Kane and Kanaloa, Wakea and his wives, the Maui brothers and their father Akalana all occur, but the gods Ku and Lono are not mentioned. In the four-teenth era, the stars are hung out and 81 star names are enumerated. The task accomplished, the bard sings:

> The heavens did swing,
> The earth does swing
> In the starry space.

This recital, after finally reaching human ancestors, ends with Lono-i-ka-makahiki, the high chief in whose honour the chant was composed. The bard had accomplished a wonder-ful feat in assembling over 2000 proper names in sequence and memorizing his composition. The fact that the chant was orally transmitted for over one hundred years until an introduced alphabet allowed it to be written gives an insight into the power of memory exercised by the Hawaiians.

The major gods of Hawai'i are Kane (Tane), Ku (Tu), Lono (Ro'o, Rongo), and Kanaloa (Ta'aroa, Tangaroa), derived directly from Tahiti. The reduction of the pantheon to four had led the modern Hawaiians to interpret the gods in terms of the Christian religion. Kane, Ku, and Lono have been selected to represent the Trinity, and Kanaloa has been conveniently relegated to Hades as the Devil. The selection of the Devil has been unfortunate in view of the concept held in the motherland of Tahiti that Ta'aroa was the Supreme Creator. This modern rationalization is contradicted by the older myth that the Underworld is presided over by Milu (Miru in central Polynesia and southern New Zealand).

The origin of the gods is clothed with the confusion characteristic of the Hawaiian genealogies. The Kumulipo states that Kane and Kanaloa were born together as the children of Kumu-honua (Foundation-of-the-earth) and Haloiho (Peer-beneath). Nineteen pairs later, in the same list, Wakea appears. This placement is directly contradicted by the chant of the priest, Pakui, who is described as a lineal descendant of historians from the very darkest ages. He states that Wakea lived with Papa, and born to them were Kane and Kanaloa. In the New Zealand myth, Rangi (Sky) takes the place of Wakea (Space) and, by marrying Papa, gave birth to Tane and Tangaroa. The origin of the gods Ku and Lono apparently did not stimulate the literary efforts of the Hawaiian bards. All bards agree that Wakea was the son of Kahiko (Ancient-one) and his wife Kupulana-ke-hau (Growth-of-power).

The origin of man shares in the general confusion of conflicting records. In the Kumulipo, Ki'i (Ti'i, Tiki) was born a man, and La'ila'i a woman in the eighth era, which ushered in the Day ending the long period of profound Night. Wakea, the father of islands and of the gods, Kane and Kanaloa, does not appear until the twelfth era. Thus man was born before the gods, which is probably as it should be, but is not supported by the myths of other parts of Polynesia.

In the lengthy genealogy of Opu'u-ka-honua it is stated that Opu'u-ka-honua came to Hawai'i from Tahiti with his two younger brothers and one woman, and found the islands already inhabited by human beings. On analysis of the generations from Opuʻu-ka-honua to Kamehameha I, who died in 1819, it has been estimated that Opuʻu-ka-honua landed in about 225 B.C. and that Wakea was born of human stock in 125 A.D. Thus Opuʻu-ka-honua came to an already populated Hawaiʻi 350 years before the islands were born of Wakea and Papa.

Another myth states that Wakea committed incest with his daughter, Hoʻohoku-ka-lani, and produced Haloa from whom the human stock is descended. This myth has affinity with central Polynesia where Hoʻohoku appears as Faʻahotu or Hakahotu. In Tongareva Atea married Hakahotu and produced the ancestors of the chiefly lines of that atoll.

To make confusion even greater, the Hawaiian historian Kepelino, after conversion to the Christian faith, revised Hawaiian mythology. He states that the major gods, Kane, Ku, and Lono, who were gods without source, creating earth and sky, the celestial bodies, and the living things of earth, created man to rule over the things they had made. They fashioned a man out of earth, breathed into him the breath of life, and named him Kumu-honua (Earth-foundation). They fashioned from the side of the man a woman named Lalo-honua. These two were placed in a fertile land and for-bidden to eat the sacred mountain apple of Kane (*ohia kapu a Kane*). A sea-bird deceived the woman and she ate of the apple, as did her husband. When Kane saw what had hap-pened, he sent them away. The trees parted to make a path for them and, as they passed, the vegetation closed in behind them, forever closing the path to the fertile land from which they had been expelled. It is unnecessary to go into details of the flood which followed because of the wickedness of the people and the building of an ark by the one righteous man named Nuʻu. This neo-myth finds no confirmation in the other Polynesian areas, and its nearest affinity is with the Book of Genesis with which Kepelino was evidently saturated when he wrote his version of the 'Traditions of Hawaii'.

The leaders of the early expeditions from Europe kept logs from which they wrote up their impressions when they returned to their homes. These accounts are interesting for the descriptions of what they actually saw, but their interpretations of native culture are inaccurate. The whalers and traders who came afterward were illiterate people who did not appreciate the oral literature of a people whom they regarded as ignorant savages. The missionaries who followed in their wake were too busy substituting their own mythology to take an immediate interest in the exact details of the mythology they sought to destroy. The Hawaiians were given new standards of value in which their native myths and traditions had no commercial or spiritual recognition. The continuity of their teaching was broken.

Later when men like David Malo, Kepelino, and Kamakau were encouraged to write up their native myths and traditions, they attempted to translate the Creation and Flood of Christian teaching into Hawaiian myth. The most extraordinary example of interpreting native lore into a Christian form is provided by the native historian, Kamakau. It so happens that in the Hawaiian cycle of thirty night names for the lunar month, the name of the god Kane was given to the 27th night from the new moon, and a series of four nights named after the god Ku commenced with the third night from the new moon. The Hawaiians had established four taboo periods in each month, and one of them was the taboo of Ku. Kamakau states that the world was created by Kane and that he commenced work on the 27th, the night named after him. He worked on the 27th, 28th, 29th, and

30th, and on into the 1st and 2nd of the following month. In these six days he completed the work of creation and rested on the seventh day, which was the third of the month, or the first Ku. He therefore hallowed that day and declared it 'the first Sabbath, the great Sabbath of the god Ku'. Kamakau was apparently so intent on making Hawaiian creation conform to the Biblical story that he overlooked the fact that he made Kane work through his own taboo period, which was imposed on the night of the 27th and not lifted until the morning of the 29th. Abraham Fornander, who recorded many of these later versions, said, 'The Polynesian legend of the creation of man shows too remarkable an accord with the Hebrew account to be lightly passed over.' As a result of his simple faith, he linked the Polynesians with a Hebraic civilization in distant Asia, whereas the unbelieving student of today links these local versions with the Book of Genesis as expounded in Hawai'i.

In spite of contradictions, inclusion of Biblical teaching, and dislocation in the time sequence of gods, heroes, and ancestors, Hawaiian mythology has retained certain elements that belong to a widely distributed Polynesian pattern. Such are the long period of darkness succeeded by light, the presence of Wakea and Papa as the parents of the gods, the existence of Kane, Ku, Kanaloa, and Lono as major gods, the association of Ki'i with the first male being, and the appearance of the culture heroes Maui, Kaha'i, and Laka in the sixteenth era of the Kumulipo.

Legend states that Hawai'i was first settled by Hawai'i-loa, who dwelt on the eastern shores of the land of Kapakapa-ua-a-Kane. His grandfather and father were Aniani-ku and Aniani-ka-lani. I mention them because we find them as lands in New Zealand where the name Hawai'i-loa occurs as

Hawaiki-roa, an ancient land. Hawai'i-loa and his navigator Makali'i (Pleiades) made many fishing trips to a sea on the east named the Sea-where-the-fish-do-run. On one of his long trips his navigator urged him to sail farther on. They sailed in the direction of the Pleiades and the planet Jupiter (Iao) as a morning star. They sailed into another sea named Many-coloured-ocean-of-Kane. They passed on to the Deep-coloured-sea, where they came to an island. The discoverer named the island after himself, Hawai'i. Pleased with his discovery, Hawai'i-loa returned to his home, picked up his wife, family, and retinue, and sailed back to Hawai'i, where he remained to become the first settler.

Much speculation has arisen among modern students as to the interpretation of this legend. Some hold that the Hawai'i referred to in sailing east was Havai'i in the Society Islands. Others hold that the land of Kapakapa-ua-a-Kane was located in Indonesia and that Hawai'i-loa sailed northeast through the Carolines and the Many-coloured-ocean-of-Kane, studded with the shallows of coral atolls and lagoons. Passing along to the Marshall Islands, the navigator sailed 2100 miles over the Deep-coloured-sea to Hawai'i. Still others hold that Hawai'i-loa lived with his brother Ki in the Society Islands, whence he sailed to Hawai'i. The date of his settlement has been placed at 450 A.D. and, until some other writer has the temerity to propose another date, we may accept it with reservations. Certain it is that some Polynesian leader arrived early with his followers, and the name of Hawai'i-loa may be used as a symbol for want of a better. Hawai'i is such a widely used place name that the theory that the first settler named the island after himself does not stand inspection. It is more likely that the name of the first settler was forgotten, and the historians gave him the name of the island in order to establish their claim that he was the first settler.

Legend merges with tradition when we come to the later influx of people from Tahiti. These voyages of exploration and settlement were led by chiefs who became distinguished ancestors of the chiefly families of Hawai'i. In all these traditions, recognition is given to the fact that there were people here before them, descendants of the people who came with Hawai'i-loa. They are referred to as the Menehune people (*ka poe Menehune*). Myth states that they were the descendants of Menehune, the son of Lua-nu'u, who appears in the chiefly genealogies of other areas as Ruanuku.

The Menehune people were probably well distributed over all the Hawaiian islands, but myths and traditions concerning them cling more thickly to the island of Kauai. It is probable that the later invaders pushed them gradually out of other islands so that they congregated in Kauai, the last of the large islands, at the northwest end of the chain. From there they apparently withdrew to the barren and rocky islets of Nihoa and Necker, as evidenced by numerous terraces, stone implements, and stone images. Nihoa, the nearer of the two, was known to the later Hawaiians through fishing expeditions, but Necker with its stone images is not mentioned in the later tales. The type of terrace with raised platforms and upright stone pillars is reminiscent of the inland temples of Tahiti, attributed to the Manahune people of that island. This similarity favours the theory that the Hawaiian Menehune came from Tahiti and not through the Marshall Islands. They must have led a bare existence on Nihoa and Necker, owing to the lack of water and vegetable foods. The absence of skeletal material argues that after subsisting for some time, they launched out on the deep again and disappeared into the unknown.

In the Kauai tales, the Menehune were credited with being skilled artisans who made many of the famous open temples and fishponds. They worked only under cover of darkness. Some of the temples were alleged to have been completed in one night, the workmen stretching in a continuous line between the stone quarry and the temple site, and passing huge stones from hand to hand. A chief of the later people employed a group of Menehune, and when the work was completed, he paid the labourers with a single fresh-water shrimp. A neighbouring hill was named Shrimp Hill to celebrate the occasion, and there it stands as a memorial to the parsimony of employers in those days. The one shrimp was probably introduced into the tale to stress the magic power of the Menehune who could feed the multitude on one small crustacean. The Menehune ditch at Waimea in Kauai is also attributed to these master craftsmen. The ditch, which carried water to irrigate a large taro flat, was led past a perpendicular cliff by building up a wall and waterway with smoothly cut stone blocks to form a structure which is unique in Polynesia.

Legend states that the only foods available in Hawai'i on the arrival of the Menehune were the fruit of the pandanus, the pith of the tree fern, the root of the *Cordyline* (*ti*), and the berries of the *ohelo* and *akala*. In Kauai, the stronghold of the Menehune, there are two forms of stone pounders which are not found in any of the other islands of the group. They are termed 'ring pounders' and 'stirrup pounders' because of their shape, and they have comparatively narrow, elliptical pounding surfaces which form a marked contrast to the large, convex, rounded surfaces of the pounders used in the other islands to pound the taro tuber into the *poi* paste that formed the staple food of the later inhabitants. It is intriguing to associate the large round-surfaced pounder with the later people who introduced taro and other cultivable food plants, and to attribute the ring and stirrup pounders of Kauai to the Menehune who originally made them for use in the preparation of food from the fruit of the pandanus or perhaps a coarse variety of taro.

The Menehune pioneers have come to be regarded as gnomes and fairies. It is even said that they were a race of dwarfs, an erroneous description similar to that given by the later story-tellers to their Manahune kinsmen in Tahiti. It seems to be a Polynesian characteristic to laud one's own family ancestors and to belittle those who preceded them in exploration and settlement. The Menehune were real, live people of Polynesian stock, and they are entitled to the honour and glory of being the first to cross the ocean wastes to Hawai'i.

Somewhere about the beginning of the twelfth century of the Christian era, there was a great influx of adventurous leaders to Hawai'i. Puna-nui settled in Kauai; Newa-lani and Maweke in Oahu; Kalana-nu'u, Hua, and others in Maui; and Hika-po-loa in Hawai'i. Some of them are referred to as contemporaries who came together, and it is evident that they separated for settlement purposes so as not to clash with each other. Perhaps some adventurous voyagers sailed north from the central Havai'i and rediscovered the lands originally found by Hawai'i-loa. This explorer must have returned to the homeland and given sailing directions to those who came later as settlers and brought with them their womenfolk, cultivable food plants, and domesticated animals.

The land whence these settlers came is named Kahiki, the Hawaiian form of Tahiti. Various specific districts in the homeland, such as Pali-uli, are referred to in song:

O Pali-uli, hidden land of Kane,
Land in Kalana-i-kauola,
In Kahiki-ku, in Kapakapa-ua-a-Kane,
Land with springs of water, moist and plenteous,
Land greatly beloved of the gods.

However, the details of locality given in legend cannot be accepted as accurate. Similar local details have been inserted by each island group in the general tales of Maui and other culture heroes. The Hawaiian tale of the famous beauty, Lu'ukia, is further evidence of the inaccuracy of place names in legend.

Lu-ukia is said to have been the granddaughter of Hika-po-loa, who settled in the island of Hawai'i. She married a man named Olopana and they lived in the Waipio valley in Hawai'i. A great flood inundated the Waipio valley, and Olopana and Lu'ukia sailed to Tahiti, where they settled down. Olopana appears in Tahiti as Oropa'a, a noted chief who was the ancestor of the Oropa'a tribe of Tahiti. His wife was Ru'utia, which is the Tahitian form of Lu'ukia. Among the ancestors of the Maori in far-south New Zealand are Tu-te-Koropanga, whose wife was Rukutia. Koropanga and Rukutia are the Maori forms of Olopana and Lu'ukia. From such evidence we must conclude that these two ancestors really belonged to Tahiti and that their descendants went to both New Zealand and Hawai'i from the central area of distribution. If Lu'ukia belonged to Tahiti, one wonders if her grandfather, Hika-po-loa, ever lived in Hawai'i. The Hawaiian historians brought Lu'ukia to Hawai'i on the wings of fancy, but they conveniently returned her to Tahiti to fit in with the tale which follows.

Lu'ukia was a very beautiful woman and captivated a powerful chief in Tahiti named Moikeha. Lu'ukia succumbed to the advances of Moikeha and became his mistress.

The Hawaiian story has it that Moikeha was an elder brother of Olopana, who was agreeable to the sharing of his wife. If so, this follows the Hawaiian custom of *punalua* in which two friends may share the same wife by a mutual agreement which removes from such relationship the European idea of immorality. All went well until another chief, whose advances had been rejected by Lu'ukia, sowed the seeds of discord in her mind by lies that Moikeha had been defaming her to others. Lu'ukia, in order to deny her favours to Moikeha, had a chastity kilt plaited with sennit braid. It reached from her waist to her thighs, and report says that the ends of the braid were so cunningly concealed that the garment could not be removed except perhaps by the craftsman who had invented the form of lashing. The garment was termed the *pa'u-o-Lu'ukia* (skirt of Lu'ukia), and the complicated lashing technique was later used in lashing outrigger booms to the hull of a canoe. A native fisherman in Hawai'i, showing me a very neat lashing on a pearl-shell hook, said that the pattern was termed the *pa'u-o-Lu'ukia*. The pattern was produced by figure-of-eight turns, but the inviolability of the lashing has probably been exaggerated to embellish the tale.

Moikeha, finding that Lu'ukia had turned against him, decided to go on a long sea voyage in order to forget her. He ordered his foster son and navigator, Kama-hua-lele, to fit up his voyaging canoe, saying, 'Let us sail for Hawai'i because I am agonized for love of this woman. When the ridgepole of my house, Lanikeha, sinks below the horizon, then I shall cease to think of Tahiti.'

Kama-hua-lele sailed the ship north under Orion's Belt, and one fine morning they lowered their matting sail in Hilo Bay. The navigator became bard as, standing on the deck of the double canoe, he raised his voice in salutation to the new land in the chant whose opening lines form the heading of this chapter. Moikeha took up his residence in the island of Kauai, where he married the two great-granddaughters of Puna-nui. He had a son named Kila whom he sent back to Tahiti to invite his son La'a, by a Tahitian wife, to visit him in Hawai'i. Kila, with the veteran navigator, Kama-hua-lele, duly accomplished the voyage and returned with La'a, who was named La'a-mai-Kahiki (Raka-from-Tahiti). La'a brought with him a famous drum whose beat Moikeha recognized as his son's ship approached Kauai. After remaining with his father for some time, La'a went to Maui and finally returned to Tahiti. He set sail from a channel between Maui and the small island of Kahoolawe and, in memory of that returning point, the channel was named Ke Ala-i-Kahiki (The Way-to-Tahiti). Traditions state that on the death of Moikeha, La'a-mai-Kahiki returned to Kauai and carried off the bones of his father that they might rest beside those of his ancestors in the homeland of Tahiti.

The legends of this period recount many voyages to and from Tahiti. In sailing south from Ke Ala-i-Kahiki, the course was maintained by keeping the North Star (Hokupa) directly astern. When the Navel-of-Space (Piko-o-wakea) was reached, the North Star sank into the sea behind but the star Newe was taken as the southern guide and the constellation of Humu was overhead. A significant voyage was that of Kaha'i, who sailed to Tahiti and returned with breadfruit which were planted at Kualoa on Oahu.

The last voyager mentioned in Hawaiian traditions is the priest, Paao, who came from Havai'i (Ra'iatea) in about 1275 A.D. He arrived in Hawai'i and, finding that the prestige of the high chief Kapawa had degenerated, he returned to Ra'iatea to procure some chief who would restore the prestige of rank. He first selected Lono-kaeho, whom he invited to return with him to Hawai'i-of-the-green-back. Lono refused and Paao then prevailed upon Pili-kaaiea to settle in Hawai'i. The line of Pili, by intermarriage with the older lines, became powerful in the islands. Paao, as a priest of Havai'i (Ra'iatea) with possessions in Vavau (Pora-pora), is credited with introducing into the Hawaiian islands the form of temple (*heiau*), human sacrifice, and the red feather girdle used in the investiture of kings. Many writers have held that Paao came from Savai'i in Samoa and held possessions in Vavau in Tonga, but as the three things introduced by him are characteristic of central Polynesia and are absent in western Polynesia, the Samoan theory must be abandoned.

The voyages between Hawai'i and Tahiti ceased with Paao. The islands became stocked with food plants, and pigs, dogs, and fowls. Taro became one of the staple foods and was mashed with stone pounders with rounded knobs at the top unlike the ornamentation of Tahiti. The mashed taro was thinned with water to form a paste termed *poi* that entered into the daily menu of the people. In other parts of Polynesia the taro could be served on leaf platters, but the *poi* of Hawai'i required containers that would not leak. Large gourds with the tops cut off were used for serving bowls and smaller ones for individuals. Gourds cut shorter were also used as covers. The wood craftsmen were evidently influenced by the gourd containers, for they made wooden bowls of like shape with covers. Hence it is that Hawai'i is characterized by round bowls rather than by the 'beaker' type with legs that are common in central Polynesia. Some Hawaiian bowls had an inner projecting flange which served as a finger wiper.

To transport quantities of mashed food, the general carry-nets had to be made to support the bowls. The nets and carrying poles of Hawai'i are the most elaborate in Polynesia, the retaining knobs of some of the poles being carved as human heads. Thus the form in which food was served initiated developments that created local differences in the crafts.

The paper mulberry was brought from Tahiti and the manufacture of bark cloth received various local innovations. A departure from the usual parallel lines on the bark cloth beaters was made by carving various patterns upon them and thus impressing different watermarks on the cloth. Bamboo splints were also carved with different patterns, dipped in dye, and stamped on the cloth to produce a rich variety of design. Capes and cloaks of fine meshed netting were covered with red feathers that marked chiefly rank in Polynesia. Later yellow feathers were added to create designs and, as the yellow feathers were more scarce, yellow became the chiefly colour in Hawai'i. Rich designs of golden triangles, crescents, and even circles on a bright red background made these regal garments a peak of achievement in the use of colour. Helmets with a median ridge like those of ancient Greece, also covered with feathers, are unique both in design and technique. Wickerwork heads with pearl-shell eyes and mouths fringed with dogs' teeth were covered with feathers as worthy representations of the gods of war.

Hereditary chiefs ruled over districts and acquired great power. They owned the land and collected taxes through subsidiary chiefs at stated times, particularly at the Makahiki festival held after the principal crop was garnered in November. In some exclusive families, brothers married sisters as an arrogant assertion that no other family was sufficiently aristocratic to produce a fitting spouse. This custom was unique in Polynesia. The issue of such marriages were regarded with the deepest possible reverence. The Hawaiians created such a number of taboos that an official executioner was appointed to inflict the punishments that the gods might have overlooked.

After a powerful chief had gained control of an entire island, the people were grouped by families in districts rather than tribes named after common ancestors. Men did the cooking, and the two sexes were not allowed to eat together. The sanctity of this taboo was weakened by the many unrecorded white men who had been living with Hawaiian women since the days when foreign ships began to visit the islands. These men not only did not observe the taboo themselves but must have scoffed openly at it. Finally the taboo was broken by the Queen Dowager Kaahumanu, who ate with her son in public. Kaahumanu brought about the equality of the sexes in Hawai'i over a century before the suffragette movement started in England.

The major gods that came from Tahiti were worshipped in walled enclosures of stone that were termed *heiau* instead of *marae*. A local feature was the three-story tower from which the will of the gods was made known by the high priest. The temples were decorated by large wooden images of the major gods and smaller ones in wood and stone of the lesser gods that were created locally. The temple ceremonies were rich and elaborate and the ritual chants are full of poetic imagery. Hula dances were both secular and religious, and offerings were made to Laka, the deity of the dance. Human sacrifices were made to Ku, the god of war, but human flesh was not eaten.

In the fertile northern islands the Hawaiians became strong and vigorous, elaborating a culture founded on that of central Polynesia. They derived happiness and contentment from their perfect adjustment to environment and the balance maintained between land and sea. Pigs, dogs, and fowls were the food of the wealthy; fish remained the mainstay of the people. The land provided sweet potatoes and taro to eat with fish, and the raw material for making canoes, nets, and fishlines. Boundaries of districts did not stop at high-water mark but ran out into the sea; for land and sea were complementary to each other and only together could they form a complete setting for human existence.

Legend and tradition grew up about the hills and valleys of Hawai'i. The urge for deep-sea adventure decreased and interest narrowed to the coastal seas. Voyaging canoes ceased to sail out from the channel of Ke Ala-i-Kahiki (Road-to-Tahiti) and trim their course for the Equator. The long sea voyages of the northern rovers had ended—Hawai'i had become home.

19. THE SOUTHERN ANGLE

I found a great land covered with high mists in
Tiritiri-o-te-moana, the open sea that lies to the south.
KUPE'S DISCOVERY

My mother was a full Maori of the Ngati-Mutunga tribe
of North Taranaki in New Zealand. She had the arresting
name of Ngarongo-ki-tua (Tidings-that-reach-afar). I hope
for the sake of her memory that, by gathering tidings from
afar, I may be worthy the honour of being her son. She was
the first-born of the senior family of the Ngati-Aurutu sub-
tribe, and I absorbed pride of race from her. Her only
brother was named Te Rangi Hiroa after an ancestor who
had lived two centuries before. I was told that Hiroa was a
contraction of Ihi-roa and that the name meant the Heavens-
streaked-with-the-long-rays-of-the-sun. My uncle became
seriously ill during a visit to a distant village and commanded
that he be moved in order that he might die at home. Unfortunately he died on the way, and I was given my first name
of Te Mate-rori (Death-on-the-road), a wretched name because 'rori' is the modern Maori form of road. I was greatly
relieved on reaching my teens to be given my adult name
of Te Rangi Hiroa in more classical memory of my uncle.

My father belonged to a north of Ireland family that lived in Armagh, so I am entitled to his family name. I am binomial, bilingual, and inherit a mixture of two bloods that I would not change for a total of either. I mention this brief family history to show that from my birth I was endowed with a background for the study of Polynesian manners and customs that no university could have given me. My mother's blood enables me to appreciate a culture to which I belong, and my father's speech helps me to interpret it, inadequate though the rendering be at times.

My maternal grandmother was a wonderful old lady. She had lived so long that she had acquired more wrinkles than anyone I have ever seen. She had seen many of our tribe die, and she had mourned over them all. It used to be the custom when wailing over near of kin to incise the skin with a flake of obsidian so that the flow of blood and tears might mingle to the fullest expression of grief. Sometimes charcoal was rubbed into the cuts and left indelible marks. My grandmother's breast was covered with such grief marks; and for her very dear ones, she had made the record on her cheeks. I was particularly proud of her tattooing. She had the orthodox pattern for women on both lips and her chin was covered with an artistic curved design. But in addition she had beautifully executed double spirals on either nostril and short curved lines on her forehead that arched upward from the inner angles of her eyes. When I was chastised at home for some error in conduct, I ran away to the Maori village and took refuge with my grandmother. She told me tales of happenings in her girlhood, and I learned tribal history from her as well as from my mother.

When I went to Te Aute College after my mother's death, I spent some of my vacations with my tribe. In spite of the protestations of my relatives with houses of sawn timber, I insisted on sleeping beside my grandmother on the earthen floor of her native hut with its walls of tree-fern slabs. She grew her own tobacco outside her hut, and, as she smoked her pipe beside her charcoal fire in the evenings, she told her college grandson stories that it was a privilege to hear. She had been an eyewitness of so much that had passed that she belonged to another age. With each parting, she wept the longer, and we both realized that the end of our companionship was approaching nearer and nearer. She has passed away to join her daughter in the Polynesian spirit land, and I would that our myths of that land were true. Her name was Kapuakore which means Cloudless, an apt name for one who in her long life brought no cloud of sorrow to any living soul.

After graduating in medicine in 1904 and spending a year as a hospital interne, I obeyed the call of my blood and joined the government service as a Medical Officer of Health to the Maoris. I visited various villages and was received in all with the courtesy that still takes the form of old-time ceremony. The people gathered in the open space before the village assembly house, and tears were shed for those who had recently passed away. The Maori *tangi* (weeping) and the Irish wake are similar in fundamental principle, and on such occasions my two halves could unite as one. Speeches of welcome couched in archaic form were made by the local chiefs to which I replied as best I could. Five years' study at a medical school with a year in hospital had made a serious break in the continuity of my Maori education. My Maori words unconsciously flowed along an English channel of grammar, and I was horribly conscious that I was talking to my own people like a foreigner. The speeches were followed by the ceremony of pressing noses with all and sundry. This form of greeting, at one time universal throughout Polynesia, now survivies as a regular custom only in New Zealand. It says much for our generation that we never tried to evade the custom because we did not wish to give pain to our elders. After these nasal contacts, the taboo of the stranger was lifted and one could mix freely and talk informally.

The visitor was the guest of the village, and the best food was provided for him during his stay in the tribal guest house. Different districts have local foods which are a great asset to the people not only for their own sustenance but for the entertainment of their visitors. Fish, crustaceans, and shellfish in the coastal districts, eels and whitebait in the river regions, pigeons and parrots in the forest areas; all had their particular season when they were at their best. My own district was famous for its lamprey eels in June or July. The sea eggs (echinoderms) were fat at Te Araroa when the golden flowers of the *kowhai* blossomed in spring. Sharks came into the fishing grounds off the Taranaki coast when the new growth of bracken fern began to straighten out its curled shoots. I learned to know the food seasons of the various parts of the island, and I tried to make my visits of inspection coincide with the native food calendar, not only because I liked native foods but because native hosts were so genuinely pleased to lay before their guests the foods for which their district was noted. Economic embarrassment was avoided, and host and guest shared a common satisfaction.

I early realized that to gain the interest and support of chiefs and leaders older than myself, I must overcome the handicap of youth by an exhibition of Maori scholarship that would not only earn their respect but indicate clearly where my sympathies lay. I commenced an intensive study of Maori mythology, legends, traditions, and the details of customs, manners, and etiquette. I learned the pattern of ceremonial speech and the forms of metaphor and simile that went with it. The more speech is illustrated with quotations from myths and ancient traditions, the better a Maori audience likes it. Old songs and incantations with an apt bearing on the subject matter are necessary because a speech is regarded as incomplete without them. I was never good at rendering songs, but I acquired a host of chants and incantations to illustrate speeches. I combed the printed literature, and I learned at first-hand from the experts of various tribes who were only too pleased to impart their knowledge to an appreciative student of their own blood. With others of the younger leaders, I became a homemade anthropologist—not to obtain a university degree, but to gain an inner understanding of our own people in order that we might the better help them through the problems and trials created by civilization.

In the Maori houses of learning, the creation of the world was recorded in evolutionary stages in genealogies which were recited and taught by experts. Such teaching was referred to as the Kauae-runga (Upper-jaw), in contrast to knowledge of things terrestrial termed Kauae-raro (Lower-jaw). Things celestial commenced appropriately enough with the Void (Kore) and went on to the unknown, personified as Night (Po). Elsdon Best, in describing this early period, says, 'The unknown æons of time before the heavens, earth, and heavenly bodies came into being was the Po—intangible, unknown, unseen, unknowable.' The quotation sums up the position, but the Po period cannot be dismissed lightly by one general term. It was drawn out to a count of ten Nights or given various descriptive terms, such as Po-tangotango, Po-kerekere, and Po-tinitini, names that were used by the philosophers at Taputapu-atea in central Polynesia.

The Unknown was followed by periods of growth that were expressed in terms of plant and human development. The botanical evolution was personified as the Tap-root, Side-roots, Rootlets, Stem, Branches, Twigs, and Leaves. Human evolution was personified as Conception, Swelling, Birth, Mind, Thought, and Desire, which preceded the two primary parents, the Sky-father and the Earth-mother. We have already met the primary father under the name of Space rendered as Atea, Vatea, and Wakea. In New Zealand, he appears as Rangi (Sky) which nevertheless is Space. The primary mother retains her original name of Papa (Earth-stratum) which is qualified as Papa-tu-a-nuku, the Stratum-which-assumed-the-form-of-land.

Rangi and Papa clave together and children were born to them. Some recitals list no less than seventy children who were confined between the bodies of their parents, and the closeness of Rangi to Papa precluded space and light. Some of the children, led by Tane, planned the separation of their parents in order that they might stand erect and that light might be admitted into their world. The plan was bitterly opposed by Whiro, who led the first conservative party in the South Seas. Tane's policy received the majority vote and was carried into effect. The Maoris seem to have lost Ru, the Propper-up-of-skies, so the task of pushing the Sky-father up into his present position devolved upon Tane. He tried pushing with his hands in vain, and then stood on his head and pushed with his feet. Trees, which are the children of Tane, represent the position of their parent, for Maori myth says that their heads are down in the ground and their feet push upward. By Tane's effort, the Sky-father was raised on high, the Earth-mother remained below, and light came flooding in the space between. The tears of Rangi fell as rain upon the bosom of the Earth-mother, and Papa's grief at their separation rises as mist.

Some of the children of Rangi and Papa became the major gods of the Maori pantheon, as they were in other parts of Polynesia. Tane, the most powerful, presided over forests and bird life. Tangaroa was the god of the sea and fish. Tu had the portfolio of war. Rongo directed horticulture and peace. Raka gave way to the local Tawhirimatea as director of winds and rain. A department of uncultivated food to include the local fern root was created, and Haumea was placed in charge. Whiro, who led the opposition against the separation of Earth and Sky, went off in a huff to the Under-world to abide in the darkness that he preferred. The characters Te Tumu and Fa'ahotu, who were associated with other cosmogonies, are missing in New Zealand. Like their island kinsmen, the Maoris deified certain ancestors and created lesser spirits from family abortions and miscarriages as need arose.

The creation of man was associated with the god Tane and with Tiki. In some myths, Tiki was the first man, but in others he was regarded as a personification of the pro-creative powers of Tane. Tane, having hung the stars in their places and given the sun and the moon their appointed courses, sought for the human element to people the earth. With the advice of his colleagues, he moulded some red earth at Kurawaka into the form of a woman. The figure was vitalized into the first living woman and named Hine-ahu-one, the Earth-formed-maid. Ancient chants deal with the primary ignorance of the sexual act, but ignorance was eventually overcome and Tane took the Earth-formed-maid to wife. A daughter named the Dawn-maid was born, and the inevitable incest took place. The Dawn-maid, on learning that Tane was her own father, retired to the Underworld where she exercised a beneficent care over the souls of mankind who ultimately sought that place of abode.

The evolutionary pattern described is simple and straightforward. It appears to have been the version evolved by the priests at the religious seminary at Opoa in Ra'iatea at the time that the Maori ancestors left the central area. But, just as the priests of Opoa later changed their theology to make Ta'aroa the Creator, so some of the schools in New Zealand also elaborated their beliefs to include a creator of all things. This exalted personage was Io, who created all the processes of nature and caused the already existing gods to be. He was given various titles of which Io-matua-kore (Io-the-parentless) indicates that he himself was the very beginning. The old theology had a sky of ten successive levels, but the new version added two more and placed Io in residence in the highest heaven. He was provided with a house named Rangiatea, and the assembly place before it was named Te Rauroha. A staff of Celestial Maids (Mareikura) was provided, and Guardians (Pou-tiriao) were appointed to the different floors which were given individual names. Messengers were engaged to carry on communication between the upper sphere and the major gods.

As the name Io has some resemblance to the Hebrew form of Jehovah, some have thought that the cult of Io was evolved after contact with Christian teaching. However, references to Io occur in the native literature that was composed before the Old Testament was introduced into New Zealand. An example is the lament of an old chief, composed over two hundred years ago for a favourite grandchild, in which he directs the path her soul should take:

Grasp with thy hand the guiding vine
By which the god Tane ascended to the highest heaven,
That thou mayest be welcomed by the Celestial Maids
Assembled on the courtyard of Te Rauroha
And so enter within the palace of Rangiatea.

Then and only then shall all desire for this world cease,
Ah, little maid of mine.

In Tahitian myth there is an account of a war between Tane and Hiro. The Maori theologians have introduced this contest into the myth of Io. Tane set out to obtain the three baskets of knowledge from Io in the twelfth heaven, but Whiro by an alliance with Tawhiri-matea arrayed against Tane the forces of rain, hail, winds, and intense cold. He also let loose the various forms of disease grouped together under the name of Maiki. Tane overcame them all and so the knowledge of good, of evil, and of ritual were brought down to this world of ours and transmitted to mankind through the ancient houses of teaching.

Passing on to the period of legendary heroes, we have the widespread story of the Maui family and the fishing-up of islands. The usual deep-sea fishing voyage was made by five Maui brothers. The youngest Maui by magic art caught his hook in the land beneath the sea. In spite of the protests of his brothers, Maui hauled up a huge land fish. The fish was the North Island of New Zealand, and the canoe was raised high on a protuberance that became Mount Hiku-rangi. Maui's hook is represented by the curve of the coast line of Hawkes Bay between Mahia Peninsula and Cape Kid-napper. The fish, termed the Fish-of-Maui (Te Ika-a-Maui), was likened in shape to a sting ray. The southern end repre-sents the head, the western extension of Taranaki and the eastern extremity of East Cape are the two wings or flappers, and the thin part forming the North Auckland Peninsula is the tail. The seat of the British government is, oddly enough, situated at Wellington in the head of the fish. The parts of the fish are still used in Maori oratory. I belong to Taranaki, and the Ngati-Porou tribe of the East Coast used to welcome me as coming from the other flapper of the fish of Maui. I have heard members of parliament being flattered with the sentence, 'You come from the head of the fish where all wisdom lies.'

The myth states that Maui left his brothers with the fish while he returned to the homeland to get a priest to perform the requisite ritual over the new land. His brothers cut up the fish and, in its writhing under the pain of the surgical operation, the hills and valleys were created. Many hold that the earliest inhabitants of New Zealand were descended from the Maui family but, apart from the fact that the tale is a myth, it is difficult to understand how an early population could have arisen from a fishing expedition that was not accompanied by women.

As in other island groups, Maui obtained fire from the Underworld and snared the sun. New Zealand legend has a quest for immortality which differs from the Tuamotuan myth of the sea-slug already related. Maui sought to slay Hine-nui-te-po (Great-goddess-of-night) while she was asleep in her cave. He took with him a number of birds as companions. He enjoined upon them the necessity for absolute quiet while he entered into the body of the goddess to remove her heart and so end the cause of death. Unfortunately he committed an error of judgment in including the flycatcher, or fantail, in his retinue. This bird cannot remain still, and when it saw Maui entering the body of the goddess it twittered with laughter. The goddess awoke and Maui was strangled. An old lament says:

Death overtook the leaders of men
When Maui was strangled by the Goddess of Death,
And so death remained in this world, alas!

I could throw a stone at the descendants of that flycatcher, but perhaps I had better not, for problems of overpopulation might have arisen had the flycatcher not laughed.

The real discovery of New Zealand is generally attributed to Kupe in about the middle of the tenth century. The legend states that he was so angered at squids that took his bait while fishing that he swore to kill their leader known as the Wheke-a-Muturangi. He chased the chief squid over the sea, and it led him to the far south where he encountered a land with high hills covered with mist. He finally overtook the squid in the strait between the two main islands of New Zealand and slew it. He returned to central Polynesia and reported his discovery of land inhabited only by birds. The sailing direction in the lunar month of November-December was a little to the left of the setting sun. From various traditions, there is little doubt that subsequent voyages were made on these sailing directions that were handed down orally in central Polynesia.

Some time after Kupe's discovery, people making a voyage between islands in the Pacific were driven out of their course by a storm and reached New Zealand. They became the first settlers and were subsequently referred to as the people of the land (*tangata whenua*). They had their women-folk with them, but any cultivated food plants or domesticated animals that they may have had with them were disposed of on the unexpectedly protracted voyage.

In the twelfth century, an ancestor named Toi sailed south from central Polynesia in search of his grandson, Whatonga, who had been blown away by an offshore wind during a canoe race in central Polynesia. Toi made New Zealand and settled down at Whakatane in the Bay of Plenty. Whatonga, who had landed safely at another Pacific island, returned home and in turn set out in search of his grandfather. He also made New Zealand and found his grandfather. Both Toi and Whatonga had set out on search expeditions with ample sea provisions but had taken no cultivable food plants to grow in a new home, no domesticated animals, and no women. They took wives from the previous settlers and became the ancestors of mixed tribes.

In the fourteenth century, owing to conflicts in the homeland of Hawaiki, the Maori form of Havai'i, a number of voyaging canoes set out on Kupe's sailing directions with the definite object of colonizing the land that lay to the south. Most of the voyagers made their landfall in the Bay of Plenty near Cape Runaway in November or December when the Christmas trees (*pohutukawa*) were in bloom. One of the chiefs, on seeing the scarlet colour of these trees, took off his red feather headdress and hurled it into the sea, saying, 'The chiefly colour of Hawaiki is cast aside for the chiefly red of the new land that welcomes us.'

The leaders of the canoes and their followers settled on sections of the coast apart from each other so as to avoid the conflict that they had left behind them. These landing places formed centres of development and, as the groups increased and spread to meet adjoining groups, boundaries became established. The newcomers came into conflict with the first settlers and with the descendants of Toi. After many wars, the earlier settlers were absorbed into the more dominant groups of the later comers. The Maori people are grouped into tribes, which trace their descent and take their names from ancestors who came in the various canoes of the fourteenth-century migration. Some claim that their chieftainship came from the later canoes but that their right to land was derived from the earlier settlers. The traditions and history of the earliest settlers have been overlaid by tales of the later arrivals, and honour and prestige is traced to the voyaging canoes. Pride in canoes finds expression in many songs of which the following is an excellent example:

> Behold Tainui, Te Arawa, Mataatua, Kurahaupo, and Tokomaru,
> All afloat on the ocean vast.
> The tree trunk was hollowed in Hawaiki
> And so Takitumu took form.
> A night was spent at Rangipo
> And Aotea took the sea at dawn.
> These are the canoes of Uenuku
> Whose names resound unto the heavens.
> How can their fame be e'er forgot
> When they float for aye on memory's tide!

Oh, poet's faith! How indeed, unless our blood becomes so diluted that it fails to stir at the sound of our own speech? The names of the seven canoes enumerated are famous, but others, such as Horouta, deserve their meed of praise. The fame of particular canoes depends upon whether or not they have been recorded in song and story by bards and historians. A continuity of dominant chiefs and supporters is further required to bring the record down to modern times.

The Tainui canoe under the leadership of Hoturoa prepared to sail from Hawaiki on the Orongo night (27th) of the lunar month corresponding to October-November. But the old men advised Hoturoa to delay sailing until the stormy Tamateas (6th to 9th nights) of the following month had passed. Hoturoa replied, 'I will sail out now and meet the Tamateas on the open sea.' He surmounted all storms and trials to make safe landfall at Cape Runaway. The Tainui worked north to what is now known as Auckland Harbour and paddled up the Tamaki branch. Scouts reported a branch of the sea stretching away to the west. The Tainui canoe was hauled over the intervening ridge into Manakau Harbour, sailed into the western sea, and worked south to Kawhia. Her descendants peopled the area from Manakau to the Mokau River in the south, and other branches spread east to the Thames.

In Hawaiki, a chief named Tama-te-kapua and his younger brother stole fruit at night from a tree that grew back of the house of the high chief, Uenuku. As a result of the theft, Tama-te-kapua and his people left on the Arawa canoe for the land of the high mists in the south. In the popular account, the fruit tree was said to be a *poporo*, which is a species of *Solanum* in New Zealand that has no economic value. Fortunately an ancient dirge records the original name of the tree:

> Sacred tree of Hawaiki
> That grew on the farther side of Great Tahiti,
> It was the *kuru* that shaded the house of Uenuku.

It is evident that the Maoris in their popular version had substituted the local *poporo* for the fruit tree termed *kuru*. No Maori could explain what the *kuru* was like, but in central Polynesia *kuru* and its dialectical forms is the name for the breadfruit. The breadfruit will not grow in New Zealand but in central Polynesia it is a most important food.

Tama-te-kapua kidnapped a learned priest named Ngato-roi-rangi, and under his guidance the Arawa canoe made New Zealand at Cape Runaway. The canoe turned up the coast, its passengers landing at Maketu and spreading inland. The tribes that occupy the coast and the thermal district of Rotorua are descended from Tama-te-kapua, and those that spread farther inland to Lake Taupo claim descent from Ngatoroirangi. The tribes descended from the crew of the Arawa say that the carved bow of their canoe rests at Maketu, and the stern piece is formed by the mountain of Tongariro.

The Mataatua commanded by Toroa paddled into a river in the Bay of Plenty and beached on the shore. The sea-cramped crew scattered inland to view the new land. Toroa's daughter, who was ill, lay down on the beach near the grounded canoe. The rising tide began to float the canoe away, and the sick chieftainess said, 'I must act like a man'. Exerting all her strength, she managed to prevent the canoe from floating away, and to record her action the river was named Whakatane (Act-as-a-man). The people in time spread along the coast to the historic landing-place near Cape Runaway and inland over the Urewera country.

The Kurahaupo under various chiefs went north and its people settled not only in the north Auckland district, but made their way to Taranaki and to the district between Wanganui and Lake Horowhenua.

The Tokomaru is my own canoe which left Hawaiki because of wars. One version of the tradition states that Manaia was the captain. An old song states that Tokomaru was owned by Whata, captained by Tama-ariki, and navigated by the priest, Rakeiora. The canoe made Cape Runaway, sailed around the North Cape, and beached at the Mohakatino River in north Taranaki. An assembly house named Marae-rotuhia was built on the bank of the river. The people spread from the Mokau River in the north to a boundary named Onuku-taipare, some miles south of the present town of New Plymouth. The southern boundary lay between the Tokomaru people and descendants of the Kurahaupo canoe, who took their tribal name of Taranaki from the native name given to Mount Egmont. The Tokomaru tribes united in the confederation termed Ati-awa, to which belonged my two tribes of Ngati-Mutunga and Ngati-Tama.

The Takitumu canoe under Tamatea peopled the east coast of the North Island from Gisborne to Wellington. Parties crossed the Cook Straits and settled in the South Island.

The Horouta canoe peopled the east coast from Cape Runaway to Gisborne. The dominant tribe of Ngati-Porou take their name from their ancestor Porou-rangi, and the Ngai-Tahu tribe of the South Island is said to be descended from Tahu, a younger brother of Porou-rangi.

The Aotea canoe came from Hawaiki, known as Ra'iatea to its present inhabitants but as Rangitea to the Maoris, who do not drop the *ng* consonant. The Aotea tribes carry the memory of the homeland in the saying, 'We can never be lost, for we come of the seed that was sown from Rangitea.' The Aotea left in an off-season and was driven west to the Kermadec Islands, which were named Rangitahua. The Kermadecs are uninhabited, but a broken adze and some sling-stones found there bear witness to a Polynesian visit. The Aotea must have landed in the Kermadecs in March when the *karaka* (*Carynocarpus laevigata*) was covered with its golden berries, for the Aotea is generally credited with having introduced the *karaka* into New Zealand. The storm-tossed crew of Aotea, after enjoying the ripe berries, probably took the kernels on to New Zealand only to find that the tree was a native of the country. The canoe landed at an inlet on the west coast of the North Island named Aotea after the canoe. The crew marched south to the Patea River, whence their descendants spread north to form the Ngati-Ruanui tribe and south toward Wanganui to form the Nga-

Rauru tribe. The sea voyage was made the theme of a deep-sea chanty, in which the names of the canoe, captain, and steering paddle are recorded. The following translation was made by James Cowan:

THE PADDLE SONG OF THE AOTEA CANOE

Aotea is the canoe,
Turi is the chief,
Te Roku-o-whiti is the paddle.

Behold my paddle!
It is laid by the canoe side,
Held close to the canoe side.
Now it is raised on high—the paddle!
Poised for the plunge—the paddle,
Now we leap forward.

Behold my paddle, Te Roku-o-whiti!
See how it flies and flashes,
It quivers like a bird's wing,
This paddle of mine.

Ah, the outward lift and the dashing,
The quick thrust in and the backward sweep,
The swishing, the swirling eddies,
The foaming white wake, and the spray
That flies from my paddle.

The voyagers of the fourteenth century came to settle, and they probably brought all the available food plants of central Polynesia with them. However, they sailed to a cold land where the coconut, breadfruit, and banana would not grow. The voyagers to the south evidently feared the effect of the cold on their plants, for an Aotea legend states that Rongo-rongo, the wife of Turi, kept some sweet-potato tubers in a double belt around her waist to keep them warm against her body. This incident gave rise to an honorific name for the sweet potato, the 'Belt of Rongorongo'.

Although the sweet potato, taro, yam, and gourd grew in the new land, they produced but one crop a year as against a succession in the tropics. Larger cultivations had to be made for the annual crop, and local need led to storage in underground pits or sunken houses with roofs covered over with earth. Such storage houses are absent in central Polynesia where the need did not exist. The sweet potato was the most prolific of the introduced plants, and its economic importance created a new ritual during planting. A god to promote the fertility of the sweet potato was added to the Maori pantheon and represented by images in stone. Even the ordinary digging stick was improved by lashing a carved step to it and carving the top of the handle.

The paper mulberry plant was introduced to provide bark cloth, but the plant did not thrive and bark cloth was not suited to a cold climate. The need for warmer clothing led to trying out the twined technique of fishtraps on a new fibre discovered in the leaves of the native flax. Capes and cloaks were made with an outer thatch of flaxen tags that shed the rain like a shingled roof. Women with alert minds and skilful fingers invented a succession of improvements that resulted in a variety of garments. The early thatched cloaks remained in ordinary use, but dress cloaks with ornamental dyed cords, feathers, and coloured borders were produced for the upper classes. Women, in developing a form of finger weaving, blazed a trail that was to lead them far from the arts and crafts of their tropical homeland.

One must be saturated with the atmosphere of tropical Polynesia to fully appreciate what the first Maori settlers lost and what they gained in their new country. They lost certain prolific food plants, and somehow the pig and fowl were left behind or died on the voyage. The dog alone of three Polynesian domesticated animals landed in New Zealand. The Polynesian name of the fowl, *moa*, was evidently applied to a large wingless bird which became extinct. The forests teemed with bird life and new processes were invented for catching, preserving, and storing. The decoy water trough, the carved snare, the bone-pointed bird spear, and receptacles for preserved pigeons are all local developments not known elsewhere in Polynesia. The rivers, lakes, sea beaches, rock reefs, and the sea all provided a supply of food that more than made up for the cultivable foods that would not grow in the colder climate.

The greatest wonder of all must have been the forest trees that grew larger than any others in Polynesia. The canoe builders must have gazed awestruck at the great trunks of the *totara* and the *kauri* pine. I can see them offering up a ritual formula to Tane and spanning the tree trunk with admiring arms. As practical geologists, they must have enjoyed cracking and testing rock until the best basalt indicated where adze quarries should be located. With larger and heavier adzes, the forest giants were felled and dubbed into canoe hulls. The dugouts could be made so wide that they floated like boats without need of a side prop, and so the outrigger attachment was abandoned.

The Maoris had to adapt their houses to the climate of New Zealand. The simple structures of tropical Polynesia were of no use where cold winds had to be kept out, so they sank the floor below the ground surface and made thickly thatched walls to keep the houses warm. For large community houses the usual round poles were replaced by dressed timber. In central Polynesia, the artistic sense of the builders was expressed in lashing designs made with sennit braid. In New Zealand, the Maori craftsmen carved the main posts and the wall posts with conventional forms of the human figure. With an instinct for balance in art, they painted the upper woodwork of rafters and ridgepole with scroll designs in colour and thus prevented carving from running riot. The decoration of the Maori community house followed a line of local development that was stimulated originally by cold.

In addition to a rich supply of basaltic stone, New Zealand gave her settlers the gift of jade. It was found as boulders in the rivers of the west coast of the South Island, and that island consequently received the name of Te Wai-pounamu (Water-containing-jade). Jade was used to make ornaments and short war-clubs that became priceless heirlooms, but more wonderful were the chisels and adzes that took an edge almost as keen as steel. The *totara* timber was durable but soft, and with good wood and excellent tools, the Maori carvers developed a craft into an art that was unique not only for Polynesia but for the Pacific.

Our appraisal of Maori art motifs has been unduly influenced by the theory that they must have originated somewhere along the trail traversed by our ancestors in centuries gone by. We have given insufficient attention to the possibility of breaks occurring, due to lack of wood and stone and the necessity of developing other crafts. The time spent in the atolls of Micronesia would be long enough to erase the memory of former arts. The art of wood carving apparently made little progress in central Polynesia at the time of the dispersal of voyagers and settlers, else art motifs would have been shared by various islands in the same manner as myths, legends, religion, and the social pattern. The only motif that the Maoris appear to have brought from Hawaiki was the human figure with flexed legs and hands clasped on the abdomen.

The *manaia* figure that has the appearance of a bird-headed man in profile has given rise to speculation as to its origin. The bird-headed man of Easter Island was derived there from the sooty petrel. The bird motif of the Solomon Islands with a scroll pattern of interlocking beaks was taken from the man-of-war hawk. In New Zealand, there is no myth extant as to what bird the *manaia* represented. Studies by Mr. Gilbert Archey, Director of the Auckland Museum, have shown conclusively, I think, that the birdlike appearance was produced by carving one half of a human head with the middle part of the upper lip unduly prolonged. The *manaia* was thus derived from a human figure and not from a bird. Evidence has been brought forward by Mr. Archey to show a local origin for the double spiral that plays such a prominent part in Maori art. The development of carving patterns influenced tattooing patterns, so that curved lines were used instead of the straight lines of central Polynesia. High chiefs did not deem it beneath their dignity to wield the mallet and the chisel. Picture the master craftsman before a large slab of wood on which the human figure has been roughed out with stone adzes—in his left hand a chisel of jade and in his right a mallet of whalebone. With such a field and with such tools, is it any wonder that he was able to execute work undreamed of in his former home?

But the cold climate affected not only the raw material and its treatment, but also the man himself. He was imbued with a vigour and a stamina that developed during the process of adjustment to more trying conditions. He became more aggressive. The tribes built up a war record and kept an honour ledger. Victories were balanced against defeats, and each tribe strove to acquire a credit balance. There were no coconut or breadfruit trees to protect against theft, and the people congregated in villages for protection. The open village invited attack, and so the engineers selected hills and promontories in which nature aided the defence. Most Polynesians living on volcanic islands selected some natural spot difficult of access to which they retired for protection. The Tongans, owing to the lack of hills, dug trenches and built fences around defensive villages. The people of Rapa terraced commanding hilltops to form forts. It remained for the Maori to combine terrace, ditch, and palisade in his system of defence and to occupy such forts permanently. In times of doubt, sentries were posted in lookout towers. During the night, they recited watch alarms in a loud voice, not so much to keep their own warriors awake as to inform night attackers that the fort was on the alert. Though brief and cryptic in text, the alarms were nevertheless rich in imagery derived from natural surroundings. The following example translated by James Cowan belonged to a fort built on a cliff-girt promontory on the coast of Kawhia:

> O Soldiers of the fort, arise,
> Lest ye go down to death.
> High up, high up, the thundering surf
> On Harihari's cliffs resounds,
> And low the wailing sea
> Croons on the Mokau coast.
> But here am I, on guard,
> Watching, seeking, peering,
> As on those rugged rocks
> The sea hawk sits
> And watches for its prey.
>
> Soon will the sun
> Rise flaming o'er the world.

The cliffs of Harihari, to the north of the fort, jutted out into the sea and took the full force of the ocean breakers. The crash and roar symbolized war with the shouts of contending captains and the anguished cries of the wounded and the dying. To the south, the coast line curved in to form a sheltered sandy bay into which the Mokau River flowed. Though there was apparent peace, the unending moan of the waves against the sand represented the wailing of women, weeping for their dead. The last two lines are a prayer and a wish. Most attacks were made at dawn when there was enough light to see the battlements. The rising of the sun ended the watchman's vigil and ushered in a day of peace and life.

The fortified village necessitated a departure from the religious pattern of Hawaiki. The sacred raised platform or *ahu* was detached from the open court or marae proper and relegated to the outside of the fort. In a secluded grove, the priest erected a stone pillar or a wooden post, and there, alone or with a few assistants, he took council with his gods. No multitude watched the proceedings, and therefore the *ahu* platform dwindled to a shrine, often represented by a natural outcrop of rock yet retaining the ancient name of *ahu* in the Maori form of *tu-ahu*.

The marae court was retained in the village as the open space where tribal gatherings were held. In place of the *ahu* platform, a large carved house was built that served as meeting house and guest house. The meeting house was usually named after an ancestor, and when the tribe met within its walls, they gathered within the bosom of their ancestor. The marae space in front received a name in important villages and was the centre of social life. There visitors were welcomed, all important functions took place, the dead were laid in state, and the funeral ceremonies were held. Ceremonies were held on the marae by day, and in the evening they were continued within the tribal meeting house. In the Tuamotu, the spaced upright limestone pillars on the religious marae were named after ancestors, and in the Maori meeting house the spaced wall-posts, carved in human form, were also named after ancestors. In central and eastern Polynesia, the marae, because it carried a religious as well as a secular function, was dismantled and abandoned on conversion to Christianity; but in New Zealand, the marae still functions as the social centre of the people. Today, in spite of the breaking up of village life because the Maori population is engaged in farming and dairying, the meeting house and the marae remain the nucleus to which the scattered tribe returns to welcome visitors, weep for its dead, and discuss tribal welfare. May the marae long continue to function, for so soon as it is abandoned, so soon will the Maori lose his individuality.

The people descended from different canoes probably carried on culture differences that were brought from various islands in central Polynesia. When the seafaring men of the Pacific settled in New Zealand, they became landsmen. As they developed local traditions, they cut off for ever the sea roads to Hawaiki. Yet the memory of a maritime past rings out in the welcome to visitors, whether they came by foot in the past or come by motor car in the present.

> Draw hither—the canoe!
> Haul hither—the canoe!
> To its pillow—the canoe!
> To its bed—the canoe!
> To the place where shall rest—the canoe!
> Welcome, thrice welcome!

Having followed the Maori branch of the Polynesians to

the land of high mists and indicated some of the problems that they overcame, let us leave their descendants to work out their own salvation in the firm conviction that the stamina and mentality inherited from their stone-age ancestors will enable them to make good in a changing world. Fate and the courtesy of American institutions have so ordered it that I take part in the task of gathering together and recording the fragments of Polynesian culture. I bid farewell to the land of my birth in the words of an old lament:

Dirge for a Chief

Alas, the bitter pain that gnaws within
For the wrecked canoe, for a friend who is lost.
My precious heron plume is cast on Ocean's strand,
And the lightning, flashing in the heavens,
Salutes the dead.

Where is authority in this world, since thou hast passed
By the slippery path, the sliding path to death?

Lone stands Whakaahu mountain in the distance,
For thou art gone, the shelter of thy people.
Flown has my singing bird that sang of ancient learning,
The keel of Tainui, the plug of Aotea,
Now bewailed by women's flowing tears.

Beautiful lies thy body in thy dogskin tasseled cloak,
But thy spirit has passed like a drifting cloud in the heavens.
All is well with thee who liest in state on chieftain's bier.
Ah, my precious green jade jewel, emblem of departed warriors!
The dragon emerged from his rocky fastness
And sleeps in the house of death.

20. THE BASE OF THE TRIANGLE

The heavens are swinging
And touching the earth.

SAMOAN PROVERB

THE eighth and last trail from central Havai'i turns west
toward the setting sun and leads to the important island
groups of Samoa and Tonga, set in the middle of the base of
the Polynesian triangle. These two groups, because of their
size and large population, dominated the west and developed
local features in their culture that differ greatly from those
of the islands on the seven trails we have hitherto explored.
Samoa and Tonga have been alluded to in literature as central
Polynesia and nuclear Polynesia. Neither geographically nor
culturally are they central or nuclear. They form the centre
of distribution for a western Polynesian area.

Included in the western area are the atoll group of Tokelau and the atoll of Pukapuka, lying respectively north and
northeast of Samoa. East of Tonga is Niue, or Savage Island,
where I once spent six months as relieving medical officer.
The peaceable and industrious people of Niue object strongly
to having their island called Savage Island just because an
ancestor threw a spear at Captain James Cook. The spear
missed—and why should an individual failure be perpetu-

ated on the descendants of a bad marksman? In the ocean stretch between Tonga and Samoa lie Niuatobutabu (Keppel Island) and Niuafou, colonies of Tonga. Niuafou is popularly known as Tin-can Island after the one-time method of floating the mail ashore from passing liners in a sealed kerosene tin. The tin represented western civilization, but the swimmer who guided the mail ashore through the sharks was a Polynesian. West and north of Samoa are the volcanic islands of Futuna, Alofi, Uvea, and the atolls of the Ellice Islands. Farther west still are a number of islands in Melanesia, already referred to as marginal islands, where the Polynesian language is spoken.

The volcanic islands of Samoa are divided into two groups: Western or British Samoa now administered under mandate from the League of Nations, and Eastern or American Samoa in possession of the United States. Western Samoa includes the large islands of Upolu and Savai'i with the small islands of Manono and Apolima in the straits between them. Eastern Samoa consists of the large island of Tutuila with Aunu'u off its coast and the Manu'a archipelago of Ofu, Olosega, and Tau. Tau rises to 3000 feet and is the largest and most easterly island in Manu'a. Allusions to Manu'a in myth and legend refer to Tau.

My first field work for Bishop Museum was in 1927 on Tutuila and Aunu'u with A. F. Judd and Bruce Cartwright. After my colleagues returned to Honolulu, I visited the Manu'a islands, Upolu and Savai'i. My study was concentrated on material culture. The social organization of the Manu'a had previously been studied by Margaret Mead, whose work was published by Bishop Museum.

Before dealing with mythology, let us allude briefly to the Samoan dialect. The *k* is replaced by the glottal stop represented by an inverted comma in the written word; *g* represents the *ng* sound, and *s* and *f* take the place of the *h* in other dialects. Of the interchangeable consonants, *v* and *l* are used instead of *w* and *r*.

The Samoan cosmogony commences with Leai (Nothing), which corresponds to the Kore (Void) of New Zealand. This is followed by personified rocks, winds, clouds, and heavens. and culminates in Tagaloa. Tagaloa-lagi (Tagaloa-of-the-heavens) existed in space but he did not know how or whence he came. He threw down stones that became various islands of the Samoan group. Before the lands consolidated, he sent down his daughter in the form of a snipe (*tuli*), but she could find no resting place. She made further visits at his command and successively reported spray, lumpy places, water breaking, land above surface, and finally a dry place where she could rest. Later she reported the extending surface of land and the growth of a vine. Had she taken back a sprig of the vine, the affinity with the dove that Noah sent out from the ark would have been more striking. The vines withered, rotted, and swarmed with maggots and worms which grew into men and women. Some myths say that the evolution from worms took place on Manu'a.

Influenced by mythology and local legends, the Samoan regards himself as truly autochthonous. At a kava ceremony in Tau, I was welcomed by a talking chief in the stilted phrases of his office. In my reply, I alluded to the common origin of the Polynesians somewhere in Asia and the wonderful voyages our ancestors had made in peopling Polynesia.

The talking chief replied, 'We thank you for your interesting speech. The Polynesians may have come from Asia, but the Samoans, no. We originated in Samoa.'

He looked around with an air of infallibility, and his

fellow scholars grunted their approval. In self-defence, I became a fundamentalist.

I said, 'The good book that I have seen you carrying to church three times on Sundays says that the first parents of mankind were Adam and Eve, who were created in the Garden of Eden.'

In no way disturbed, the oracle replied, 'That may be, but the Samoans were created here in Manu'a.'

A trifle exasperated, I said, 'Ah, I must be in the Garden of Eden.'

I took the silence which followed to be a sign of affirmation.

Returning to Tagaloa, we have a series of Tagaloa-of-the-heavens, Tagaloa-originator-of-man, Tagaloa-the-explorer, and Tagaloa-dweller-in-lands. The sequence is an excellent illustration of the Polynesian cryptic form of historical narrative that time has converted into myth. Tagaloa or a descendant of Tagaloa came from a distant horizon, metaphorically alluded to as the heavens (*lagi*), on an exploring expedition and settled in the land of Samoa. He first touched earth at Tau in Manu'a and came in contact with the first settlers. The chiefly stock of Samoa descended from Tagaloa, and their historians disposed of the prestige of the first settlers by making them the lowly descendants of worms. In the course of time, the human voyager was regarded as a god who descended directly from the heavens. Hence the Samoans consider themselves as originating in Samoa.

The mythical form of historical narrative states that the first chiefly house was built on Tau and named Fale-ula. Owing to the first settlement of the Tagaloa family in Manu'a, those small islands have enjoyed honour out of all proportion to their size and population. The Tui Mahu'a, or ranking chief of Manu'a, received precedence over many chiefs ruling over larger districts. Nothing annoys the people of the larger island of Tutuila more than to be reminded of the Manu'a myth that Tagaloa made Tutuila as an afterthought to provide a stepping stone between Manu'a and western Samoa.

Turning to western Samoa, we find that a descendant of the Tagaloa family, named Pili, established himself in Upolu. He is credited with great power, for he divided Upolu into three districts which he gave to three of his sons, whose names were given to the districts. He gave the western part and the spear to Ana, the middle portion and the fly whisk to Saga, and the eastern end and the planting stick to Tua. The spear represented war, the fly whisk oratory, and the planting stick horticulture. In his last exhortation to his sons, he said, 'When you wish to fight, fight; when you wish to talk, talk; and when you wish to work, work.'

Genealogies place Pili in the year 1000 A.D. but a great deal of human activity must have taken place in Samoa before that uncertain date.

Samoan myths contain some stories concerning the hero Maui. He occurs as Maui-ti'iti'i-a-talaga, which we recognize as the New Zealand form of the name. In Samoa, however, Talaga is the father, whereas in New Zealand Taraga is the mother. Maui obtained fire in the Underworld from Mafui'e but his exploits in fishing up islands were replaced by the stone-throwing activities of Tagaloa.

Turning to traditions, we find that there are no tales of long sea voyages. Percy Smith believed that the Polynesians reached Samoa in about 450 A.D. Whenever it was, the Samoans have been so long in residence that, like the Tahitians, the records of the first ancestors who came by ship have been overlaid by the mass of succeeding events. The theory

of a local origin from worms is a mythical substitute for forgotten human history.

In place of voyagers by canoe, there are myths of long-
distance swimming. An ancestor named Ui swam from the
Tokelau group to Tau, a distance of over 300 miles. I was
shown the rock that represented his petrified body. Two
women named Taema and Tilafaiga swam back to Samoa
from Fiji, where they were supposed to have observed the
Fijian custom of tattooing the women but not the men.
Owing to their long immersion in the sea, they landed in
Samoa shivering with cold and through chattering teeth they
delivered the following inverted message:

> When the men grow up, tattoo them.
> When the women grow up, let them bear children.

Before leaving the realm of myth and legend, let us turn
south to Tonga. The Tongan islands are composed of three
groups: Vavau in the north, Tongatabu in the south, and
Haapai between. Vavau has wooded hills rising to a height
of between 500 and 600 feet and a landlocked harbour studded with islets. Haapai consists of several low-lying islands
of which Lifuka is the most important. To the west of Haapai lie the volcanic cones of Kao and Tofua. Tongatabu, seat
of the government, is low, but Eua rises to over 1000 feet.

In 1912, my wife and I passed through the Tongan islands
on our way to Niue. At Tongatabu, the Prime Minister,
Tui Vakano, took me to call on King George Tubou II. He
was six feet eight inches tall and a magnificent type of the
Polynesian high chief. At Vavau, I met Tugi, the governor
of the island. He is now Prime Minister and the husband
of Queen Salote, who succeeded her father.

I had time to absorb only a little of the Tongan atmosphere. The Tongan dialect retains the consonants *k* and *h* that are absent from Samoan, but some words have the *s* sound. In some words *b* is used instead of *p*, as in tabu. The *j* is used to represent the sibilant *ch* sound before certain vowels. The modern field work in Tonga was conducted by E. W. Gifford and W. C. McKern, members of the Bayard Dominick Expedition sponsored by Bishop Museum. Useful information has also been supplied by the Reverend E. E. V. Collocott.

Tongan myths are contradictory, and I have made an arbitrary selection to provide an outline. Abandoning cosmogony and coming to the origin of the islands, we meet the Maui family of grandfather, son, and grandson in the persons of Maui-motua, Maui-atalaga, and Maui-kisikisi. The three came to Manuka (Manu'a) in Samoa to obtain a magic hook from Tonga-who-fished-up-lands. Tonga is a substitution for Tagaloa. Tonga, though he was averse to parting with his magic hook, could not avoid the custom of allowing visitors to view his hooks and of selecting one as a present. The hooks were all made of pearl shell but the magic hook, on account of its dull colour and poor lashing, was the least attractive in the collection. Tonga spread out his whole kit of hooks, confident that Maui-kisikisi would select the wrong hook.

Maui-kisikisi, however, with the cunning attributed to him throughout Polynesia, had made love to the fickle wife of Tonga. She secretly told him the appearance of the magic hook and hence she was named Whisper-in-Manuka. Maui unerringly selected the right hook and, with his grandfather, father, the woman, and the hook, voyaged forth and fished up the islands forming the Tongan group. The following verse, translated by Collocott, records the episode:

> The canoe that came from Manuka
> Was manned by a crew from the gods,
> Maui-atalaga, Maui-motua,
> Maui-kisikisi the wise.
> He brought the woman
> Known as Whisper-in-Manuka.
> He brought the wondrous hook,
> He came and drew up lands,
> And so Tonga and Eua were given (to mankind).

Other myths state that Maui also fished up Haapai, Vavau, and Naua. He stamped upon them and flattened out the fertile lands for cultivation.

An alternative theory of the creation of some of the islands follows the Samoan myth but substitutes the god Hikuleo for Tagaloa. Hikuleo dwelt in the west at Pulotu, but he seems to have visited the upper regions above Tonga, for the volcanic islands of Kao and Tofua were formed of 'land stones' thrown down by Hikuleo. The people of Vavau give credit for the fishing-up of their island to Tagaloa-lagi.

The heavens were arranged in ten stories. The first sky was so low that it touched the upper end of the stick with which Maui-motua spread out the heated stones of his cooking oven. Annoyed with the lowness of the ceiling, Maui-motua placed the lower end of his stick against the first sky and pushed it up out of the way. The charred end of the stick left marks on the sky. The myth is a western version of the tale of Ru-the-propper-up-of-the-sky.

The origin of the first human beings in Tonga follows the Samoan myth of local creation from worms that developed from a rotting vine. The descendants of the worms were Kohai (Who), Koau (I), and Momo (Crumb) names which indicate the gropings of the human mind for a beginning. Kohai was said to be the first king of Tonga.

As in Samoa, the Tagaloa family now enters the stage. Tagaloa Eitumatupua in the upper regions evinced an interest in mundane affairs. He descended to earth by an ironwood tree that had its roots on an islet in the lagoon of Tongatabu and its branches against the sky. He saw the woman Ilaheva fishing nearby and, as was the wont of gods in dealing with the daughters of men, he appropriated her. In due course, Ilaheva gave birth to a male child whom Tagaloa named Ahoeitu (Day-has-dawned).

When he grew up, the boy Ahoeitu asked his mother who his father was and where he lived. Following his mother's instructions, he ascended into the sky by the ironwood tree and found his father on a mound netting wild pigeons. The recognition was mutual and parental acceptance immediate. Ahoeitu was slain by his jealous half-brothers, sons of a celestial mother, but his father restored him to life. Tagaloa sent Ahoeitu back to earth to rule over the Tongan islands as the first Tui Tonga (high chief) of a new dynasty. The descendants of worms seem to have raised no opposition, and the dynasty of Kohai ceased to function. Ahoeitu was of divine origin through his father and of earthly descent through his mother. The dynasty he inaugurated in about 950 A.D. ruled for thirty-five generations to end with Laufilitoga in 1865.

In Tonga and Samoa we find a complete absence of the concept of creation that spread out from central Polynesia. Atea and Papa, as primary parents, are unknown. The major gods—Tane, Tu, and Rongo—are absent, and their brother Tagaloa, though present, is not the son of the Sky-father and the Earth-mother. He functions more as a mythical ancestor from whom chiefly rank was inherited than as a god who was worshipped as such. The origin of man from worms takes the place of the creation of the first woman from earth by the god Tane. Tiki, who is associated with the first created woman in the other parts of Polynesia, is absent in the west. In Samoa and Tonga, there were district gods and lesser family gods. There were no great national gods that presided over special departments, such as forest, sea, agriculture, peace, and war.

The Tongan god Hikuleo and the Samoan Si'uleo, unknown in the rest of Polynesia, dwelt at Pulotu in the west, whither the souls of the dead returned. The gods were represented by incarnations of living things and in the temples by inanimate objects. In Tonga, images were carved in wood; in Samoa, but one carved image is known. Stone images that form such a marked feature of the rest of Polynesia have not been recorded for the west.

The western temples were houses built on the same plan as dwelling houses set on a raised platform and surrounded by a fence. The paved stone marae with its raised stone platform is conspicuously absent. The Tongan and Samoan *malae* is the village green where purely social events were conducted. Long ritual chants and extended marae ceremonies were evidently unknown. People seeking benefit from the gods brought presents of food and goods before the house temple, where they sat on the ground while the priest took the material representative of the god out of its basket, unwrapped the bark-cloth covering, and exposed the shell, stone, or weapon to the faithful. In sickness the relatives sometimes cut off a finger joint as an offering, which may be an attenuated form of human sacrifice. The Samoans have been referred to as the 'godless Samoans', and, from the lack of awe-inspiring ritual, the statement has some justification.

Samoa and Tonga became centres for the development and distribution of a western Polynesian culture. Bishop Museum field expeditions to Uvea and Futuna were conducted by E. G. Burrows, to Tokelau by Gordon Macgregor, to Puka-puka by Ernest and Pearl Beaglehole, and to the Lau Islands of Fiji by Laura Thompson. The traditions and culture of these smaller islands indicate that after an early settlement they were influenced by incursions from Samoa or Tonga. The Tongans were the more daring sailors and maintained communications with their nearer colonies. Many of the Tongan voyages are related in connection with the Tui Tonga dynasty, whose line serves as a chronology of historical events. The Tui Tonga had double voyaging canoes built for their own use, and these were placed under the direction of expert pilots who were also expert fishermen. The crews were selected not only for their physique but for their skill in games and the use of weapons.

In the reign of Momo, the tenth Tui Tonga who lived at the end of the twelfth century, the invasion of Samoa was commenced by the Tongans. The occupation of Samoa continued until the reign of Talakaifaiki, the fifteenth Tui Tonga, when the Samoan chiefs Tuna and Fata defeated the Tongan forces. The Tongans withdrew to their ships in orderly fashion while the Samoans watched the great war canoes hoist sail to depart. The double canoe of Talakaifaiki was the last to leave and, as it began to move, the Tongan leader, standing in the stern of his ship, shouted his meed of appreciation to his valiant opponents across the widening waters: 'Malie tau, malie toa' (Clean fight, brave warrior). The descendants of Tuna and Fata, who rule the district of Tuamasaga, assumed the title of Malie-toa from the above incident.

A voyage that intrigues the imagination is that of Kauulu-fonua to avenge the murder of his father Takalaua, the twenty-third Tui Tonga, who lived about the year 1450 A.D. He and his younger brothers followed the two murderers to Haapai, Vavau, Niuatobutabu, Niuafou, Futuna, and Uvea, where they captured them and brought them back to Tonga to be executed. Kauulufonua, a warrior as well as a king, went into a battle, leaving his back to be protected by the gods while he defended his front. He was wounded in the back and shouted above the stress of battle, 'The gods are fools'.

Society was based on the general Polynesian system of rule by chiefs whose titles were hereditary in the male line. The people were grouped in families (*aiga*) allied in villages and districts. The chiefs were graded according to power over family groups, villages, and districts. Matters of importance were settled in councils (*fono*) and, as etiquette and procedure grew more complicated, the high chiefs delegated their administrative powers to lesser chiefs termed talking chiefs or orators. In Tonga, the Tui Tonga dynasty created the Tui Haa Takalaua title for a junior member of the family to conduct administrative functions. Later the Tui Haa Takalaua established the Tui Kanakupolu title for a younger brother to carry on administrative work. In the course of time, the Tui Kanakupolu absorbed the two senior titles but the power was retained by high chiefs.

In Tonga, the *fono* (council) was called together in order that the talking chiefs might announce the policy of the high chiefs. In Samoa, the talking chiefs attained such power that in the *fono* they practically dictated their policy to their superior chiefs. They influenced the succession of titles so that it was awarded to the son of the wife whose family group would give the talking chiefs the greatest reward in food and goods. In Samoa, the party in power was termed the *pule* (rule) and the party in opposition, the *mau*. In western Samoa today the government officials are termed the *pule*, and part of the native population opposed to the government forms the *mau*. The high chiefs of the rest of Polynesia, though they had orators and councillors, never allowed administrative powers to get out of their own hands.

An important social element in Samoa was the guest house. The architecture of the house is unique in that the roof has a convex curve from the ridgepole to the eaves and has rounded ends. The curve is produced by using pliable rafters and strutting them with a series of transverse beams to maintain the curve. The rounded ends are formed of oblique arches composed of short curved sections of wood fitted with locking joints. The status of a chief was indicated by the number of cross beams in his guest house. The higher the rank, the greater the number of beams and consequently the greater the height of the house and the greater the number of arches in the rounded ends. The walls were open in Samoa but the wall posts were important socially, for they formed backrests for both hosts and guests who were assigned to the posts which distinguished their rank. Feasts preceded by the kava drinking ceremony usually took place within the guest house, and all ranking chiefs had to have guest houses to maintain their dignity.

The guest houses were built by expert carpenters united in a guild, which had a mythical origin from a conference convened by the god Tagaloa to discuss how a house should be constructed. The assembled carpenters built the first house in the upper realms and afterward repeated the pattern on earth in Manu'a. The guild of builders which subsequently developed called themselves the Sa-Tagaloa (Family-of-Tagaloa). The guild formed societies in different islands and the societies in turn claimed origin from some charter member who had attended the first conference. My studies of the Samoan house were conducted under the auspices of the Aiga-sa-Sao (Family-of-Sao) of Manu'a. I was invited to ascend the scaffolding and watch the ridgepole being lashed in position with sennit braid in the elaborate pattern termed *le sumu o le 'au'au*. I was able to study houses in various stages of construction and to attend social functions connected with their construction. I received detailed instructions from master craftsmen, not only of the Family-of-Sao but also of the Family-of-Malama on Tutuila. It was Malama who advised Tagaloa that the appropriate timber for a chief's house was breadfruit wood. Hence it is that a child of chiefly descent may shame a commoner by saying, 'Have you lived in a house made of breadfruit wood?'

Owing to the social necessity for a guest house that could be built only by expert carpenters, the Family-of-Tagaloa acquired great power. They organized a trade union and formulated the terms of contract. They demanded good food with fowl and pork at frequent intervals. They drank only kava and the liquid contents of coconuts during the hours of work and required constant attention from the family of the owner. Feasts with a liberal distribution of food took place at certain stages of construction. On the completion of the framework, the builders were given a feast and paid with fine mats, goods, and food. During building, if the standard of food fell off or some breach of etiquette was committed by the owner's family, the carpenters returned to their homes. Because of the trade union, no other carpenters would complete the house. Food supplies frequently gave out when the middle section and one rounded end of the house framework had been completed. The house owner made the best of a bad job by completing the thatching of the roof and closing the uncompleted end with thatch. The family went into residence until more food and goods were accumulated to re-employ the original carpenters. An incomplete house was termed a *fale tala mutu*, a house with a cut-off end. When walking through a village in Olosega with a master carpenter, I noticed a number of houses with but one rounded end. Turning to my companion, I asked, 'Did all the pigs die out in Olosega?' He looked at me in a somewhat embarrassed manner and then laughed so heartily that I required no verbal reply.

The guild of carpenters also made the better types of canoe. Specialization took place in adzing the planks to form projecting inner flanges along the edges. After the planks were fitted together, holes were bored through the inner flanges, and the lashings that were passed through them did not show on the outside of the hull. Elsewhere the lashings passed through holes pierced through the full thickness of the planks and thus showed on the outside of the hull. A triangular matting sail was used with the lateen rig in which the apex of the triangle was down at the bow. This rig contrasts with the triangular spritsail with its apex at the foot of the mast, such as was used elsewhere in Polynesia with the exception of Mangareva.

The Tongans specialized in stonework and made tombs for their kings. Some of the coral limestone blocks were quarried on near-by islands and transported across the water by double canoes. Telea, the twenty-ninth Tui Tonga, built the finest of the royal tombs in three tiers, and two of the four corners were unique in having L-shaped corner stones.

The famous trilithon in Tongatabu consists of two large uprights of coral limestone with a crossbar of the same material mortised in to their upper ends. The larger upright is 17 feet above ground, 14 feet wide at the base, 12 feet wide at the top, and 4½ feet thick. The uprights are 12½ feet apart and McKern, who gives the above measurements, estimates that the visible portions of each weigh between 30 and 40 tons. The material was cut from a cliff face near the site. The worked blocks were dragged over skids up an inclined earth ramp and lowered into position. The trilithon was named Haamonga-a-Maui (Burden-of-Maui), the two uprights being likened to burdens supported on the ends of a carrying pole. It was built by Tuitatui, eleventh Tui Tonga, as a monument to his two sons. The form and size of the memorial are so unique that imaginative writers have advanced the theory that it was made by some archaic civilization that preceded the Tongans.

Another item in which the west differed from the rest of Polynesia was in the great importance given to kava, a beverage prepared from the root of the *Piper methysticum*. In Samoa and Tonga, no social event could take place without the preliminary serving of kava. The kava was served to chiefs from one bowl in their order of precedence with an elaborate ceremony that is absent elsewhere. Special round bowls with legs were made for the sole purpose of preparing kava. Every bowl has a suspensory lug on its outer surface below the rim, and this lug was always turned toward the person preparing the kava, except in the kava ceremony of the great Tui Tonga who enjoyed the royal privilege of having the suspensory lug turned toward him.

The following incident illustrates the method of indirection dearly loved by the Polynesians. After the death of the last Tui Tonga, two of the greatest supporting chiefs of the Tui Tonga dynasty came to George Tubou, who had been gathering the reins of temporal power into his hands, and informed him that they wished to make kava for him. They conducted him into the guest house and, seating themselves behind the kava bowl, proceeded to prepare the kava. George Tubou sat down opposite and waited. He looked casually across at his companions and saw what to a Tongan must have been a soul-stirring sight. The suspensory lug of the bowl was pointing toward him. The chiefs had not spoken, but the speechless bowl was announcing a king.

In the process of making cloth from the bark of the paper mulberry, the west differs from the rest of Polynesia. In the western area, the individual strips of bark were well scraped with shells, beaten into separate pieces of thin cloth, and pasted together to obtain the desired thickness and size. Designs were sometimes painted in freehand with vegetable dyes, but generally layers of thin cloth were placed over a tablet design, and the cloth was rubbed with a wiper dipped in dye to bring out the design on the underlying tablet. In the rest of Polynesia, the bark was washed instead of being scraped, soaked in water for over twenty hours, and the various strips were felted together in a continuous sheet by beating with grooved beaters which left a watermark on the cloth. The cloth was painted freehand or stamped with a design.

All Polynesia used a calendar of lunar months. Except in the western area, each island group had a list of thirty names for various stages of the moon from new moon to new moon. When a lunar month had only twenty-nine nights, one of the thirty names was dropped. Though a few local changes took place with regard to names, the similarity of the system is striking on all seven trails from central Polynesia, and its complete absence in the west is all the more remarkable. There the days of the month were counted numerically, sometimes in groups. In the rest of Polynesia, the New Year was ushered in by the morning or evening rising of the Pleiades, and the annual lunar cycle was corrected at intervals by intercalating a thirteenth month. No definite information exists as to how the calendar was corrected in the west.

Two social customs that prevail in Samoa and Tonga are not present in the rest of Polynesia. One is the brother-and-sister taboo which includes cousins bearing the same relationship term as brother and sister. After ten years of age, brothers and sisters were brought up in different houses and they ceased to play together. If one was in a house, the other might not enter or, at least, might not sit near by. This custom is incomprehensible elsewhere in Polynesia. In New Zealand, the marriage of cousins was encouraged to keep domestic conflicts within the family. In Hawai'i brother-and-sister marriage was regarded as the highest form of chiefly alliance.

The other custom was the great respect paid by men to their sisters, particularly their elder sisters. In Tonga, the sister was regarded as superior in rank to the brother, and this superiority was shared by her children. In Samoa, the sister's children were sacred (*tama sa*) to their uncle's family, and they were feared because it was believed that their mother possessed magic powers that she would use if her children were offended. In Tonga, the sister's children were *fahu* to their uncle and his children, and the term meant that they could demand food and goods from them. A male *fahu* could appropriate even his uncle's wife. This custom contradicts the general Polynesian pattern of descent and prestige on the male line.

The differences between western and eastern Polynesia may be attributed to three causes: local development, diffusion from Fiji, and early separation from central Polynesia.

Local development affected the arts and crafts, such as the building of houses and canoes and the making of bark cloth. Local variation is evident throughout Polynesia, which indicates that craftsmen and artists were not entirely inhibited by older patterns of technique. The Tagaloa guild of carpenters received inspiration from within and gave the credit to the god Tagaloa.

Diffusion from Fiji was responsible for the brother-and-sister taboo, widespread throughout Melanesia, and the power of the sister's children. This power is present in Fiji as the *vasu* custom, and it is evident that the Tongans adopted not only the custom but also the term under the Tongan form of *fahu*. The Fijian *vasu* is based on the Melanesian system of descent through the mother. The husband is practically a guest in his wife's household, and his children are provided for by his wife's brother. The husband, in turn, provides for his own sister's children. Such a system is as strange to the rest of Polynesia as it is to Europe and America. Intercourse with Fiji is also responsible for certain relationship terms particularly affecting relationship by marriage, and probably accounts for the social importance of kava. In material things, Fijian influence is seen in some of the head rests and weapons. James Hornell has pointed out that both Tongans and Samoans adopted the Fijian form of double canoe though in comparatively recent times. In the realm of myth, the Fijians provided the souls of the dead with a resting place at Pulotu, called Bulotu in Fiji and unknown in central and eastern Polynesia.

Early separation between the west and the centre accounts for differences in myth and religion. The widely spread Maui myth may be associated with the 'descendants of worms' or the pre-Tagaloans. An early communication between Samoa and Ra'iatea must have existed to account for the spread of food plants and domestic animals with which we shall deal in the next chapter. The voyagers who came west to Samoa were evidently descendants of a deified Tagaloa to whom they attributed the creation of the Samoan islands. The Tagaloa group that remained in Ra'iatea had to compromise with other groups by including their deified ancestors in a richer pantheon. At a later period in Ra'iatea, the supporters of Ta'aroa (Tagaloa) became influential enough to raise him to the position of a supreme deity but with a wealth of detail that is absent in Samoa. The Samoan Tagaloa and the Ra'iatean Ta'aroa have little in common beyond the name and the general idea of creation. Communication between the west and the centre must have ceased before the social assembly place termed *marae* was given a religious significance and before the priests at Opoa had systematized the theology of the Sky-father and Earth-mother, and of Tane, Tu, Rongo, and Tangaroa as departmental gods. Thus in Samoa and Tonga the *malae* remained the secular village green, but in Ra'iatea the *marae* evolved into a sacred assembly place where men sought communion with powerful gods that were unknown in the western pantheon.

It may be argued that Tagaloa could have travelled east to the centre with the plants and animals, but my belief is that he accompanied the other great voyaging ancestors direct from Micronesia to central Polynesia. If the volcanic islands of Samoa and their great resources had been the first encountered after the long passage through atoll islands, they would have been the main centre of the development of Polynesian culture. The religious seminary of Opoa would have been in Samoa had the gods come that way.

21. THE TRAIL OF PLANTS AND ANIMALS

*Plant my head and from it will grow a
tree whose fruit will remind you of me.*

SAMOAN MYTH OF TUNA

TUNA, the eel lover of Sina, was killed by jealous suitors,
but at his last meeting he had told Sina of his impending
fate. He commanded her to cut off his head after he was
slain and to plant it. From his head would grow a tree
with a fruit that would furnish her with both meat and
drink. On the fruit itself she would see the two eyes that
had adored her and the mouth that had spoken tender words
of love. So it came to pass that Sina planted the head of
Tuna and from it grew the coconut palm.

The myth is found throughout Polynesia, and outside of
Samoa the dialectical form of Hina replaces Sina. Even
now, the Polynesian who husks a drinking nut for a stranger,
delights to point out the eyes and mouth of Tuna represented
by three depressions on the top of the shell. The mouth
depression is the only one that pierces the full thickness of
the shell, and it is closed with soft material. It is through the
mouth of Tuna that the shoot passes to the outside of the
nut to grow into a tree to provide food and drink for the
descendants of Sina.

Myths add a halo of romance to the origin of food plants which played such an important part in the economic life of the Polynesians. The ethnologist, however, cannot rely on myths as indicating a local origin for plants. He must consult the botanists who have studied the origins and spread of food plants into Polynesia.

The plants that were present in Polynesia when man arrived offered little in the way of food. On volcanic islands there were certain berries, roots, the pith of the tree fern, the curling young shoots of ferns, the growing ends and stems of creeping plants, and seaweed. All edible plants have been used on various islands during famines in recent times, and were certainly eaten by the earliest settlers before other plants were introduced. On atolls, the only edible plants were purslane (*Portulaca* sp.) roots of the *Boerhaavia*, and seaweed, and perhaps the pandanus on the islands to which pandanus seeds may have preceded man. Pandanus, which grows luxuriantly on atolls as well as on volcanic islands, has a large fruit divided into keys like a pineapple. The fleshy basal part of the keys forms a nourishing food, and the outer, hard part contains seeds in a watertight compartment. When dry the keys are light and could be conveyed long distances by ocean currents to become established on islands without the aid of man. Professor St. John, botanist at Bishop Museum, informed me that there are scores of species or varieties of pandanus on the various tropical islands of the Pacific. Most of them occur on only one or a few islands, but a very few of them are widely distributed. Hence the genus must have spread so long ago that many local species have had time to develop. The pandanus doubtless invaded the Pacific long before the Polynesians, though these people certainly carried the cultivated, long-leaved varieties with them and established them on many island groups. The pandanus was of the greatest economic value' to the Polynesians not only for the fruit as food but for the leaves to make baskets, mats, and sails, and to thatch houses.

The important fruit-bearing trees present in Polynesia on first European contact were the coconut, breadfruit, banana, and plantain. The main tuberous plants were the taro, yam, arrowroot, turmeric, and sweet potato. Of other plants useful to man, I shall mention only the paper mulberry used for the making of bark cloth and the small gourd (*Laginaria vulgaris*) used for containers. The botanists tell us that all these plants, with the exception of the sweet potato, originated in the Indo-Malayan region. They were all established in Polynesia before Columbus discovered America, and hence could not have been introduced by later Spanish vessels. The journey of the plants from Indonesia to Polynesia is clothed with as much romance as that of the Polynesian voyagers.

There is divided opinion among botanists as to the original home of the coconut palm. Some believe that it was America; others maintain that it was Asia, and the latter seem to have the best of the argument. Though the dry, mature coconut will float until waterlogged and must have been carried to islands by currents and storms, there is a doubt as to how long the living embryo within the nut can survive. There is a possibility that coconuts drifted to near-by islands and rooted, but there is little or no evidence to indicate that coconuts have floated to and established themselves on remote islands. The spread of the coconut throughout Polynesia must be attributed to man. Indeed, all the food plants and the paper mulberry were undoubtedly introduced by man.

However, the transference of plants from one island to another was more difficult than that of the human beings in whose voyaging canoes the plants were carried. Man was captain of his soul and carried food and water to sustain his creature wants. The plants were helpless passengers with a varying resistance to sun, wind, and salt water. On arrival at an island, whether coral or volcanic, man could adjust himself to his environment, but the plants that survived the voyage could grow only in soil that suited their particular needs.

The only introduced plants that will grow on atoll islands are the coconut and a coarse variety of taro which was grown in trenches dug down to the subsoil brackish water. Fine varieties of taro require volcanic soil. Another atoll plant used occasionally for food was the *noni* (*Morinda citrifolia*), and it may have been aided by man in its diffusion. All other cultivable food plants require volcanic soil, and hence could not possibly travel into Polynesia along an atoll-studded route. The Micronesian route, therefore, would not be taken by the plants, for the volcanic islands end at Kusaie, or at most at Banaba and Nauru Islands. The distance from Kusaie in the Carolines to Ra'iatea in the Society Islands is over 3000 miles and to Samoa about 2500 miles. The intervening atolls were peopled gradually over a long period of time during which only the coconut, coarse taro, pandanus, and *noni* could have been relayed from atoll to atoll to central Polynesia.

The other food plants had to advance eastward into the Pacific by a route on which volcanic islands formed growing stations that were within voyaging distance of each other. Such a passage is afforded by the southern route through Melanesia. I am not an ethnobotanist, but I feel that, though the Polynesians travelled into central Polynesia by the Micronesian route, such important food plants as the breadfruit, banana, yam, and finer taro were carried from Indonesia to

New Guinea and relayed by Melanesians to their eastern outpost at Fiji.

The earliest scouting parties of the Polynesians who came direct from Micronesia to Ra'iatea in the centre, Hawai'i in the north, and Samoa on the base of the triangle, could have carried only the coconut, pandanus, *noni*, and the coarse taro. On Oahu in Hawai'i, there is a deep, wide trench at Kualoa so ancient that there is no Hawaiian explanation as to its purpose. Things that cannot be explained by the later culture usually belong to an earlier culture that has ceased to function so far back in time that they remain a mystery. May it not be that the deep excavation down to subsoil water is a witness of the coarse taro cultivation brought by the earliest settlers direct from atolls and abandoned when the better varieties of taro reached Hawai'i at a later date?

The richer food plants which reached Fiji had to be relayed to central Polynesia through volcanic islands. The first relaying station in western Polynesia was provided by Samoa or Tonga. Gifford has pointed out, however, that the Tongan myths regarding the origin of plants associate them with Samoa, the skies and Pulotu, vaguely situated beyond Samoa. The first stage of the passage of plants from Fiji to Polynesia thus centres on Samoa.

The breadfruit that came into Polynesia was seedless and could be propagated only from young shoots that sprang up from the spreading roots of growing trees. Similarly the banana was grown from shoots that grew up around the base of the parent trunk. Neither of these plants could cross sea channels unless they were carried by man. As they could not be used for sea provisions, it may be accepted that the presence of the breadfruit and banana prove definitely that the plants were carefully brought by people who were seeking to settle on a volcanic island. Handy collected a Marquesan tradition concerning an expedition which set out for Rarotonga with a ship loaded with young breadfruit plants. The taro and the yam were grown from tubers and had no seed mechanism by which they could fly by air or float by sea. Hence we repeat that the plants could reach Samoa from Fiji only by canoe.

Human contact between Fiji and Samoa must have commenced at a very early period. Probably the vanguard that dropped south from the Gilberts also reached some of the Fijian islands. These early scouting parties were daring and courageous, and they must have handled such vessels as they had with consummate skill. The Fijians had good double canoes which they handled skilfully within the confines of their own archipelago. They did not go east, however, except on later, occasional voyages after Samoa had been peopled by Polynesians. Had the food plants been brought eastward by Fijians, Samoa would have been a Melanesian colony.

From Samoa, the plants were carried to the Polynesian centre of distribution at Ra'iatea and Tahiti, also at a very early period. Both the introduced plants and animals were a necessary factor in the great social development that took place in the centre. Communication between Samoa and Ra'iatea ended before the priests at Opoa had elected the various deified ancestors to a common pantheon, and hence Tagaloa-lagi carried a restricted mythology to Samoa.

Forest B. H. Brown found so many varieties of breadfruit in the Marquesas that he was led to the conclusion that the groups must have been inhabited for a very long time to allow such a number to develop. Similarly there are many varieties of sweet potato in Hawai'i. Either varieties develop quickly in tropical islands or Polynesia has been inhabited for a longer time than we think. A variety of sweet potato and one of taro flower and seed in Hawai'i, and one variety of breadfruit in Tahiti has seeds. Were the present seedless varieties developed from early plants that seeded, and were the first plants carried by means of seeds? It is a problem for the ethnobotanist.

Associated with the food plants are the domesticated animals. Here again the zoologists tell us that the pig, dog, and fowl found in Polynesia had their home in the Indo-Malayan area. The animals reached America via the Atlantic long after they had found their way into Polynesia. It is significant that none of these three animals was found on coral atolls in Polynesia when first visited by Europeans. There is a Tuamotuan version of the origin of the dog, but this comes from Anaa, which had frequent communication with Tahiti. We must remember that the coconut was carried along by the early settlers and until the plants became established in quantity there was little food on an atoll for pigs and fowls. Dogs could have subsisted on fish or become vegetarians, but their chances of surviving times of drought or famine were small, especially as they could be eaten by their owners. The animals now found on atolls were introduced in post-European times when the coconut trees were numerous and trading schooners brought food from the outside world. Coral atolls thus formed a barrier to the spread of domesticated animals. They must have been relayed along the Melanesian route and passed from Fiji to Samoa.

A Samoan legend has a bearing on the transport of the pig. A Samoan voyager visited Fiji and was feasted on pork. He naturally desired to take pigs back with him to his own country. The Fijians, however, refused to allow any live pigs to leave their shores, but they raised no objection to dead pigs being taken as food for the voyage. The Samoans thereupon procured two very large pigs which they killed and dressed. Unknown to their hosts, they stole some young ones and concealed them in the abdominal cavities of the dressed animals which they covered with leaves. Carrying the dead pigs on poles, they successfully eluded the vigilance of the Fijian customs officers, and so pigs were introduced to Samoa.

The importance of Fiji as a trade centre cannot be over-estimated. The western triangle of Samoa, Tonga, and Fiji became an important area for exchange and diffusion. Commercial relationships were favoured by intermarriage, and Fijian customs that were of use to the Polynesians were readily adopted. Intermixture took place between chiefly families and as a result a higher Fijian culture that absorbed certain Polynesian elements was developed at the places of contact. This mixed culture was marked by patrilineal descent, powerful chiefs, and much elaborate ceremony which contrasted with the earlier Melanesian culture retained in those parts of Fiji that did not come under Polynesian trade influence. The Samoans and Tongans incorporated some of the Fijian customs such as the power of the mother's brother and brother-sister avoidance into their own culture. The business methods acquired in dealing with Fijians affected the psychology of the western Polynesians, for cloak it with ceremony as they may, they have a keenness to acquire goods and a hard commercial instinct that is absent in the rest of Polynesia. The cultural changes that took place in the western triangle were initiated primarily by exchange and barter for food plants and domesticated animals. Communication was continued, for both Samoans and Tongans desired red feathers from Fijian parrots to adorn their fine mats and ornaments, and the Tongans required big timber for their canoes and sandalwood to burn as incense to their dead.

The plants and animals were carried to central Polynesia, but the Fijian customs remained in the west. From the centre, the plants and animals and the polytheistic mythology were carried along the various radials by the later voyagers of the tenth to the fourteenth century. On the northern route, all the plants and animals reached Hawai'i. To the northeast, all except the dog reached the Marquesas. From the Marquesas, all the plants arrived at Mangareva, but the fowl dropped out and only the pig gained temporary foothold. In far-off Easter Island, the coconut and breadfruit are lacking and of three animals only the fowl survived. South and southeast, the Australs had all the plants and all three animals, but in southerly Rapa, the breadfruit would not grow, the coconut did not bear, and the animals were absent. Southwest in the Cook Islands, all the plants are present. The animals, however, have a varied distribution, for the pig, though important in Rarotonga, Atiu, Mauke, and Mitiaro, was absent in Aitutaki and Mangaia. I am not sure of the distribution of the dog and the fowl in the Cook Islands. In New Zealand in the south, the taro, yam, and small gourd obtained a footing, but of the three animals only the dog was present at the time of first European contact.

The paper mulberry reached all the volcanic islands including Hawai'i, Easter Island, and New Zealand. The spread of plants and animals to all parts of Polynesia indicates clearly that though the earliest scouting parties may have reached islands by lucky chance, there was a later period extending from the tenth century when voyages of exploration were made and followed up by deliberate voyages to settle the lands discovered. Apart from legendary evidence, it does not seem logical that people would carry the tender shoots of breadfruit and banana over 2000 miles to Hawai'i and banana shoots over 1000 miles to Easter Island unless they had some idea of where they were going.

A problem is caused by the presence in Hawai'i of a large calabash apparently not found in other parts of Polynesia. From its size it formed an excellent container (*ipu nui*) for carrying clothing, and it was also used for storing quantities of pounded taro. Botanists termed the plant *Cucurbita maxima* and placed it in the pumpkin group, which differs from that of the smaller gourd (*Lagenaria vulgaris*) widespread throughout Polynesia. The original home of pumpkins, squashes, marrows, and melons is in America. The question is, how did the large gourd get to Hawai'i? It could not have come in with the sweet potato for then it would be found in other parts of Polynesia. Hawaiian informants state that the large gourd was also called *hulilau* and that its leaves and flowers could not be distinguished from those of the other gourds, of which a number of varieties served different purposes. There is a possibility that the large gourd has been wrongly placed with the pumpkins and that it may belong to the true group of Lagenaria. If so, the problem is clarified for it could have come as an ordinary gourd from central Polynesia and have been developed into a large variety in Hawai'i.

Let us now consider the sweet potato (*Ipomœa batatas*) which entered Polynesia from the east and not from Asia. Botanists have determined the original home of the sweet potato as South America. The theory of a German scientist that it was introduced into Polynesia by Spaniards is based on inaccurate data and is untenable. From traditional history we learn that the sweet potato was in Hawai'i by 1250 A.D. and in New Zealand by 1350 A.D. at the latest. As there are no traditions of later contact with the outside world, it is evident that the Polynesians themselves carried the sweet potato from central Polynesia to the northern and southern angles of the Polynesian triangle. Hence the sweet potato had reached the Society Islands before the final Polynesian voyages were made to the north and the southwest.

The late Professor Roland B. Dixon was convinced that the sweet potato was in Polynesia before Columbus reached America and that the claims that the Spanish distributed the plant were untenable. He says, 'The plant could only have reached Polynesia from America by the aid of human hands, and since we have no evidence that at any time the Indians of the Pacific Coast of South America, where the sweet potato was grown, had either the craft or the skill for making long sea journeys, we are forced to conclude that the transference of the plant was carried out by Polynesians. At some time a party of these intrepid sailors must have reached the Peruvian coast, and have taken this valuable plant back with them to their island home.'

The Peruvian coast is specified because in the Kechua dialect of north Peru the name for the sweet potato is *kumar*. As the general Polynesian name for the plant is *kumara*, the tuber must have been obtained from an era that used the name *kumar*.

Some time before the thirteenth century an unknown Polynesian voyager sailed east in search of a new land. Though Easter Island is the nearest Polynesian island to America and the distance of 2030 miles well within the accepted compass of a Polynesian voyaging canoe, no expedition could have been inaugurated from that island because of the lack of timber to build a suitable canoe. It is also improbable that Easter Island was used as port of call, because any voyager who had come over a thousand miles from the nearest land in eastern Polynesia would have settled there and not gone on. I believe that the expedition hoped to find land within fair distance of their place of departure and that, because of the empty eastern sea, they were forced to go on until they reached the South American coast.

The nearest islands from which the expedition could have set out are Mangareva and the Marquesas. The Tuamotu atolls are eliminated, because there is a possibility that the seeds of the gourd (*Lagenaria vulgaris*) were introduced into South America from Polynesia in pre-Columbian times; and such gourds do not grow on the Tuamotu. An expedition from Mangareva is likely to have encountered Easter Island and stayed there. But, even if a canoe had gone on from Easter Island, the probability is that it would have touched the American coast south of Peru where the sweet potato name of *kumar* was unknown. The clear open sea between the Marquesas and north Peru offered no interruption, and hence we will assume that the expedition set out from the Marquesas.

The distance from the Marquesas to the north Peruvian coast is just over 4000 miles. Dixon estimates that the voyaging range of a Polynesian ship was 2500 miles, but this estimate was based on the voyages accomplished within Polynesia. Allowing a canoe with a favourable wind a speed of seven miles an hour, the voyaging from the Marquesas would have taken a little over three weeks, which is not too long a period for sturdy men to endure. The voyage was exceptional and probably was made only once. Had the leader of the expedition suspected that the distance to the nearest land toward the east was so great, he probably would have waited until the westerly winds were over and then sailed in a different direction.

I will not attempt to interpret the feelings of the voyagers as they sailed day after day without sighting land. When hope ebbed, a huge land with mountains piercing the sky loomed up over the horizon. What a sight it must have been to people accustomed to oceanic islands! They landed but had to go warily among a strange people. Fearing a conflict against larger numbers, they decided to return to the homeland in Polynesia.

Contact was too short to make any lasting exchange in religious or social ideas. Of material things the Polynesians may have passed on the seeds of the gourd, and they certainly received the sweet potato.

The Polynesian commander refitted and provisioned his ship. He laid aboard a supply of the new tubers, and, when the winds were favourable, he sailed for his homeland in the west. The gods were good as evidenced by the arrival of the sweet potato in Polynesia. From whatever part of Polynesia he may have left, he evidently arrived on his return at the Marquesas, where his plants grew. Later they were carried eastward to Mangareva and Easter Island and westward to the Society Islands in the centre.

The unknown Polynesian voyager who brought back the sweet potato from South America, made the greatest individual contribution to the records of the Polynesians. He completed the series of voyages across the widest part of the great Pacific Ocean between Asia and South America. Tradition is strangely silent. We know not his name or the name of his ship, but the unknown hero ranks among the greatest of the Polynesian navigators for he it was who completed the great adventure.

EPILOGUE

The old net is laid aside;
A new net goes afishing.

MAORI PROVERB

THE old world created by our Polynesian ancestors has passed away, and a new world is in the process of being fashioned. The stone temples have been destroyed and the temple drums and shell trumpets have long been silent. Tane, Tu, Rongo, Tangaroa and the other members of the divine family of the Sky-father and the Earth-mother have left us. The great voyaging canoes have crumbled to dust, and the sea captains and the expert craftsmen have passed away to the Spirit-land. The regalia and symbols of spiritual and temporal power have been scattered among the museums of other peoples. The glory of the Stone Age has departed out of Polynesia.

The old net is full of holes, its meshes have rotted, and it has been laid aside.

WHAT NEW NET GOES AFISHING?

325

BIBLIOGRAPHY

CHAPTER 1
Gregory, H. E.: *Geography of the Pacific*, in *Problems of the Pacific*. Proc. 2nd Conf. I.P.R. Honolulu 1927, Chicago 1928.
Jones, Frederic Wood: *Australia's vanishing race*. Sydney 1934.

CHAPTER 2
Buck, P. H.: *Maori somatology: racial averages*. Jour Polynesian Soc., Vols 31-32, 1922, 1923.
Shapiro, H. L.: *Physical characters of the Society Islanders; based on field records by E. S. C. Handy and W. C. Handy*. B. P. Bishop Mus Mem., Vol. XI, No. 4, Honolulu 1930.
Shapiro, H. L., and Buck, P. H.: *Physical characters of the Cook Islanders*. B. P. Bishop Mus., Mem., Vol. XII, No. 1, Honolulu 1936.
Sullivan, L. R., *Contribution to Samoan somatology; based on field studies of E. W. Gifford and W. C. McKern*. B. P. Bishop Mus., Mem., Vol. VIII, No. 2, Honolulu 1921.
Sullivan, L. R., *Tongan somatology; based on field studies of E. W. Gifford and W. C. McKern*. B. P. Bishop Mus., Mem., Vol. VIII, No. 4, Honolulu 1922.
Sullivan, L. R.: *Marquesan somatology: with comparative notes on Samoa and Tonga; based on field studies of E. S. C. Handy*. B. P. Bishop Mus., Mem., Vol. IX, No. 2, Honolulu 1923.
Sullivan, L. R.: *Observations on Hawaiian somatology*. B. P. Bishop Mus., Mem., Vol. IX, No. 4, Honolulu 1927.

CHAPTER 3
Fornander, Abraham: *A Account of the Polynesian race: its origin and migration and the ancient history of the Hawaiian people to the time of Kamehameha I*. Three volumes, London 1878, 1880, 1885.
Smith, S. Percy: *Hawaiki: the original home of the Maori*. Fourth ed., New Zealand 1921.

CHAPTER 4
Hornell, James: *Canoes of Oceania*. Vol. I, *Canoes of Polynesia, Fiji, and Micronesia*. B. P. Bishop Mus., Spec. Pub. 27, Honolulu 1936.

CHAPTER 5
Haddon, A. C.: *Canoes of Oceania*. Vol. 2, *Canoes of Melanesia, Queensland, and New Guinea*. B. P. Bishop Mus., Spec. Pub. 28, Honolulu 1937.

327

CHAPTERS 7, 8

Emory, K. P.: *Stone remains in the Society Islands*. B. P. Bishop Mus., Bull. 116, Honolulu 1933.

Handy, E. S. C.: *History and culture in the Society Islands*. B. P. Bishop Mus., Bull 79, Honolulu 1931.

Handy, E. S. C.: *Houses, boats, and fishing in the Society Islands*. B. P. Bishop Mus., Bull. 90, Honolulu 1932.

Handy, W. C.: *Handicrafts of the Society Islands*. B. P. Bishop Mus., Bull. 42, Honolulu 1927.

Henry, Teuira: *Ancient Tahiti*. B. P. Bishop Mus., Bull. 48, Honolulu 1928.

CHAPTER 9

Buck, P. H.: *Material culture of the Cook Islands (Aitutaki)*. Board of Maori Ethnol. Research, Mem., Vol. 1, New Plymouth 1927.

Buck, P. H.: *Mangaian Society*. B. P. Bishop Mus., Bull. 122, Honolulu 1934.

CHAPTER 10

Buck, P. H.: *Ethnology of Tongareva*. B. P. Bishop Mus., Bull. 92, Honolulu 1932.

Buck, P. H.: *Ethnology of Manihiki and Rakahanga*. B. P. Bishop Mus., Bull. 99, Honolulu 1932.

CHAPTER 11

Emory, K. P.: *Archæology of the Pacific Equatorial Islands*. B. P. Bishop Mus., Bull. 123, Honolulu 1934.

CHAPTER 12

Handy, E. S. C.: *Native culture in the Marquesas*. B. P. Bishop Mus., Bull. 9, Honolulu 1923. (Out of print.)

Handy, E. S. C.: *Marquesan legends*. B. P. Bishop Mus., Bull. 69, Honolulu 1930.

Handy, W. C.: *Tattooing in the Marquesas*. B. P. Bishop Mus., Bull. 1, Honolulu 1923. (Out of print.)

Linton, Ralph: *Material culture of the Marquesas Islands*. B. P. Bishop Mus., Mem., Vol. VIII, No. 5, Honolulu 1923.

Linton, Ralph: *Archæology of the Marquesas Islands*. B. P. Bishop Mus., Bull. 23, Honolulu 1925.

CHAPTER 13

Aitken, R. T.: *Ethnology of Tubuai*. B. P. Bishop Mus., Bull. 70, Honolulu 1930.

Stokes, J. F. G.: *Ethnology of Rapa*. B. P. Bishop Mus. (Ms.).

CHAPTER 14

Emory, K. P.: *Tuamotuan stone structures*. B. P. Bishop Mus., Bull. 118, Honolulu 1934.

Stimson, J. F.: *Tuamotuan religion*. B. P. Bishop Mus., Bull. 103, Honolulu 1933.

Stimson, J. F.: *Legends of Maui and Tahaki*. B. P. Bishop Mus., Bull 127, Honolulu 1934.

Stimson, J. F.: *Tuamotuan legends*. Part 1, *The demigods*. B. P. Bishop Mus., Bull. 148, Honolulu 1937.

CHAPTER 15

Buck, P. H.: *Ethnology of Mangareva*. B. P. Bishop Mus., Bull. 154, Honolulu 1938.

Laval, Honoré: *Mangareva*. Braine-le-Comté, Belgium 1937.

CHAPTER 16

Lavachery, Henri: *Contribution à l'étude de l'archéologie de l'île de Pitcairn*. Société des Américanistes de Belgique, Bull. 19, Bruxelles 1936.

CHAPTER 17

Métraux, Alfred: *Easter Island*. B. P. Bishop Mus., Bull. 160, Honolulu (in press).

Routledge, Mrs. Scoresby: *Mystery of Easter Island: the story of an expedition*. London 1919.

CHAPTER 18

Beckwith, Martha W.: *Kepelino's traditions of Hawaii*. B. P. Bishop Mus., Bull. 95, Honolulu 1932.

Beckwith, Martha W.: *Kamakau's history of Hawaii*. B. P. Bishop Mus. (Ms.).

Fornander, Abraham: *Hawaiian antiquities and folklore*. B. P. Bishop Mus., Mems., Vols. 4, 5, 6, Honolulu 1916-1920.

Malo, David: *Hawaiian antiquities*. B. P. Bishop Mus., Spec. Pub. 2, Honolulu 1903. (Out of print.)

CHAPTER 19

Best, Elsdon: *The Maori*. Polynesian Soc., Mem., Vol. 5, Wellington 1924.

Buck, P. H.: *The coming of the Maori*. Cawthron Inst. Lectures, Vol. 2, No. 2, 1925.

Cowan, James: *The Maoris of New Zealand*. London 1910.

Grey, Sir George: *Polynesian mythology*. London 1855.

Skinner, H. D.: *The Morioris of Chatham Islands*. B. P. Bishop Mus., Mem., Vol. IX, No. 1, Honolulu 1923.

CHAPTER 20

Beaglehole, Ernest and Pearl: *Ethnology of Pukapuka*. B. P. Bishop Mus., Bull. 150, Honolulu 1938.

Buck, P. H.: *Samoan material culture*. B. P. Bishop Mus., Bull. 75, Honolulu 1930.

Burrows, E. C.: *Ethnology of Futuna*. B. P. Bishop Mus., Bull. 138, Honolulu 1936.

Burrows, E. C.: *Ethnology of Uvea (Wallis Island)*. B. P. Bishop Mus., Bull. 145, Honolulu 1937.

Collocott, E. E. V.: *Tales and poems of Tonga*. B. P. Bishop Mus., Bull. 46, Honolulu 1928.

Gifford, E. W.: *Tongan myths and tales*. B. P. Bishop Mus., Bull. 8, Honolulu 1924. (Out of print.)

Gifford, E. W.: *Tongan society*. B. P. Bishop Mus., Bull. 61, Honolulu 1929.

Hocart, A. M.: *Lau Islands, Fiji*. B. P. Bishop Mus., Bull. 62, Honolulu 1929.

Macgregor, Gordon: *Ethnology of Tokelau Islands*. B. P. Bishop Mus., Bull. 146, Honolulu 1937.

Mariner, William: *An account of the natives of the Tonga Islands*. Two vols., London 1818.

McKern, W. C.: *Archæology of Tonga*. B. P. Bishop Mus., Bull. 60, Honolulu 1929.

Mead, Margaret: *Social organization of Manua*. B. P. Bishop Mus., Bull. 76, Honolulu 1930.

Thompson, Laura: *Southern Lau, Fiji*. B. P. Bishop Mus., Bull in Ms.

Turner, George: *Samoa a hundred years ago and long before*. London 1884.

CHAPTER 21

Dixon, R. B.: *The problem of the sweet potato in Polynesia*. American Anthropologist, Vol. 34, No. 1, 1932.

Dixon, R. B.: *The long voyages of the Polynesians*. American Philosophical Soc., Vol. LXXIV, No. 3, 1934.

Hillebrand, William: *Flora of the Hawaiian Islands*. Heidelberg 1888.

INDEX

PHOENIX BOOKS
in Sociology

PHOENIX BOOKS
in Anthropology

PHOENIX BOOKS
in Archeology